Sri Lankan Housemaids in Lebanon

IMISCOE
International Migration, Integration and Social Cohesion in Europe

The IMISCOE Network of Excellence unites over 500 researchers from European institutes specialising in studies of international migration, integration and social cohesion. The Network is funded by the Sixth Framework Programme of the European Commission on Research, Citizens and Governance in a Knowledge-Based Society. Since its foundation in 2004, IMISCOE has developed an integrated, multidisciplinary and globally comparative research project led by scholars from all branches of the economic and social sciences, the humanities and law. The Network both furthers existing studies and pioneers new research in migration as a discipline. Priority is also given to promoting innovative lines of inquiry key to European policymaking and governance.

The IMISCOE-Amsterdam University Press Series was created to make the Network's findings and results available to researchers, policymakers and practitioners, the media and other interested stakeholders. High-quality manuscripts authored by IMISCOE members and cooperating partners are published in one of four distinct series.

IMISCOE RESEARCH advances sound empirical and theoretical scholarship addressing themes within IMISCOE's mandated fields of study.

IMISCOE REPORTS disseminates Network papers and presentations of a time-sensitive nature in book form.

IMISCOE DISSERTATIONS presents select PhD monographs written by IMISCOE doctoral candidates.

IMISCOE TEXTBOOKS produces manuals, handbooks and other didactic tools for instructors and students of migration studies.

IMISCOE Policy Briefs and more information on the Network can be found at www.imiscoe.org.

Sri Lankan Housemaids in Lebanon

A Case of 'Symbolic Violence' and 'Everyday Forms of Resistance'

Nayla Moukarbel

IMISCOE Dissertations

AMSTERDAM UNIVERSITY PRESS

Cover design: Studio Jan de Boer, Amsterdam
Layout: The DocWorkers, Almere

ISBN   978 90 8964 051 2
e-ISBN   978 90 4850 636 1
NUR   741 / 763

My deepest gratitude goes to Professor Russell King
who has accompanied me during this journey,
first as a dedicated DPhil supervisor, and second,
as a priceless help in editing the thesis into its final book version.

Table of contents

1   Introduction

'La banalisation de l'insolite se fait par répétition, donnant un statut
de "normalité" au déraisonnable ou d'"habitude" à l'exceptionnel.'
'The "normalisation" of the unusual is brought about by
repetition, giving a status of "normality" to the
unreasonable or of "habit" to the exceptional.'
Mounir Chamoun (*L'Orient Le Jour*)

My interest in Sri Lankan housemaids[1] working in Lebanon began a
few years ago, initiated by a class project on foreign labour when I was
a student at the American University of Beirut, and subsequently pursued as a DPhil thesis at the University of Sussex. I chose domestic
work as my subject because I have always been puzzled by the blurred
boundaries that exist with this particular form of employment, where
private life and work are indistinctly connected.

But there is a more personal reason, too. Ever since I can remember,
I have been surrounded by maids. I not only witnessed but 'lived'
through every nationality change that took place in Lebanon within this
form of occupation, from Syrians and Egyptians to Sri Lankans and Filipinas. Whether in my parents' household or those of friends and relatives, maids were always there, cooking, cleaning, feeding, running
after children ... and, some of them, after me. I was almost raised by a
Syrian maid, Jamileh, who came to work and live with us as a child
(she was ten) and left as an adult of 22. At that time, it was common
for young Syrian girls to be sent to Lebanon by their families to work
as maids. Jamileh used to tell me stories at the kitchen table so that I
would finish my plate, play with me, watch over me. My mother
worked and Jamileh was there. I used to love playing with water and I
often asked Jamileh to let me do the dishes. But she never did; it was
her role, not mine. Even years later, when my mum had no permanent
help, my numerous races to the kitchen sink, trying to get there before
her, were unsuccessful. She'd always push me away saying: 'You'll do
plenty of that when you get married'. My answer was precise and systematic: 'But I will have a maid when I get married'.

I was a few months old when Jamileh arrived and twelve when she
left. I still remember to this day the pain and frustration I felt the moment she said goodbye. I could not even imagine her need for a life
elsewhere. For me, she simply belonged with us. She was 'part of the
family', people sometimes mistook her for my big sister. I can still see
the look on her face when one of us would answer: 'No, she is our
maid'. I never saw her again, never knew what had happened to her, if

she got married as she hoped for, if she forgot about me and us. If she was indeed 'part of the family' wouldn't she, wouldn't we, stay in touch? Or does her 'belonging', in fact, end with the job?

When Jamileh left, 'to get a life' as she confided in me at the time, my mother hired an Egyptian maid who, as I remember, was lazy but cheerful. She was fired after a few months. After that, and to this day, my mother employs freelance[2] Sri Lankan housemaids. Some have worked on a monthly-wage basis, coming six days a week, and some on an hourly basis, only working two or three times a week. I have witnessed, up close, many of the problems encountered by my mother with her successive housemaids, and their impact on the family as a whole as one gets easily 'dependent' on outside help. But more importantly, I have watched my mother build different relationships with her maids. Just as I have, being the daughter of the employer. I have become, for the past five years, an employer myself. Since I moved out from my parents' house, a Sri Lankan freelancer (Komari is the third one in five years) cleans my flat once a week.

For this research, I decided to limit my scope to Sri Lankan housemaids, as they were (and still are) the largest female migrant group in Lebanon, estimated to number around 100,000. But there is another reason, a rather subjective one, behind my choosing this community and not another. I have always felt closer to this migrant community than to any other. Since Arab maids stopped 'living in' and working within our household, they were replaced by Sri Lankan freelancers who, one after another (Shanti, Mali, Soma, Ramia, Lata), took care of my family and me. Did my mother prefer Sri Lankans over other nationalities? The answer is no. In fact, Sri Lankans almost hold the 'monopoly' of freelancing work. I never came across a Filipina freelancer. Sometimes, recruitment agencies have women from various countries (the Philippines, Sri Lanka, Ethiopia, etc.) 'on hold' to 'bail out' Lebanese families for a short period of time (one to three months) while they await the arrival of the newly 'ordered' housemaid or during their vacation spent in Lebanon. But I have never seen a Filipina housemaid (or any other nationality, for that matter) offering freely and directly her services to Lebanese employers on a freelance basis.

This brief background is useful to put things in context, and to clarify, right up front, my positionality. The researcher, after all, comes from a particular setting; one that carries with it a load of '*vécu*' or life experiences that give him or her a unique insight to the subject studied. 'When one does research it is highly unlikely ever to be "clean" experience ... researchers bring to their research different kinds of baggage, which has consequences for the research process and final product' (Hockey 1996: 12). It is hard for researchers to reflect on the baggage they carry into their own work. But it is important to do so in order to avoid some biases as well as acknowledge others. My own baggage, as shown above, is rather heavy.

In a very few words, this book is about Sri Lankan housemaids in Lebanon – my home country. My actual research covers years of gathering and analysis of data (qualitative as well as quantitative) made up by 90 in-depth interviews with Sri Lankan housemaids and twenty with Lebanese female employers, plus other key interviews with various actors in the field (30 in all) and several years (in a sense, a lifetime) of participant observation. Although the research embodies in an obvious way the study of migration, gender, racism and domestic work, its two conceptual frames are the *symbolic violence* (Bourdieu 1991) vaunted by the employers on the housemaids, and the *everyday resistance* (Scott 1985, 1990) deployed by the latter to improve their living and working conditions.

My key research aim is to give a deeply ethnographic and even personal appraisal of the situation of Sri Lankan housemaids in Lebanon. I attempt, if I may use this imagery, to take the reader by the hand and guide him/her through the complex journey which has been my research trajectory.

Throughout this book, and beginning with this chapter, examples from my data will be used in an attempt to 'bring to life' the subjects discussed. It is my belief that a pure theorisation of issues relevant to domestic work could appear arid, failing to seize the 'essence' of a private and controversial subject. Many of the issues I focus upon in this research, namely gender, violence, resistance and racism, are not, in my view, clear-cut, exclusive categories (just as the problems housemaids face are not merely unidirectional as one might presume, i.e. stemming mainly from employers). These concepts are, rather, interwoven; almost 'feeding' on one another to subsist.

The feminisation of migration and domestic work

Although human migration has existed throughout time, it is considered as one of modern history's most important social phenomena. The shift to post-industrial economies and the general phenomenon of globalisation have resulted in a greater demand for cheap labour from overseas. Added to this, the great changes in transport and communication and a bigger disparity between rich and poor countries have, along with other factors, led to the creation of 'transnational' communities. Numbers of international migrants have more than doubled since 1960. There are now 200 million international migrants worldwide, half of whom are women. But already in 1960, 47 out of 100 migrants were women. Since then, the female proportion has risen to reach 48 per cent in 1990 and 49 per cent in 2000. Despite the fact that women have represented for a while now a significant portion of the global migrant population, migration was considered to be a male phenomenon until the mid-1980s (IOM 2005a). The 'feminisation' of international migration has only recently begun to receive the attention it merits, as researchers start to look more closely at the role of women in the new composition of migrant populations across the world. Migrant women are no longer seen as subordinate to men, nor are they limited to their reproductive function (Sharpe 2001). The term 'feminisation' of migration was coined to note not so much an increase in the proportion or numbers of female migrants but the emergence of a new form of female migration in the early 1980s: women were migrating independently to seek jobs abroad (rather than joining their husbands) and were becoming the main income provider for their family. '*The diversity* of the new forms of migration has therefore gone hand in hand with *feminization*' (Anthias 2000: 20; emphasis in original). Moreover, the employment of migrant women has undergone a shift from the industrial to the service sector and to the informal economy. While it is easier now for women to migrate independently, the labour markets available to them in the countries of destination are still limited and remain sex-segregated. Women provide low-cost and flexible labour within various service sectors, especially in the 'hidden labour market' (Anthias 2000). 'They assist the elderly and the handicapped in the crumbling welfare state, or work as nurses; they find employment in restaurants, in tourism, in the sex industry and as maids for western women seeking their own autonomy' (Campani 1995: 548). Traditional female jobs like domestic work and prostitution, previously marginalised, have now to be reconsidered within this new economic context. These workers, Campani (1995) asserts, can no longer be considered as marginal subjects, but as 'social actors' in their own right.

One form of female labour migration within the 'hidden market' has received a significant amount of attention lately: domestic work. Domestic work is a particular form of employment where housemaids not only work for, but also, in many cases, live with their employers. Private life and work become intertwined; labour, a way of living in itself. This type of labour, usually occupied by women, is undervalued and underpaid. Moreover, it is often the arena for serious human rights abuses, increasingly revealed around the world.

Paid domestic work emerged as an important feminist issue in the 1970s. This rising interest grew to encompass sociologists, anthropologists, historians, journalists, NGOs, international organisations and human rights activists. Numerous scholars (Anderson, Brochmann, Constable, Ehrenreich, Gamburd, Hochschild, Hondagneu-Sotelo, Lutz, Narula, Romero and many others[3]), too, have concentrated on the migratory experiences of women who leave their countries (the Philippines, Sri Lanka, India, Ethiopia, etc.) to seek employment as housemaids in cities in Europe, the Middle East or North America. Books published with a focus upon domestic work in developed countries have been growing in number in recent years: for example, Tilly and Scott (1987) on pre-industrial and early twentieth-century Britain and France; Rollins (1985) on domestics in the United States; Palmer (1989) on the shift from local to migrant women in domestic employment from the late nineteenth century to the early twentieth century in the US; Sanjek and Colen's (1990) edited collection of essays on household workers in a number of countries such as Nigeria, Nepal, Zambia, Martinique and Malaysia; Romero (1992) on Chicanas in the US; Constable (1997) on Filipinas in Hong Kong; Anderson (2000) on countries of the European Union; Andall (2000) specifically on Cape Verdean women in Rome; Chang (2000) on migrant domestics in the US; Hondagneu-Sotelo (2001) on Latinas in the US; Parreñas (2001) on Filipinas in Rome and Los Angeles; and Lutz (2008) for the latest edited collection on migration and domestic work in Europe. Studies of domestic workers in other countries are numerous and there is no space here for a full review; contrasting cases might include Chin (1998) on Indonesians and Filipinas in Malaysia and Zontini (2002) on Filipinas and Moroccans in Bologna and Barcelona. Other social scientists focus upon the role of exploitative labour relations as part of the developmental process in capital accumulation (see Castles 1995), while Ehrenreich and Hochschild (2002) published an edited collection of studies on the transfer of services within globalisation from poor countries to rich ones. Others have provided excellent overviews of domestic work and migration, linking the relevant concepts and practices across space and through time – see Moya (2007) for the most recent of these which have come to hand. A recent anthropological study looked at return migrants in Sri Lanka who had worked in the Middle East (Gamburd 2000); this is an important reference point for my own study – Brochmann's (1993) book on Sri Lankan migration to the Gulf (again, looked upon from the returnees' side) had led the way. International organisations such as the International Labour Organization (ILO) and the International Organization for Migration (IOM) have also taken an interest in the subject (see Esim & Smith 2004; IOM 2005b). Other studies on domestic workers have concentrated on the gender aspect and reproductive role of women who serve other women (Carling 2005; Jolly & Reeves 2005; Kofman, Phizaclea, Raghuram & Sales 2000; Momsen 1999; Parreñas 2005; Piper 2005).

What is interesting about all these studies is that the conditions and treatment of migrant housemaids are virtually identical across time and space. No matter where the job is taking place, by what nationality it is held, the experiences are very much alike.

The need for a study on Sri Lankan housemaids in Lebanon

Most studies regarding labour migration to the Middle East over the past few years have concentrated upon the flow of migrant labour from Asian and Arab countries to the Gulf States as a significant new destination of temporary migration following the oil boom in the 1970s. Further, most of these studies have been rather economistic in their focus, concentrating on structural factors such as wage differentials, remittances and the supply and demand characteristics of international labour markets (see Birks & Sinclair 1980; Castles & Davidson 2000; Castles & Miller 2003). Some research has also addressed the political dimensions relating to migration in a region that has witnessed many conflicts and wars (Choucri 1986; Fargues 2002; Russell 1990). While these conceptual approaches are important, there is a tendency to ignore the social interactions between these migrant housemaids and their employers. These interactions are extremely difficult to research, but provide the *raison d'être* for my own study.

A few specific studies on the treatment and conditions of Asian housemaids working in the Middle East have been produced: Kahale (2003) on Syria; Najjar (2004) on Bahrain; Godfrey, Shah & Smith (2004) on Kuwait; and Sabban (2004) on the United Arab Emirates.

Limited material relating to foreign domestic work in Lebanon has been produced, such as NGO reports (see for example Caritas 2005; McDermott 1999) as well as numerous newspaper and magazine articles. In his book *Migrant Workers in Lebanon*, Young (1999) does give a general overview of the problems migrant housemaids encounter in Lebanon. While I am in no way questioning this book's valuable input, I do believe that Young's general (and rather journalistic) appraisal of the subject of migrant housemaids leaves room for further in-depth analysis of the subject. The only academic studies available on Sri Lankan (or any other nationality for that matter) housemaids in Lebanon derive from my early work carried out at the American University of Beirut, before I transferred my research to the University of Sussex. The first phase of research yielded a number of conference papers with my then supervisor, and culminated in a formally published paper which explored the concept of 'contract slavery' in the context of Sri Lankan housemaids in Lebanon, 70 of whom I had interviewed at that time (Jureidini & Moukarbel 2004). An ILO report (Esim & Smith 2004) includes a chapter on Sri Lankan housemaids in Lebanon (Jureidini 2004) which is almost entirely based on my early-stage research mentioned above. Despite the considerable scale of my first-stage field research, I felt that there were many conceptual and practical questions still to be answered. This book, therefore, represents a further development of that earlier research, with more interviews and new theoretical angles explored. Above all, the experience of housemaid migration to such 'intermediate' Mediterranean/Middle Eastern locations as Lebanon remained *terra incognita* waiting to be further studied.

Research questions: symbolic violence and everyday resistance

As I began my research on Sri Lankan housemaids in Lebanon, I became very quickly aware of the substantial amount of interest the subject of migrant housemaids received, whether in Lebanon or worldwide. As mentioned above, international organisations, various NGOs, scholars and journalists have all highlighted the exploitative and abusive working and living conditions migrant women face in foreign countries and households. Many commentators have viewed these women as vulnerable victims; others as empowered women who, driven by the need to improve their lives, face difficult circumstances with stoicism. All studies, papers, articles, reports, etc., blame the employers (whether directly or silently) for their reprehensible treatment of housemaids. Many talk about new forms of slavery taking place within modern households. While I agree with most of the issues raised and condemnations voiced, the dichotomous approach generally adopted left me wondering: were things as simple as they were portrayed or were the dynamics at stake more complex and in need of further decoding?

It goes without saying that Sri Lankan women working as housemaids in Lebanon are, in general, treated inhumanely by their employers (particularly women employers or 'Madames'[4] who are the ones 'in charge' of the housemaid). But are employers the only party responsible, or is there a consensus (or 'conspiracy of silence') amongst the Lebanese society and government, the Sri Lankan government and maybe even housemaids themselves, that allows for this mistreatment to endure and become rooted inside so many households? Do housemaids 'participate' somehow in this domination/submission dynamic and why? Is it simply, as many have suggested, because they are poor and vulnerable women who are 'forced' into accepting harsh labour and living conditions in order to improve their situations back home? Is the general picture limited to a capitalist approach with the rich exploiting the poor, the strong, the weak? Is it also, perhaps, because they are 'black' and therefore demeaned by racist 'white' Lebanese employers? And why are Sri Lankans viewed (and preferred by Lebanese employers) as more submissive and 'easier to break' than (for instance) their

Filipina sisters? But more importantly, why do Madames from all social classes (high- or low-class Madames, those who have careers, who are doctors or architects or those who have never had paid employment, Madames with a higher education or those who barely made it through high school) think it is 'normal' to control and dehumanise their housemaids? Why do they think they have the right or even the obligation ('One simply *cannot* be nice with these women') to keep the housemaid under a solid grip? And why do Sri Lankan housemaids give them this 'right'? All Madames (at least, all I know of) portray themselves as 'ideal employers' ('I treat her like my daughter') having to deal with 'ungrateful housemaids'. As one Lebanese employer told me: 'In the end they are all *ingrates*. Have you seen a maid saying good things about her employers, maids who were thankful? No. Because all the good things are forgotten if the employer shouted at her one second only. Praise the Lord. This is the truth for every servant. This is normal'. Is this 'normal'? What is true, in fact, is that what has become 'normalised' is a type of behaviour that is highly controlling towards housemaids.

This book unravels, beyond making accusations, the real dynamics at stake within this particular form of labour held by Sri Lankan housemaids within Lebanese households. Issues of *violence and domination* (by the employer), *resistance* (by the housemaid in an attempt to limit the domination), *racism* (the Sri Lankan housemaid is a woman of colour), *gender roles* and renegotiations (as we are dealing with two women who are supposedly challenging traditional gender roles, one by 'delegating' her household responsibilities to a housemaid and the other by getting 'empowered' by her own migratory experience) are at the core of this employer/housemaid dynamic.

I argue that regular and insidious forms of violence (or 'symbolic violence' as defined by Bourdieu 1991) used by employers to control their housemaids constitute the 'norm'. These disguised strategies of domination are very efficient in keeping the housemaid cornered where she belongs, in her quarters, costume, role and being (one Lebanese employer commenting on her friend's refusal to let her housemaid sit in the living room with her; she could, however, sit behind her in the annex dining area: 'It's normal, each one in her place'). Symbolic violence is not about physical violence (beatings, slapping and hair-pulling do occur but remain the exception rather than the rule); rather, it is displayed through constant belittling and criticism, calling the housemaid names (*hmara* (donkey) or *habla* (stupid) are used frequently), not allowing her to prepare her own food ('The smell of curry is disgusting') or simply giving her leftovers ('Here, eat this so that we don't throw it away'), holding on to her passport, not paying her on time or indeed at all, locking her in, not allowing her outside the household except rarely and under some sort of supervision, not giving her one day off per week, threatening to take her to the agency to be 'taught a lesson', controlling every aspect of her life and personhood ('Madame cut my hair very short. She no like my hair long. I cry'). Domination is maintained through interpersonal relations in a family setting where work is not defined as such but rather as a 'service', a position of care and subservience. Symbolic violence is hijacking the housemaid's personhood and fitting her into a mould, it is claiming to have allowed her to be 'part of the family' while denying her every right any 'real' member of the family is entitled to.

Symbolic violence is efficient and lasting, it takes unexpected routes and is very hard to resist, especially on the part of Sri Lankan housemaids ('the easiest to break') whose baggage or 'habitus' (Bourdieu 1991) predisposes them to such forms of exploitation. For 'symbolic violence' to work, it needs to be performed on people predisposed in their habitus to accept it. I will attempt to prove that the baggage or habitus Sri Lankan housemaids carry with them is one that is more likely to adhere to forms of symbolic violence administered by Lebanese employers.

Even if 'symbolic violence' is the principal drive within this dynamic defining its process and outcome, housemaids do try to limit (yet not reverse) the employers' domination patterns by using 'everyday forms of resistance' (as defined by Scott 1990). These tools used by the 'weak' take (just as 'symbolic violence' does) indirect and 'safe' routes, away from direct provocation, in an attempt to avoid first-hand repercussions. These strategies of resistance stretch from playing sick and lying about family matters, to pleasing the employer and abiding by the rules. The 'negative' forms of resistance, however, such as lying, stealing, etc., can 'backfire' on housemaids. Lebanese employers can in fact perceive them as 'natural' traits pertaining to Sri Lankan women in general, hence giving them further 'excuses' to tighten even more their control patterns.

I also argue that gender issues are essential in understanding the dynamics at stake within the Madame/housemaid relationship (women are, in this particular case, controlling other women). Furthermore, I believe that gender-role renegotiations (for both women: the Madame and the housemaid) remain limited. Despite the fact that the Madame has 'liberated' herself from household chores and succeeded in upgrading her role into a 'managerial' one, she is still trapped in traditional gender roles whereby she is responsible for the 'private' well-being of her family. As for most housemaids, who may be relatively empowered by their migratory experience and their new role as sole breadwinners within their families, they easily revert back to their roles as wives and mothers upon return.

Finally, I will show that the problematic between the Madame and her housemaid goes beyond cultural and racial differences. Lebanese and Arab maids in the past were treated with the same disdain and control. I believe that race is used as yet another 'excuse' for further exploitation but is not at the core of the abuse.

To illustrate some of the points I raise above (and many more), issues relating to symbolic violence (control of the – very private – living and working conditions of housemaids) and to means of resistance (in this case pleasing the Madame) are narrated below as parts of a taped interview I held with a Lebanese employer. This Madame had recently acquired the services of a Sri Lankan housemaid. I will let the text speak for itself:

> We [the employer and her husband] went to the agency. I went there because my neighbours told me about her. And she was cheap, $900. Other agencies you pay more but you get better quality. We went to the agency, me and my husband. I wanted her to have worked before, in Saudi Arabia or Jordan. Speaking Arabic at least a little so I did not have a hard time with her. Because they told me if you bring her and she doesn't know anything, it's too much of a hassle for you. And I have no time, no time to leave my work and sit with her. So we picked her because she's supposed to have worked in Jordan. It turned out she knows a little Arabic, just a few words. I didn't pay the agent. I told her I will only pay you after she comes and stays with me a month and I test her and all her tests are good then I will pay you, and more if you want. But that I pay and then have a hard time, I won't do it. She agreed. We went to get her from the airport. We waited almost three hours. It was exhausting. They told us she arrives at 2:30. They let them out only at five o'clock. General Security gave me her passport at the airport. She came out with a plastic bag only. She didn't smell, I don't know if she was dirty. From the airport directly to the bath. The bath was hot, ready for her. I bathed her, I had prepared a shampoo for her against lice. Her clothes all of them I took them and threw them in the garbage. Because she was skinny I gave clothes from my daughter before I could buy her new ones. I taught her how to take a bath. I think that they take a bath with their clothes. When she stepped into the bathtub she had still her panties and bra on. I closed the curtain and told her to take them off, and I gave her shampoo and a sponge to clean her body. She was shy, trying to hide her breasts and ... you know... I also taught her how to brush her teeth. She took her bath. After the bath, I made her clean the bathroom. After we had dinner and I taught her how to do the dishes. She's supposed to

know how but it wasn't to my liking. She did the dishes, me standing in the kitchen beside her. Then I did her bed and she slept. *Haram* (Poor her), she was tired. The next day, I started teaching her, little by little. I took three or four days off work to train her. My boss was angry with me, he said: 'You are missing work because of a Sri Lankan'... She wasn't dumb but she wasn't too smart either. Her husband is dead. She missed her kids but she was happy that we didn't have any small kids. In the morning before she started working I told her: 'I don't want you to work before you drink your Nescafé or tea and eat cheese and *labné* [type of Lebanese yogurt]'. She didn't eat, she didn't eat cheese and *labné*. She likes jam and banana. She made a sandwich of strawberry jam with banana. My daughters liked her, whatever they ate they gave her, they told her come and eat. I taught her how to do things. On Saturday, she started working at six am. My husband was mad and asked me to make her stop, it was too early, she woke us up. I told her on Saturdays and Sundays she shouldn't move before 8:30 or nine am because Mister was asleep and needed his rest... After I trained her for four to five days, I went back to work. I told her: 'Clean here, clean there'. When I came back home, I checked to see if it was clean. Now she noticed me twice looking to see if it was clean. The third time when I came she took my hand and told me: 'Madame, come and see' and she showed me under the bed... To tell me that she worked so that I am happy. For lunch I tell her: 'This is what you have for lunch because in the evening I'll be coming for dinner'. I called home yesterday and my daughter told me that she [the housemaid] fried one egg. It's OK for this one time, but I won't let her take the habit of preparing food for herself, she should eat the food that is already there. At first my husband put her on the dining table with us. I told him, *haram* (poor her). First of all the house is small... Then she took a table to the balcony and told me: 'Madame I like sitting there'. She took her plate, when we served, all of us, she took her plate and sat outside. She was great. But their odour!! She doesn't remove the hair under her arms. In the beginning, as she is always wearing a T-shirt, I did not notice. Then I cut her underarm hair with scissors. If my husband sees them, he'll go crazy, he will kick her out! How is she going to smell in the summer? She [the housemaid] did not react. Then the next day, I told her: 'Take, this is shaving machine, go shave'. She said: 'No Madame' and I don't know what... I replied: 'Go shave because this hair brings bad odour of sweat'. So you have to go into disgusting details. For instance, she does not remove the hair on her legs. And they look scary! I told her: 'Stop wearing skirts, we are not ob-

liged to be confronted with this sight, wear pants'. [Laughing]. I
like to be presentable. I tell her: 'You are beautiful'. I like her to
look smart. I tell her to tie her hair in the morning. It is so long,
disgusting. I want her to cut her hair but I think, this one, she will
go crazy if I cut her hair, crazy. I make her wash her clothes every
day. I told my husband that, later on, I would let the maid pay for
her own things (deodorant, et cetera) from her salary. He replied
that this poor widow, with only $100 per month, should not have
to, he will pay for her things. The man I have is so weak and tender. She is lucky to have such a Mister... I do not like having a
live-in maid but I have to. Believe me, one shouldn't get a maid if
there is no real need for her. It is an invasion of privacy. Lebanese
maids ask for $300 a month, not even to live in. It is much, much
cheaper to get a Sri Lankan, it is also much cheaper to get a Sri
Lankan live-in than to employ a Sri Lankan freelancer... One day,
she woke up as normal. I was standing in my kitchen preparing
my Nescafé. I had prepared her tea and was eating a cup cake.
Then I heard something fall. I turned around and saw her on the
floor. My husband and daughter were home. My husband carried
her. I poured water on her, slapped her face so that she wakes up.
She woke up and passed out again, six times. Within two hours.
Then she had like a nervous attack, her hands were squeezed
tight. I called the agent. I hadn't paid her yet. The maid was there
for fifteen days only. So I didn't pay her. The maid the day before
broke a vase. It must be that she felt dizzy and fell and nobody
knew because she was alone in the house. So I called the agent.
She said her insurance is at Najjar hospital. But three days before
this incident, my husband was sick, his ear was hurting, I took
him down, she told me: 'Madame, me too ear'. My husband said:
'Let's take her too'. The doctor who checked him checked her too.
He told me her ear has a hole in it. She needs an operation. I
didn't believe the doctor. He took out all the pus from her ear; it
was disgusting. He gave her some medication, I bought them for
her and she took them. She started getting better. But the third or
fourth day this happened. I took her to Najjar. He told me the
same thing like the university doctor, this is due to a very long infection or she fell at one point. It cannot heal unless she has an
operation because she has no balance. She gets dizzy, she falls on
the floor, she shouldn't for example take too many showers because water in her ear might give her an infection. Or she has to
close her ear at all times. I didn't want to keep her because it's a
responsibility. I was scared that at one point, while alone for instance, the gas is on, she's cooking for me or doing something,
she gets dizzy and falls. Responsibility. I'm scared that she dies or

something happens to her because six times she passed out. I put her on the plane the same day. I brought her from the hospital and I told the agent: 'I am not taking her home with me, I'm taking her to your place and tonight you have to send her back to Sri Lanka, I forbid you to let her sleep at your place tonight'. I myself took her to the airport and sent her because I got scared that she might keep her and give her to someone else. Because she told me: 'We can give her to someone else and I'll get you another maid'. I told her: 'No, I want her to go back because she came under my name and I don't want problems'. The agent was good, I can't say she wasn't good. But she was under pressure by us. She wasn't happy that we sent back the maid, she didn't want her to be sent back. Saying no, she doesn't want to work and she didn't believe that her ear was damaged. I told her I was like you I didn't believe, even the university doctor I didn't believe him. She said maybe the university doctor is the one who damaged her ear. I said impossible, on the contrary, he took all the pus out, he relieved her, her ear was hurting a lot. After, under pressure she accepted. And she tried to give me someone else but I refused because I didn't want one anymore, it was a bad experience. My husband got very angry. You see, Nayla, my luck is damned. God help me.

Note that the Sri Lankan housemaid (a widow) and the employer are of almost the same age (34 and 35) and both are mothers (the housemaid has three children and the employer two). These demographic data come as a bit of a shock after reading the narrative, in which the relationship appears to be very different from one between two women at very similar life-course stages.

Asian migration to the Middle East

Large-scale flows of labour migration from Asia to the Middle East are relatively recent and are directly linked to the oil boom which started in the early 1970s. Earlier migration flows included small numbers of Indian divers to work on a seasonal basis in the fishing and pearling industry. Trade involving textiles and gold existed for centuries between the Arabian peninsula and India, Sri Lanka and South-East Asia. In the nineteenth century, there was a notable presence of Indian civil servants in areas under British control. Then, and following the OPEC's decision to massively increase oil prices in the autumn of 1973, labour migration into this region of the world increased dramatically, shifting from Arab workers from neighbouring countries to Asian sources of labour (Abella 1995; Baldwin-Edwards 2005; Brochmann 1993; Castles & Miller 2003). The number of Asian workers grew from 65,000 at the beginning of the 1970s to nine times more by the end of the decade (Abella 1995). Following the big increase in oil revenues, the GCC (Gulf Cooperation Council) oil-rich states (Kuwait, Oman, Bahrain, Qatar, Saudi Arabia and the United Arab Emirates) faced a shortage of labour, much needed to help in the realisation of their ambitious development plans. In fact, the workforce participation rate of these states was low, a high proportion of the population was under working age and the female labour participation remained very low due to religious norms and traditions (Russell 1990). Moreover, very few within this workforce had the expertise to help in the implementation of modern development projects. Labour demand, therefore, had to be met from abroad.

In the early years of the oil boom (1970s to early 1980s), the majority of the foreign labour force was recruited from neighbouring Arab countries, mainly from Egypt, Yemen and Palestine (Baldwin-Edwards 2005). Some, though not many, Asian workers were recruited too, mainly from India and Pakistan. But it is not until the decade from the mid-1980s to the mid-1990s that the Asian presence became important. Movements grew to include the Philippines, Indonesia, Thailand, and later Bangladesh and Sri Lanka. In 1985, Asian workers comprised 63 per cent of the total Gulf labour force (Kapiszewski 2006).

Arab workers were replaced by Asian workers for various reasons (Girgis 2002). First, the 1985 collapse of oil prices led to necessary cuts in private and public costs (less-skilled Asian workers accepted lower wages and did not benefit from social support services). Second, Asian workers were unlikely to settle and bring their families; they were also easier to lay off as well as viewed as more efficient and obedient. Third, Asian countries (unlike Arab ones) were actively engaged in the placement of their workers. And finally, and more importantly, Arab workers (specifically Egyptians and Yemenis who overthrew their monarchies, and Palestinians who could drag the receiving countries into their own Pan-Arabic struggle) were considered to be a possible threat to the existing political order within the receiving GCC rich countries. Following the 1990 Gulf crisis, many Arabs became even more undesirable (especially those whose governments backed Saddam Hussein, such as the Yemenis and Palestinians – Abella 1995). In fact, two million Arabs and their dependants lost their jobs in the GCC countries following Iraq's invasion of Kuwait (Baldwin-Edwards 2005).

Early flows of Asian workers to the Middle East were mainly males working in various construction projects. The temporary decline in construction work in 1985 allowed a shift of labour into various service sectors, from hotels to personal services. Moreover, and following the rapid accumulation of wealth and shift in the standards of living of GCC nationals, emerging needs relating to personal help (housemaids and nannies) were to be met (Brochmann 1993). With the acquired new wealth, these 'host' populations did not see it appropriate to occupy 'demeaning' positions and, therefore, imported unskilled workers from abroad. A rising demand for domestic service led to a feminisation of labour flows, principally from the Philippines, Indonesia, Thailand, Korea and Sri Lanka, while countries like Pakistan and Bangladesh did not wish to send their women to work abroad (Castles & Miller 2003). As a result of this boom in Asian domestic-worker migration, 81 per cent of migrant women present in the Middle East now work as housemaids (Chammartin 2005). According to the United Nations Population Division, the stock of women migrant workers grew rapidly in countries such as Bahrain, Oman, Saudi Arabia and the United Arab Emirates between 1965 and 2000 (Chammartin 2004: 10). GCC national statistics show that the percentages of foreign women workers in the early 2000s have doubled or tripled since the 1970s and early 1980s. For example, more than 90 per cent of Indonesian workers in Saudi Arabia and the United Arab Emirates were women in 1998. By 2001, 85-94 per cent of Sri Lankan workers in Jordan, Kuwait and Lebanon were also women (Chammartin 2004).

Context: Sri Lanka

Sri Lanka (population 20 million) has a long history of colonisation and forced labour. It was successively occupied by the Portuguese, Dutch and British. Previously called Ceylon, it attained independence in 1948. It participated in colonial and post-colonial trade networks since the sixteenth century. European administrations brought labour forces from India or China to work on plantation and mine projects on the island. The British, for example, imported Tamil-speaking labourers from South India to work on the predominantly Sinhala tea plantations.

Although Sri Lankan unskilled migrants' main destination nowadays is the Gulf region, this was not always the case. Sri Lankans started going abroad soon after attaining independence. Following economic and social pressures, Sri Lanka's educated and wealthy elites emigrated to Europe, Australia, Canada and the US as early as the 1950s. Ethnic tensions since the late 1970s between the Sinhala-speaking Buddhist majority and the Tamil-speaking Hindu and Muslim minorities developed into an ongoing civil war in 1983, costing thousands of lives. Tamil-speaking Sri Lankans fled the North-East and many Tamil plantation workers left for South India. 'As refugees, emigrants, and laborers, many different portions of the Sri Lankan community have travelled abroad, with a wide range of motivations' (Gamburd 2000: 30).

As Gamburd (2000: 54) notes, it is 'the history of Sri Lanka as a former colonial export economy under British rule (specializing in tea, rubber and coconuts) that largely explains the sophisticated economy as well as the fairly well-developed infrastructure'. Moreover, Sri Lanka has a life expectancy of 72 years, an 89 per cent adult literacy rate and a gross educational enrolment ratio of 66 per cent (UNDP 1997). However, and despite this rather positive image, a lack of opportunities and unemployment are prevalent in Sri Lanka, especially in the rural areas. Appearing to be a somewhat well-developed country, Sri Lanka is in reality very poor, ranking among the 30 poorest countries in the world.

Between 1970 and 1977, Sri Lanka was governed by a coalition, the United Front and the Sri Lanka Freedom Party. Since the early 1970s, the standard of living of the lowest strata of the population declined. The state's involvement in economic affairs amplified. Control was enforced on international trade and private companies nationalised. This led to a worsening of the overall economic situation: the GNP average growth rate for this period was less than 3 per cent (compared to almost 6 per cent after 1977). Economic stagnation was marked, and unemployment and infant mortality rates increased significantly during this government's rule (Brochmann 1993). The post-1977 government, following its introduction of a new economic policy of export industrialisation, was also facing a very high rate of inflation, a hard-currency deficit, youth unemployment and price increases (they had been controlled in the period 1970-1977). Between 1977 and 1984, rice prices increased by 158 per cent, bread by 339 per cent, milk powder by 345 per cent, and kerosene by more than 700 per cent (Brochmann 1993). So the increased demand for labour in the Gulf came at a time when Sri Lanka was facing severe economic problems.

Therefore, following the first major jump in oil prices in 1974 and the subsequent labour demand, the migration of labour from Sri Lanka to the Gulf started. As with many migrant sending countries, the Sri Lankan government encouraged its citizens to go abroad to work despite the various forms of abuse and exploitation reported and the pain of separation suffered by private households (Brochmann 1993). Earnings from employment in the Gulf became the most important component of private remittances into Sri Lanka. Remittances in 1978 financed 15 per cent of the deficit on current payments for goods and services, reaching 27 per cent by 1982 and 56 per cent in 1984 (Brochmann 1993). Workers' remittances have increased at an average annual rate of 10 per cent over the last 30 years (Lueth & Ruiz-Arranz 2007). Sri Lankan migrants remitted $1.4 billion in 2003, 8 per cent of the country's GDP (*Migration News* 2005). According to Lueth and Ruiz-Ar-ranz (2007: 5), 'In the case of Sri Lanka, persistent rural poverty, growing inequality, and ethnic tensions will continue to secure stable flows of remittances in the medium term'.

In the mid-1970s, the Sri Lankan labour force in the Middle East was predominately male construction workers. Women, however, rapidly joined the migration labour process and soon dominated the flows: in 1981, 52 per cent of Sri Lankan migrants were women; by 1994, the figure increased to 79 per cent (Gamburd 2000). Of the 200,000 Sri Lankans joining the international labour force every year, two-thirds are women heading principally to the Middle East to work as housemaids (*Migration News* 2005). This figure, equivalent to 1 per cent of the Sri Lankan population leaving annually, is gross outmigration and does not take account of return migration. There are currently between 600,000 and one million Sri Lankan women working abroad as housemaids. Aged between eighteen and 40, they usually have around ten years of education and have never held a paid job in Sri Lanka (*Migration News* 2005). Limited economic opportunities for Sri Lankan women (especially those married with children, unemployed in the formal sector, relatively uneducated and living in rural areas) are one of the main motivating factors driving them to seek employment abroad. As Gamburd points out, an interesting transposition of colonial-type relations has taken place: 'With the increased efficiency of global transportation, relations of domestic servitude that used to take place in colonial times between the visiting colonial and the native servant are now reproduced in the Middle East, with the servant now the visitor and the master now the native' (Gamburd 2000: 31).

The government of Sri Lanka's policies have generally been to promote its citizens' employment abroad (Gunatilleke 1995). As the magnitude of migration to the Middle East grew, the government created in 1985 the Sri Lanka Bureau of Foreign Employment (SLBFE) to regulate and control migration. Every migrant is required to register with the SLBFE and pay exit fees before leaving the country. The new policy, however, was not fully implemented: 'Sri Lankan authorities believe that about 40-50 per cent of labour migrants proceed abroad without registering with the appropriate authorities' (Shah 1994: 235). This registration was made compulsory in 1995 (Fernando 2001). SLBFE licences recruitment agencies and offers migrants a twelve-day training course providing general instructions relating to housework. There are over 500 licensed agencies in Sri Lanka helping nationals to find jobs abroad, while the number of sub-agents is estimated at 10,000 (IOM 2005b). The government also expanded existing embassies in the Middle East and opened new ones to assist its citizens abroad (*Migration News* 2005).

Context: Lebanon

Lebanon, historically, was associated with Phoenician rule (as early as c. 1600-800 BC), to fall later under the Roman Empire. In the seventh century AD, the Arabs conquered Lebanon, where the Maronite Christians were already established. Islam gradually spread but the country remained predominantly Christian. Invasions by the Crusaders and Mongols followed until the Ottoman Empire conquered and reunified the region. The dismantlement of the Ottoman Empire after World War I resulted in a new delimitation of the region. Greater Lebanon (*Grand Liban*) was separated from Syria in 1920 under the French Mandate into its current territorial boundaries (10,452 km^2). The Lebanese Republic (Lebanon) attained independence from France in 1943. The French created a confessional political system whereby the major religious confessions were represented in the parliament. Lebanon has always been a mixed population of Christians, Shiite and Sunni Muslims as well as Druze (there are as many as seventeen sects recognised in the country). Following a census in 1932 (Christians formed the majority of the population then: 50.03 per cent Christians, 48.71 per cent Muslims), the presidency of the Republic was assigned (and still is) to a Christian Maronite. 'Until today, the fear of major changes in the confessional equilibrium has prevented the organization of a new census' (Jaulin 2006). Current estimations of the population distribution reverse this balance: Muslim 59.7 per cent, Christian 39 per cent (CIA 2006).

Lebanon has been the scene of much inter-community (and inter-religious) fighting. In 1970, a large number of Palestinian fighters (Palestinian Liberation Organization, PLO) took refuge in Lebanon after being expelled from Jordan. This destabilised the country politically, and in 1975 what was to be known as the fifteen-year civil war emerged. The war ended in 1990 with the Taef Agreement.

The Lebanese are known for their migratory and trading spirit which some trace back to the Phoenicians and their exploratory expeditions. The sea provided trade routes in ancient times for exports and commerce. Lebanese emigration has always existed but numbers grew dramatically during the 1975-1990 civil war, during which an estimated 900,000 Lebanese emigrated (mainly to Europe and the Gulf states but also Africa, Australia, Canada and the US) and 800,000 were internally displaced (Baldwin-Edwards 2005). Many emigrants returned at the end of the civil war but no accurate data exist regarding the extent of this return phenomenon. Despite the end of armed conflict, and because of the economic depression that followed, high rates of emigration continued: almost 700,000 Lebanese were reported emigrating over the period 1992-1999 (Pederson 2003). Various estimates are given regarding the Lebanese diaspora abroad: numbers vary from one million (IOM 2004) to fourteen million of Lebanese descent (Al Khouri 2004). Lebanon is also host to many refugees, the vast majority of whom are Palestinians. Following the Arab-Israeli war in 1948, approximately 100,000 Palestinians took refuge in Lebanon. The number of Palestinian refugees present in Lebanon today, almost solely dependent on the United Nations Relief and Works Agency (UNRWA), is estimated at just over 400,000 by UN sources. The Lebanese constitution and successive governments actually forbid the 'implantation' of Palestinians in the country. Palestinian refugees are not allowed to work in skilled professions, cannot buy property and do not have access to health care.

Like most countries within the MENA region (Middle East and North Africa), Lebanon is at the same time a migrant receiver and a sender (Fargues 2002). Although a traditional country of emigration, it experienced an influx of low-skilled workers from South-East Asia from 1990 onwards. In 2000, more than 90 per cent of these migrants were women working as housemaids (Baldwin-Edwards 2005).

Sri Lankan housemaids in Lebanon

There is virtually no documented information about Sri Lankan housemaids working in Lebanon during the period of the civil war (1975-1990), although there is some evidence that Asian migrants were entering Lebanon in the 1970s: in 1974, 4.4 per cent of the foreign labour force was Asian, as against 73.9 per cent Arab (Nasr 1999). The huge migration programme into the Gulf states from the 1970s saw the most significant number of Sri Lankan (as well as Filipina, Indian, Pakistani and Ethiopian) women enter the Middle East labour market. Lebanese working in the Gulf, but also Lebanese agents inspired by a potential profitable market, brought back to Lebanon this now-customary practice, although only in small numbers during the civil war. The numbers gradually increased as the Lebanese demand for Sri Lankans in particular gained pace. It is only in the early 1990s that large numbers of migrant women (mainly Sri Lankans) started coming to Lebanon to work as housemaids: in 1994, 50.4 per cent of the foreign labour force in Lebanon was Asian vs. 43.8 per cent Arab and in 1997 the numbers were 64.7 per cent Asian and 22 per cent Arab (Nasr 1999). This important flow coincided with the first Gulf crisis (Iraq's invasion of Kuwait in 1990) that led to the evacuation of 450,000 Asian workers (Castles & Miller 2003) – of whom 100,000 Sri Lankans, mainly women, from Kuwait only (Rodrigo 1992). It is worthy of note, as well, that the year 1990 saw the end of the fifteen-year civil

war in Lebanon. Lebanon was, therefore, redeemed as a safe destination for foreign labour.

There are no official records of the migrant population present in Lebanon. The Central Administration of Statistics (CAS) publishes, since
1993, the number of work permits issued to migrants working in Lebanon. These renewable work permits are valid for a maximum of one
year from the date of issue. The CAS numbers include new and renewed permits, but leave out those who entered the country illegally
and those whose permits have expired. Obviously, these data are not a
valid measure to determine the exact number of migrants working in
Lebanon at any point in time. The CAS figures for the year 2002 show
a total of 88,733 work permits issued (of which 32,497 were to Sri Lankans and 10,183 to Filipinos), while the number of foreign workers present in Lebanon is estimated at up to 30 per cent of the official workforce of 1.3 million (Murphy 2006). The CAS figures are therefore
quite unreliable and should, according to the Sri Lankan embassy, for
example, be multiplied at least three times to reflect more realistic
numbers.

The number of Sri Lankan housemaids working in Lebanon, therefore, is hard to determine exactly. The number of the Lebanese population, for that matter, is also based on general estimations. Since the last
national population census in Lebanon was held in 1932, sample sur-
veys only are regularly conducted by both private and government research agencies. Calculating in estimates, therefore, Sri Lankan housemaids in Lebanon are around 100,000 (estimates go from 80,000 to
160,000 depending on the various sources used: the Sri Lankan embassy, NGOs, Lebanese government officials, the UN) while the Lebanese population is calculated at 3.6-4 million (Lebanese, UN and CIA
World Factbook sources). Just out of comparison, and to give an idea of
the importance of the Sri Lankan community in Lebanon, estimates
for Filipina housemaids vary between 30,000 and 40,000 and Ethiopians are estimated to be around 20,000.

What is certain, however, is that Sri Lankan housemaids have become part of the Lebanese scene. People are talking about 'too many'
Sri Lankans; here are some of my fieldwork notes:

A woman met at a friend's home: 'Yesterday, I went for a walk in
my neighbourhood. Sri Lankans were outnumbering us...'.

A man, co-owner of a café/restaurant in my neighbourhood,
commenting on the numerous wars Lebanon underwent from
1975 till recently (July 2006): 'First, we were attacked by the Palestinians, then the Syrians and now Israel... And next it'll be the Sri
Lankans...'

Jokes are being sent through the internet. I copied one in its original form:

> Falling in love with Srilankan woman: A man from Saudi Arabia fell in love with a Sri Lankan woman. He kidnapped her and took her to the desert. So when she saw all the sand she said: '*Ana no kanniss killo* [Me no sweep all of it]'.

Sri Lankans are given as an example in a 'lesson' on globalisation. On the beach one day, I pick up part of a conversation between a couple sitting not far away. The man was telling his female friend, while pointing at a Sri Lankan housemaid looking after her employers' children: 'This is globalisation, a Sri Lankan looking after Lebanese children'.

Sri Lankans have also indirectly entered the political arena. In one of the radio political talk shows, a Lebanese citizen intervenes by phone. Angry with Lebanese politicians who postponed the national dialogue till a later date, he said, among other things: 'If I explain to my Sri Lankan what these politicians are saying, and the reasons they gave for postponing the dialogue till Monday, even she will think it is crap'.

One pro-Syrian Lebanese politician, explaining how Syria was not the least worried about the United Nations Special Tribunal investigating Rafic Hariri's (the previous Lebanese Prime Minister) assassination, said on local television: 'Syria is concerned about the tribunal as much as she is with what's happening in Sri Lanka'. In 2005, following the assassination of the Lebanese Prime Minister, hundreds of thousands of Lebanese went on the streets to demonstrate. Footage was shown on TV of a Sri Lankan housemaid participating in this demonstration, shouting slogans too: 'Madame *badda* Syria out... *yalla!*' [Madam wants Syria out, come on!]. The snapshot of the housemaid holding the Lebanese flag next to her Madame was posted on many internet sites and the scene caught the interest of not just the local media. Kim Ghattas reported for the BBC News: 'And in one unforgettable scene an elderly lady, her hair all done up, was demonstrating alongside her Sri Lankan domestic helper, telling her to wave the flag and teaching her the Arabic words of the slogans'.

Finally I recall a scene I saw on TV (evening news) during the July 2006 war. Following the country's blockage, petrol was in short supply and people had to queue (sometimes for hours) in petrol stations to fill their cars. One middle-aged man, waiting in his car, angrily asks the journalist who was interviewing him: 'What kind of country is this, we wait for hours to get petrol; can you arrange for me a visa for Sri Lanka?'

The history of domestic work in Lebanon: from Arabs and Kurds to Sri Lankans

Long before Sri Lankans started appearing on the Lebanese scene (or inside households), Lebanese employers were 'served' by Arab maids. No proper study has been conducted on the history of domestic service in Lebanon or the Middle East generally. Anecdotal evidence, however, shows that, from the beginning of the twentieth century up to the civil war, Lebanese households employed local and foreign Arab women as well as Kurdish refugees. The term *Kerdiyeh* (a Kurdish woman) became a euphemism for 'maid', substituted in recent years by the term *Sirilankiyeh* (a Sri Lankan woman). In Lebanon, the Kurds were derogatorily stereotyped as being 'shabby'. A saying, *Haida il Kurdi ou haida il Heit* (here is a Kurd and here is a wall), indicated their reputation for being tough or stubborn. Another stereotypical impression suggested that Kurdish men preferred to lounge at home and relied upon their wives to work as cleaners and domestic workers (the same is said of Sri Lankan husbands today). During the same period, Lebanese women (mainly Shiites) were also employed as maids. They came from the eastern rural area of Baalbek, and were thus called *Baalbekiyeh*, or from poor families in the outlying districts of the main cities of Beirut and Tripoli.

In addition to the Kurds and Lebanese there were also many Syrian (mainly Alawites, called *alawieh*), Egyptian and some, although not many, Palestinian women from refugee camps in Lebanon working in Lebanese households. Syrian women (or rather girls) were frequently sent by their families to work and live in Lebanese households. Many were as young as nine to twelve years of age, such as Jamileh in my parental home. As one Lebanese employer I interviewed recalled: 'We had a Syrian maid at my parents' house. They used to come at what age... thirteen or less. They didn't even have their period when they came to work'. In this sense, the maid grew into adulthood within the employing household. Many left only to get married. Their parents would visit as infrequently as annually to collect their wages.

The political tensions during the civil war between the Syrians, Palestinians and Lebanese (and even between the Lebanese themselves from different religious faiths) became so intense that the Lebanese stopped employing Syrians and Palestinians (as well as Lebanese Shiites) in their homes. During the same period, the Egyptian government stopped the emigration of its women to Lebanon, not so much because of the war, but because of the social stigma attached to the occupation. As the General Security director related to me:

Egyptian authorities no longer allowed maids to come to Lebanon
or to another country. It is about reputation. Before if you said
Egyptian it meant maid. Like here, if a Lebanese marries a Filipina
it would be a big embarrassment for him. People would think he
married a maid. Before in Lebanon you had a lot of Egyptians,
and Syrians as maids. Now you can't have Syrians anymore. There
weren't too many Palestinian maids. They are paid in camps, no
need for them to work.

Two major reasons may be given to explain the replacement of Arabs
(and Kurds, who – for those who did not flee the civil war – had become largely assimilated by the 1990s) in domestic service in Lebanon.
First, Sri Lankan women worked for lower wages and were considered
more submissive. The second factor relates to the effects of the long
years of civil war in Lebanon, during which hostilities between all religious sects and factions were vehement and bloody. To bring local Arab
women, particularly from another religion or political faction, into
one's household after this period was to risk tension and conflict within the household. In a status-to-contract transformation, the employment of housemaids from Asia and Africa ushered in a new type of
temporary migrant worker replacing local and foreign Arab women.
The views of the Arab women who no longer undertook these positions
have not been studied as yet. It is certainly the case that domestic service is now associated almost exclusively with Asian and African women whose status and income levels are deemed unacceptable for
Arabs. When Lebanese women do accept to work as maids, they tend
to demand higher wages (up to three times those of Sri Lankans) and
refuse to live within the household of their employer. But more importantly, they are known (to employers) to be less compliant and less vulnerable than their Asian and African counterparts. As one Lebanese
employer told me when I asked her about her experience and preference for maids (whether Arabs or Asian):

At my parents' house, we had Lebanese and Syrians, but mostly
Lebanese maids. I prefer to bring somebody far from our country,
[so as] not to worry. The problems are closer to them [Lebanese],
the thinking... Foreigners feel that they are far. And abandoned.
There's no permanent contact [with their family]. I think that
those who understand your language and live a life close to yours,
they start to want to be like you in a way. There was a maid at my
parents' house, a Syrian; she used to say, when the phone rang
and my parents were out, she used to answer and pretend she was
the lady of the house... I don't know, I prefer a foreigner, someone
who is 'distant'. If you're saying something in the house they [Le-

banese] become more curious, want to know more. Their way of living is like yours, the habits and traditions are the same, everything is closer to them. She [Lebanese maid] might want to go out... they are more demanding maybe. Even if you allow this [her going out] ... you feel things being imposed on you. I think they [Lebanese maids] become familiar faster, because they already are citizens... They become too familiar quickly (byakhdo wij asrah). I remember from my mother when she used to go out the maid [Lebanese] would wear her clothes for example. As if she was like her. They had 'a kind of complex'. Whereas someone coming from far... for example if we go to work in the States, you put everything behind you and say: 'I'm coming to work', whatever the work is. When we travel and see Lebanese working outside their country we say: 'Lebanese will do any kind of job outside their country but they won't do them here'. So, I think, I prefer foreigners as maids...

There is also a status hierarchy in the labour market for foreign housemaids. Filipinas command the highest monthly salary, approximately $200-350 for those who are living in the household and where work and residency permits, insurance and airfares are borne by the sponsor/employer. This compares with $100-125 for Sri Lankans, Ethiopians and others. There is some expectation for annual salary increases of $25 per month, but it is largely at the discretion of the employer. Generally, the wages remain fixed for the period of the contract, normally two to three years. Women from the Philippines are deemed superior because they tend to be better educated, are more likely to speak English and have a reputation for being cleaner, more efficient and more trustworthy. Sri Lankan women are more likely to come from poor rural areas and have little or no education or experience with items such as household electrical appliances. Thus, more on-the-job training is required of the employers. As one Lebanese employer complains:

> Some of them [Sri Lankan housemaids] ... I had one who didn't know how to go to the bathroom. 'What's toilet paper?' She didn't know how to use it. Once, I came home, the water had flooded in the house. She stayed from morning (I was out the whole day) till the evening mopping up the water. She didn't look for the cause. All she needed to do was to turn off the tap. But she didn't think of that. To tell you how limited they are. This one. The one I have is stupid.

There does not seem to be any preference for Tamil or Muslim Sri Lankans in Lebanon. Only two housemaids in my sample were Muslim – one was originally Buddhist, she remarried a Sudanese she met in Lebanon and converted to Islam – 10 per cent were Tamil and the rest Sinhalese. Agencies do not specify such categories and it is rather unlikely that most Lebanese employers are even aware of the existence of such differences. In the Gulf region, however, the Muslim Sri Lankan population is overrepresented, up to 23 per cent (Brochmann 1993). This could be explained by the GCC nationals' preference for Muslim housemaids.

Legal and administrative arrangements pertaining to domestic work in Lebanon

Formally, a housemaid has to be 'sponsored' into Lebanon. That is, in order to be able to enter the country on a working visa, she has to be invited from the Lebanese side, either through an agency or on request by an individual employer. Lebanese agencies can either use the intermediary services of their Sri Lankan counterparts or they can work on their own, going there and recruiting women themselves.

The Ministry of the Interior's General Security Department is in charge of controlling the entry, presence and departure of foreigners in Lebanon. Migrant workers in Lebanon are classified into four categories. Category 1 encompasses skilled workers (for example, a director of a company); yearly government taxes for the residency visa amount to four million Lebanese pounds ($2,667). Sri Lankan housemaids belong to the fourth and lowest category (servants); yearly taxes amount to $550 per year. Taxes for Sri Lankan men, by comparison, are around $900 per year. They fall under Category 3 and are considered 'workers' (aamel) and not servants, even if they are employed as cleaners.

A Lebanese sponsor (or agent) should first get a pre-work authorisation from the Ministry of Labour and Social Affairs to be able to bring the housemaid into the country. He/she should have a photocopy of the housemaid's passport. Sponsors are also asked to deposit $1,000 at the Banque de l'Habitat (a government housing bank) to guarantee the payment of government taxes and an airline ticket to send the housemaid back home. This money is refundable upon the termination of the housemaid's contract. Following the Ministry of Labour's acceptance of the file, the housemaid is given a residency visa for three months by the General Security Department. The name of the sponsor is stamped on the visa. These 'three-month trials', according to government sources, are designed specifically to provide the sponsor with enough time to go through the legal procedure and paperwork and decide

whether to keep the housemaid for two or three years or not. Within those three months, the sponsor should present a full set of documentation to the relevant government departments in order to obtain the one-year residency and working visas for the housemaid (theses visas can be renewed each year) or else send the housemaid back to her country. These documents are:
- the real passport of the housemaid with the stamp of the port of entry (Beirut airport);
- a health certificate stating she is in good health following a medical check-up the housemaid has to undertake (Sri Lankan laboratory test results are not recognised in Lebanon). The check-up includes the following tests: AIDS, hepatitis, STD, tuberculosis and pregnancy; and
- one-year medical insurance (again, renewable each year).

The housemaid is required to sign a contract, drafted in Arabic, in front of a notary public (again, the initial contract signed in Sri Lanka is not recognised in Lebanon).

Agency fees in Sri Lanka are paid by the Sri Lankan women wishing to migrate. The Lebanese agency's fees are borne by the Lebanese employer if he/she chooses to use its services. There is no official migration programme in Lebanon and therefore private employment agencies, together with agencies in the sending countries, organise the flow of migrant workers into the country. Agency fees in Sri Lanka are around $200 (many women borrow the money and are therefore indebted before they even leave their home country). In Lebanon, the sponsor currently pays the Lebanese agency $1,000 to $1,200. It was only recently that these charges for Sri Lankans were reduced from $1,500 because of the economic recession and the competitive increase of agents who have entered the business. These fees cover the cost of the airfare, government charges (initial three-month residency visa) and agency commissions. In addition to these costs, the employer must pay separately for the residency and work permits, notary fees and insurance (to be renewed each year), which in total amount to $550 to $600.

Recruitment agencies in Lebanon usually have arrangements with agents in Sri Lanka. Although the costs and fees of agents may vary, as there are no price-fixing or government price-ceiling regulations in Lebanon, I will focus on one Lebanese agent here who was willing to disclose information on his financial arrangements. The agent was chosen because he is one of five elected representatives of an informal association of Lebanese agents in the industry who are lobbying for regulatory reforms; and he has a reputation for being relatively honest. This agent pays his Sri Lankan agent $500 for each 'girl'. This includes around

$260 for a one-way airline ticket to Beirut, leaving $240 commission for the Sri Lankan agent. As he states: 'Some agencies take less money but they send bad quality. I am paying a lot because I get good things (sic)'. As for his profit: 'This year, eight months have passed, I brought more than 200. We are old in this business. People trust us. We make profit for each girl: $300 net. But there are many accidents, losers...' If my calculations are right, his average monthly profit is $7,500, net as he says. Many have accused agents of being the real 'traffickers' of human beings. This issue is worth elaborating but I choose not to do so in the present research.

There are currently around 150 recruitment agents licensed by the Ministry of Labour in Lebanon and a small number who operate illegally. Licensed agents are required to lodge a $35,000 bond with the government to bring in 300 housemaids per year. In 1997, there were only twelve licensed agents with over 100 conducting business illegally. The Lebanese agencies prepare small dossiers that include various demographic details and a photograph of the housemaid so the sponsor can choose. Employers' preferences, discussed later in this book, seek to maintain power and control over housemaids.

Since 1998, General Security have enforced the following regulations to try to limit the illegal entry of housemaids, as well as trace the correspondent sponsors should problems arise with the migrants. First, the housemaid's port of entry to Lebanon has to be Beirut airport. Second, agencies cannot bring housemaids in groups; every housemaid has to have a specific sponsor to be able to come to Lebanon (agencies used to bring housemaids under fictional names and false addresses and subsequently find them a sponsor). Third, only the sponsor (not the agents and not even lawyers, as many lawyers acted as brokers for the agencies) can pick up the housemaid upon her arrival at the airport. That way, the name and address of the sponsor are recorded onto a computerised database at the airport by General Security officers.

It is important to note here that, when the employer picks up the housemaid, she is usually called by General Security at the exit gate. General Security at this point will be in possession of the housemaid's passport, but will hand it directly to the employer. In general, the employer keeps it with him/her for the length of the housemaid's stay. There is no clear law in Lebanon forbidding the confiscation of a passport. As one lawyer, who works closely with an NGO that assists housemaids in Lebanon, notes: 'It is a matter of "jurisprudence", the decision depending entirely on the judge'. The housemaids are then taken 'home' by their employers.

Three categories of housemaid

Sri Lankan housemaids in Lebanon may be classified into three categories with different living and working conditions. A housemaid may
either be a 'live-in', a 'freelancer' or a 'runaway'. A live-in resides within
her employer's household for a period of two to three years. She can be
brought into the country through an agency or by a sponsor directly.
The sponsor is responsible for all the financial costs of her stay (i.e. papers, health insurance, clothing and food). Her presence with the employer renders her living conditions harder, as she is on call 24 hours a
day, and conflicts can arise more frequently when living in this way.
The employer can (and usually does, as my research shows) control
and limit her freedom of movement, her contact with others – including her family – the quantity and quality of her food, her hours of sleep
and so on. The employer usually also keeps the housemaid's passport
and other papers, making it impossible for her to leave the country at
will. It is, as noted above, up to the sponsor to renew her work and residency papers as well as her medical insurance each year. If the permits expire, the Sri Lankan would be staying in Lebanon illegally and,
if caught by General Security or the police, could be imprisoned ('detained') and deported at a later stage. A housemaid cannot change employers, unless the employer agrees and the Lebanese authorities allow
for the 'release' to take place. The transfer of employers, allowed prior
to 1998, is illegal since that date and can only take place now under
special 'amnesty' periods arranged by General Security. The housemaid
is also obliged to finish her contract even if she no longer wishes to
work. Confiscation of the passport and the withholding of wages are
means to ensure this. The employer who has acquired the services of
an agency has the luxury of changing his or her mind and changing
housemaids within the first three months of the contract. This is the
agency's 'guarantee'.

Freelancers' living and working conditions are much less controlled.
The main difference is that they live independently (either renting, or
staying in a room in exchange for services rendered) and work on an
hourly basis (receiving between $3.30 and $4 per hour) for different
employers. They have the freedom to withdraw their services as they
wish. Of course, to remain within the law the freelancer must have a
sponsor. Most freelancers entered Lebanon with sponsored, live-in contracts. However, when the contract finished (or they 'ran away' before
it did), they decided to remain in Lebanon with the support of a 'fake'
sponsor who annually arranges their permit papers at their cost. These
remain legal. Some Lebanese have taken advantage of this as a prosper-
ous business, charging up to $1,200 annually (while these papers only
cost around $550) to act as sponsor for an individual housemaid. There

have been a number of cases where this sponsorship money has been taken, but no papers were arranged and the passport was not returned. To my knowledge, no one has been prosecuted for such fraud. It is important to note that, in most cases, the freelancer cannot prove that she had given money to get her papers regularised as these 'fake' sponsors rarely give receipts. In such cases, the housemaid is usually too scared to go to the police because of her illegal status and the risk of arrest and deportation. I tried personally to help Mali, a freelancer who used to work at my mother's house, to get her money back from a man who was supposedly going to renew her permits. I called him many times, I even tried to go to his place but I had to give up and tell Mali that the $1,000 she gave this man to act as her sponsor was simply gone. It was Mali's word against his, as no receipt was signed. Mali, at least, was luckier than others: she got her passport back. When I told a General Security officer what had happened and asked whether or not he could help, he simply replied: 'Kharja!' (Good for her!).

The third category is the 'runaway'. These women are former live-in housemaids who have decided for various reasons (mainly abuse and withholding of payments) to leave the house of their employer. They take refuge in embassies, NGOs and sometimes with their compatriots. As soon as she leaves her sponsor, the housemaid is automatically rendered illegal. The employer usually notifies General Security, as he or she is responsible for the housemaid's stay and her repatriation home. The runaway is left with two choices. She either goes back home or finds a new sponsor. In the first option, she must succeed in retrieving her passport from her employer (who sometimes 'sells' it to her or just refuses to return it) or she must get a laissez passer from her embassy. In the second option, she must again succeed in retrieving (or 'buying') her passport back in order to then find (and only during 'amnesty' periods) a new sponsor to 'live-in' with or a 'fake' one if she chooses to work as a freelancer.

Finally, foreign housemaids generally are at a disadvantage because labour law in Lebanon does not protect them. Labour laws, in general, are not applicable to the private household and do not cover occupations such as domestic work. Migrant housemaids are therefore at the mercy of the marketplace and their particular employers with regard to working conditions and treatment.

Moreover, it is worthy of note that Lebanon, despite the fact that it has contributed to the composition of the Universal Declaration of Human Rights (the preamble of the Lebanese Constitution in fact reasserts Lebanon's commitment to this Declaration) as well as ratified all major human rights conventions – such as the International Covenant on Civil and Political Rights (ICCPR), the International Covenant on Economic, Social and Cultural Rights, the International Convention on the Elimination of All Forms of Racial Discrimination, the Convention on the Elimination of All Forms of Discrimination Against Women (CEDAW), and the Convention on the Rights of the Child (CRC) – it has *not* ratified The International Convention of the Protection of the Rights of All Migrant Workers and Members of their Families nor any International Labour Organization (ILO) conventions addressing the issue of migrant workers (such as the Migration for Employment Convention or The Migrant Workers Convention). As Young (1999) points out, despite Lebanon's *laissez faire* standpoint and free market economy, the country has been reluctant to open the door to any external pressure relating to the refugees and migrants it harbours. Lebanon's government views these numerous conventions to be in contradiction with the preservation of its political and national interests.

Book structure

The next chapter covers the various research methods used and fieldwork problems encountered in this study. It describes following the two main stages of my fieldwork: before and after coming to the University of Sussex. It explains how both quantitative (SPSS) and qualitative research tools (in-depth interviews and participant observation) were fundamental to my work. It also describes the numerous problems met along the way, especially those relating to accessing Sri Lankan interviewees. Other problems (whether ethically or emotionally rooted) are raised as well. Finally, the chapter gives a general portrayal of my sample of 90 interviewed housemaids, by way of introducing these women to the reader and setting up the frame for further data analysis throughout the remainder of the book.

Chapter 3 discusses gender issues in relation to female migration as addressed in the literature and by me. The first part introduces, in general terms, the importance of gender as a social and cultural issue in need of further attention in migration studies. The second part analyses, in more detail, the gender-based power struggles and acquisitions brought about by the international migration of women entering into domestic work. It first questions whether domestic work is in fact considered as real 'work' and discusses the 'need' and demand for domestics. It then elaborates on the conflicts of interest and power struggles that arise within the household between the two women who are the key actors in this relationship, as employers try to control and 'manage' their domestics. Power acquisitions, for domestics, are also discussed as possible benefits resulting from migration. Finally, issues relating to 'transnational' motherhood are covered.

Issues of power, resistance and racism are increasingly addressed in studies on domestic work held by migrant women of 'colour'. Chapter 4 gives an overview of some of these issues present in the literature which are, again, supplemented with my own analyses and data. This chapter is divided into three parts. The first and second parts cover the forms of power female employers have over their domestics and the various means by which domestics attempt to resist this power, as raised by a number of scholars within the literature on domestic work. Racism issues, which are unavoidable in such a setting, are raised in the last part.

Chapter 5 develops the theoretical framework I base my research upon: Bourdieu's 'symbolic power', as well as the habitus concept directly linked to it. The first two parts of the chapter develop these two notions theoretically. The remaining two parts are empirically based and organised as follows: first a detailed 'profile' of the 90 Sri Lankan housemaids I interviewed in an attempt to uncover the baggage or habitus of these women and comprehend why symbolic violence seems to affect them more than others, and second a detailed and empirical description of the way symbolic violence is used by Lebanese employers to control their Sri Lankan housemaids in their daily lives.

As women exercise their power, other women resist it. Chapter 6 develops my second theoretical framework: 'everyday forms of resistance' as raised by Scott. As with the previous chapter, the first part is theoretical. The second, empirical, part shows how Sri Lankan women in Lebanon use everyday forms of resistance to limit their employers' powers. The consequences of such acts of resistance are also discussed.

Finally, Chapter 7 explores, in its first part, a number of 'solutions' aimed at improving the housemaids' living and working conditions in host countries, while stressing their limited efficiency and practice. The second part revisits the special relationship between the Madame and her housemaid.

2 My journey into the field

Approaching the field

My fieldwork officially started in 2000 and ended in 2003. It comprised two time frames (2000-2001 and 2002-2003) of information-gathering and intensive interviewing, prior to and after my DPhil registration. These time frames are in no way illustrative of 'a linear model with a beginning, a middle and an end' (Burgess 1984: 31). As I said, my fieldwork 'officially' ended in 2003. But has it really ended and does it ever? As I am writing these words, I receive a phone call from a friend who seemed upset. When I asked her what the matter was, she replied: 'I am going to kill her'. She was talking about her newly arrived housemaid, who was not properly following orders. She went on, explaining to me how difficult it was to 'train' housemaids. In this and in many other ways, I often had access to unsolicited information that was particularly insightful due, in part, to its spontaneous nature. But this was only a limited part of the 'free' access to information and knowledge I gathered. This 'invisible' community was, actually, highly visible. I saw housemaids wherever I went, on the beach sweating in the heat (they are not allowed to swim in beach resorts in Lebanon), on the streets, in restaurants (Lebanese employers sometimes take their housemaids with them when they eat out on Sundays), on balconies (for those who were hardly allowed out) or at a friend's house drinking coffee served by the Sri Lankan housemaid. I also overheard people talking about their housemaids. Housemaids, in fact, have become one of the 'salon subjects' in Lebanon. Here are two examples from my field diary.

> A night out at a friend's place for dinner. Early on, the women gathered at one side of the living room and started talking about housemaids. The hostess was complaining: 'I didn't cook, we're going to order take-out. My housemaid left me two weeks ago. She went back to Sri Lanka after eight years'. One guest acquiesces: 'Poor you. It's OK, don't worry. The important thing is that we are together. When my Sri Lankan left after eleven years, I was totally lost. I didn't even know where she put the cleaning

products. For a woman to be happy she has to have a housemaid'.
And the women went on, exchanging their experiences with
housemaids: 'Freelancers are liars'; 'You have to be careful, lock
everything because they steal'; Lebanese maids are expensive and
snobs', et cetera, et cetera. At one point, I stopped listening; this
was my night out to relax.

Another night out in a restaurant. On the table next to mine sat
three couples. At one point, I heard the word 'housemaids' so I
eavesdropped and managed to hear the last part of the conversation. One woman was telling the others: 'The Madame goes out of
the house. After a while, she phones the housemaid and tells her
what to do: "Put the vegetables in the fridge, cook some rice, et cetera". The housemaid goes: "Yes, Madame, yes, Madame" [the
story-teller was imitating the tone of the housemaid]. Then, at the
end, the housemaid asks: "Who's calling please?" Everybody at the
table laughed.

The scenes I observed did not always involve Sri Lankans but housemaids from other nationalities as well. I did not dismiss these references to other groups and took notes, believing they were rather enlightening as to how housemaids are treated in general in Lebanon.
The two incidents described below involved Ethiopian housemaids.
   I was visiting a friend who was staying in a chalet in a beach resort
outside Beirut. We were having coffee inside when her ten-year-old son
came in crying, holding his leg with one hand and shouting: 'A maid
in the alley kicked me'. My friend and I rushed outside. Three Ethiopian housemaids were standing there with a few kids (the children of
their employers). The boy pointed out the housemaid who kicked him.
My friend looked at me and said angrily: 'What should I do now? Shall
I slap her a couple of times?' I suggested she first listened to the
housemaid's side of the story. The housemaid explained that the boy
started kicking the two-year-old baby girl she was taking care of. When
she intervened to stop him he started kicking her so she kicked him
back. She said: 'I'm not scared, I tell the truth'. The boy admitted to
kicking the little girl but he did it only because 'she happened to be in
his way'. My friend said to the housemaid: 'Nobody hits my children,
you understand, nobody'. She then asked for the name of the housemaid's Madame and chalet number and declared that she was going to
ask the administration of this beach resort to forbid housemaids from
meeting outside the chalets. I tried to object: 'Why can't they meet, they
need to have fun too', but she stopped me: 'You don't know everything,
you don't know how many problems these housemaids create', and
went inside with her son (who, throughout this whole episode, was in-

sulting the housemaid in front of us). I stayed a while talking to the housemaids. One of them told me: 'Madame, it is not fair, the boy hit her. Why aren't we allowed to meet together?' I replied that indeed it was unfair but that the housemaid, instead of hitting the boy, should have looked up his mother and asked her to restrain her son, or perhaps go to her employer to let her know how a boy hit her little girl. I left wishing them good luck.

One final example: I was walking on the streets of Beirut one day when I heard shouting: across the street, a man was beating an Ethiopian housemaid. I ran towards them, as did a man who happened to be there too. We both interfered and asked the man to let go of the housemaid, but he wouldn't, he just stopped hitting her. It turned out he was the chauffeur of the housemaid's former employer from whom the housemaid had run away a few months ago. He then called his female employer on his cell phone and shouted: 'Madame, I got her, I got her...' The housemaid was pleading with us to help her get away from this man but there was not much we could do, except perhaps call the police. The police were indeed called, but by the offender, not by us. The officers grabbed the housemaid, put her in a jeep and took her away. The chauffeur was ecstatic; he claimed that the housemaid left one day with Madame's jewellery and cash. 'She was a thief and a liar, I've been looking for her for a while now'. I left the scene feeling helpless and angry. There was nothing I could do: write perhaps, as I am doing now; let people know what was really happening in my country. Yes, but what good would that do the Ethiopian who was taken away by the police? And what was the real story? Let us assume, as the man said, that she did steal and run away from her employer's household, but did she deserve such treatment? I remembered the words of a human rights activist with whom I spoke on the phone to try to set up an interview. She categorically refused to see me: 'You academics, all you do is write; we act – I have no time to waste with you'. My only comfort that day was that I was not the only one running to the housemaid's rescue.

I do not mean to say that I witnessed things worth noting every time I went out, but it was the case more often than I initially thought, or probably even wished for. I never imagined I would reach a point of 'saturation' when it came to gathering data for my work (whether sought or not), but I did. Working on the same subject for a long time (in my case, more than six years) is enlightening but also hazardous. I had to 'drop out' for periods of time and concentrate on the immense amount of data already gathered, while restraining myself from adding endlessly to it. The interest and curiosity re-emerged after these necessary small 'breaks' and I was able to reopen my eyes and ears to incidents.

Research methods

Let me now turn to the core of my research methodology. In view of
the focus of my research and its complexities, it appeared to me that
only a combination of (mainly) qualitative and (supporting) quantitative methods could create a deep understanding of the issues involved.
This study explores various aspects of labour and human relationships;
it deals with questions of gender, violence, exploitation, resistance and
many others. My research is based on trying to uncover all aspects, at
times contradictory, of the issues at stake. I needed to look at things
from the housemaid's point of view but also from the employer's, be
attentive to the exploited and the exploiter, and uncover acts of resistance as well as of violence. I also wanted to show how roles can sometimes appear to be fixed but still be intertwined and, to a certain extent,
interchangeable. I could not explore one side at the expense of the
other, nor use one method at the expense of the other. As Burgess
(1984: 3) notes, while qualitative research 'has the virtue of highlight-
ing particular dimensions of the research process it often does so at
the expense of other methods'. I relied, therefore, on a *triangulation of
method* by 'mixing qualitative and quantitative styles of research and
data' (Giddens 2001: 125). For the quantitative style, I chose the social
survey design: data from the interviews with 90 Sri Lankans were
coded and entered into the computer using SPSS. Descriptive statistics
were used in the elaboration of the data, and I present a brief statistical
profile of my interview sample at the end of this chapter. But these interviews were also at the core of my qualitative analysis. And as a
further part of the qualitative approach, I applied various research tools
such as participant observation, case studies and collection of documents. As is often found in interview-based research, people often answer in terms of what they think (or want me to think) they should be
doing. Reality, or a glimpse of it, has a much better chance of being attained through 'hard' data backed by 'softer' information, in my case
gathered mainly through participant observation. As I noted before,
this latter research tool was the easiest to use; or rather, hard to avoid.

I also interviewed twenty Lebanese housewives and analysed the data
qualitatively. I taped the interviews and transcribed them later. The difference in numbers is accounted for by the fact that the agency at stake
here are the Sri Lankan housemaids themselves; the Lebanese side is
only considered in its relation to the housemaid side. I also held 30 interviews, as well as numerous informal meetings, with other key actors
involved in the subject. I used two types of interview schedule: one for
the Sri Lankan housemaid and another for the Lebanese female employer. For all the other interviews (human rights activists, NGO staff,
embassy staff, etc.), I wrote down the relevant questions before each

meeting – depending on the person I was interviewing – following a less structured interview guide. I also met informally on numerous occasions with many of my contacts throughout the years to simply 'stay in touch' and update my data.

I started with what could be considered as a pilot study. I interviewed ten Sri Lankan housemaids, using a semi-structured questionnaire I constructed from scratch for the purpose of the study. With their permission, I taped the interviews and then transcribed them. It was easy to find ten housemaids who were willing to talk to me. I started with the housemaid who worked for us at the time and she referred me to her friends and relatives. Following the pilot study, I modified the interview schedule to its final form, as I felt that some questions needed to be omitted and others added. I also decided not to tape the housemaid interviews anymore; it took too long to transcribe them and I wanted to interview a large number to get some sort of statistical overview. Instead, I left long spaces following each question in order for the answers to be written almost word by word on the schedule. Most of the questions were open-ended. I wanted to be able to extract from these questionnaires straightforward answers that I could then code on SPSS, and also life stories that I would, later on, analyse qualitatively.

The housemaid questionnaire I used for the 90 interviews comprised 100 questions and followed the structure below. The interview followed a simplified chronological life-course perspective, starting with personal details and life in Sri Lanka, then moving to the migratory experience in Lebanon, and ending with future plans.
– Demographics of the Sri Lankan housemaid
– Life in Sri Lanka:
   • Living and working conditions, relationship with family, husband, children, etc.
   • Reasons for migrating
   • Pre-departure: travel and administrative arrangements in Sri Lanka
– Migratory experience in Lebanon:
   • Administrative arrangements
   • Living conditions
   • Working conditions
   • Contact with home
   • Contact with peers
   • Remittances
   • Details regarding Lebanese employers
   • Relationship with employers
   • Problems encountered
– Future plans

As I use the concept of habitus as a key notion framing my research questions, I needed to get as many details as possible about where the housemaids came from, their lives in Sri Lanka, violence in their households, the economic situation, etc. And as I use 'symbolic violence' as another key concept, I needed to ask as many questions as I could about the daily lives of the housemaids in Lebanese households; whether or not they had the freedom to eat, go out, etc.

The Lebanese female employer questionnaire used to interview twenty employers included 74 questions (again, mostly open-ended ones), and was set according to the following sequence:
– Demographics of the Lebanese housewife
– Relationship with her family (parents, husband and children)
– History relating to the employment of housemaids (at her parents' household as well as her own)
– Administrative arrangements in Lebanon with regards to the employment of a housemaid
– Reasons for employing a housemaid
– Working conditions of the housemaid (tasks and responsibilities)
– Living conditions of the housemaid (sleep, food, outings, etc.)
– Relationship/treatment of the housemaid.

Even though the two interview schedules followed a specific set of questions, I never abided by them completely. Depending on the person I was interviewing and the setting available, I more or less improvised as I went along, adding new questions, probing and most of the time disrupting the order (as well as the initial formulation) of the questions I had written down. I always asked all the questions I needed to ask, but I allowed myself to simply follow the flow of the conversation as it developed.

In the field: first stage

I first started (in 2000) by making contacts and interviewing most of the key actors associated, directly or indirectly, with migrant workers. This involved discussions with NGO representatives who were assisting housemaids in trouble, members of international organisations, human rights lawyers, Lebanese government officials and deputies, Lebanese economists, General Security (the force responsible for state security and in charge of controlling the 'foreign presence' in Lebanon) director and staff, Sri Lankan ambassadors (two over the years of my fieldwork), labour attachés, researchers and human rights activists engaged in the field and recruitment agencies' directors. This took some time, as I had no idea, then, that so many people were involved in the subject and, apart from a few, I did not know which doors to knock on. But the snowball method worked wonders and my informants' list grew rapidly: 'Did you see Sister Angela yet?' 'No, who's Sister Angela?' 'She's the Sri Lankan nun who heads the Laksehta centre, you should definitely meet her...'. I taped most of the conversations (I use here the word conversation intentionally as, even though I did prepare questions ahead of time, I let the interview flow naturally) conducted with the interviewees stated above, with their authorisation of course, and later transcribed them. I had, with many, a long association over the years. I saw them on many occasions, pursuing informal talks that were helpful in keeping the contacts 'alive' and the information flowing.

Of all these contacts, many were crucial in determining the course of my fieldwork: especially Father Martin, Sister Angela and the Sri Lankan ambassador at the time. The first two belonged to the Pastoral Committee of Asian-African Migrants (PCAAM), an NGO that helps migrant housemaids with the numerous problems that many encounter. PCAAM was formally established in 1997 under the aegis of Caritas, the international confederation of Catholic organisations. Under the direction of Bishop Paul Bassim and the day-to-day coordination of Father Martin McDermott, PCAAM administers social, legal and religious assistance to migrant workers. PCAAM had established a rudimentary database of the cases they had dealt with in the twelve-month period from March 1999 to March 2000. Some 406 cases of assistance were entered into a computer by Father Martin, who graciously agreed to give me a copy of his database. This seemed a great opportunity, but I was soon disillusioned. Unfortunately, the data proved to be of little use: they were too sketchy and inconsistent. Some cases, for example, comprised demographic information regarding the housemaid, while others did not; not all had the entry date of the housemaid to Lebanon, etc. Moreover, when talking to Father Martin, I soon discovered his obvious bias against Lebanese employers. According to him, the equation was simple: Lebanese Madames are the abusers and housemaids, the victims. On top of that, Sri Lankans constituted only a small proportion of the cases catered for: of the 406 cases, 234 (58 per cent) were Filipina housemaids and only 21 (5 per cent) Sri Lankans. This difference can be accounted for by the fact that Father Martin worked closely with Sister Amelia, a Filipina nun who runs the Afro-Asian Migrant Centre (AAMC) based in Beirut. I had to look for other ways to gather information. From that point on, I decided to construct my own data.

Another NGO I came across (also through Father Martin) was the Afro-Asian Migrant Centre (AAMC), managed by Sister Amelia, a nun from the Daughters of Charity order, who arrived in Lebanon from the

Philippines in 1987. This centre also helps migrant housemaids (mainly Filipinas) by providing a range of welfare services and acting as a central meeting place where religious services and recreational functions are coordinated. I thought my contact with Sister Amelia would help me get access to women for interviewing purposes. This, however, proved difficult. First, very few Sri Lankans were assisted by this centre (probably because Sister Amelia is herself from the Philippines) and, second, the appointments scheduled to take place at the centre were subsequently cancelled. I showed up for the interviews on several occasions to find out that Sister Amelia was out. Various excuses were given every time: an emergency case came up, a last-minute meeting elsewhere, etc., but I was never told upfront that I was not welcome to conduct my interviews there. I finally gave up and looked for another source for my data.

This led me to the Laksehta centre run by a Sri Lankan nun from the Bon Pasteur order, Sister Angela. She provided another refuge, more or less exclusively for Sri Lankan women in suburban Beirut. Laksehta was originally established in 1988 by a very active Lebanese Catholic priest, Father Selim Rizkallah (whom I interviewed later on), who visited places like Sri Lanka and Ethiopia to learn the languages and subsequently produce radio programmes on the Voice of Charity radio station in the Sinhalese, Tamil and Ethiopian languages. Some indication of the kinds of activity at Laksehta is provided in a detailed report that Sister Angela shared with me (Laksehta 2000). The activities vary: accommodating women within the safe house, providing legal assistance and medical care, organising mass on Sundays, retrieving passports from employers, assisting in the repatriation process (this includes the arrangement of airline ticket and tax clearances), helping women in finding employment and providing a postal service where mail may be received and sent from the premises of the centre, visiting prisons, etc. On a regular basis also, Sister Angela or another representative of the Laksehta visits the detention centre of General Security, supplying food and other necessities to Sri Lankan detainees.

The Laksehta centre was crucial in my access to information. I first met Sister Angela for a formal interview. She was a bit reluctant to meet with me again when I suggested further visits to the centre: she had more urgent matters to attend to than talk to a researcher who could only be in her way. I did manage, however, to convince her of both my discretion and my primary academic interest, and promised not to interfere with the centre's activities. Our rapport evolved positively (she even called me at times asking me to come and 'witness' the new arrival of a housemaid), though never to a point of full trust; she kept her guard at all times. She did, however, allow me to take notes from her latest annual reports detailing the centre's activities (Laksehta

2000). We agreed that I would use the centre as the locale for my field-work and interview Sri Lankan housemaids who had taken refuge there. These were 'runaways' with no place to go, who were usually directed to Laksehta by other compatriots. I managed to interview three women but, again, this experience was not wholly successful. The interviews were taking too long, privacy was impossible to attain (the centre was small, only a couple of rooms crowded with women) and I was therefore unable to conduct my interviews on a one-to-one basis. In short, I had a constant feeling of being 'in the way'. It was also my impression that I was not getting accurate information; the women were scared, tired and cautious. Moreover, I had difficulty communicating with them. This was due in part to the fact that I did not speak their language but also to my inexperience at the time. I was unable to get my message across, literally; I had not mastered the art of juggling between Arabic and English, using small sentences and simple words to make myself understood. More importantly, I did not possess at the time the art of interviewing, and was unable to create a rapport of trust between myself and the interviewee. I was simply not at ease and, therefore, nor were they. Months (and years) later, I became quite 'professional' at that task. I learned, retrospectively, that the setting (where the interviews take place) was crucial in determining the outcome of the interview. But I learned above all that, in order for others to confide in me, I needed to have confidence in myself and in what I was doing. This developed with time as I became more knowledgeable about the field and the subject I was addressing.

But going back to the interviews in question, and in an attempt to resolve the communication gap, I asked Achini (a former housemaid who became Sister Angela's assistant) to act as a translator for me. Yet again, I was quickly disillusioned. Achini would not only respond on behalf of the interviewees but would, when she did allow them to talk, summarise in very few words long sections of their answers. In short, the answers were not valid, despite my multiple probing questions. One example is given below:

Me:	Why did she come to Lebanon?
Achini:	Poor family. Living with her parents in Sri Lanka. Six brothers and sisters. She's in the middle. She's the only one in Lebanon.
Me:	Does she know of anybody who came to Lebanon before?
Achini:	She knew one lady who came to Lebanon and now is back in Sri Lanka. She was happy here.

Me:	Did she go to the agency in Sri Lanka and tell them: 'I want to go to Lebanon or I want to work anywhere?'
Achini:	No, she doesn't know what country.
Me:	When did she find out she was coming to Lebanon?
Achini:	When she came Madame told her: 'You're in Lebanon'
Me:	She didn't know she was in Lebanon?
Achini:	No.
Me:	She didn't know in what country she was in?
Achini:	No. Agency send like this.
Me:	What about a contract there? They didn't tell her?
Achini:	No. They didn't give her any detail.
Me:	She didn't have somebody with her to take her to the airport, to take her to the agency? A sister...?
Achini:	There is one Sri Lankan girl, she helped her to go to agency, airport...
Me:	Is the agency in the city or in the village?
Achini:	In Colombo.
Me:	Did her friend tell her she was coming to Lebanon?
Achini:	Yes, her friend said 'Come to Lebanon, I know Lebanon, we can work outside, we can make money'.
Me:	So her friend was coming to Lebanon with her?
Achini:	Yes.
Me:	So she knew she was coming to Lebanon?
Achini:	Yes.

This small interviewing experience at the very beginning of my fieldwork was perhaps disappointing and confusing but not fruitless. This first real contact with Sri Lankan housemaids was instrumental for it highlighted numerous mistakes I was to avoid in the remainder of my field research.

Soon after these interviews took place, Sister Angela called me to tell me that she needed to cancel our arrangement. The police had raided the centre and she felt that my presence was giving it too much exposure. The interviews stopped but not our collaboration or, I should say, the most important and beneficial part of this collaboration. Sister Angela's centre gave me a convenient 'cover' to enter the detention centre as well as the prisons where Sri Lankan housemaids were held. A detention centre is supposed to be a temporary place where foreign workers are held for no longer than a few days, awaiting deportation. The reality is quite different. Most women are left there for months, in difficult sanitary and living conditions. I drove Sister Angela and her assistant, Achini, to the detention centre on one of their visits there. For them I was providing transport, while I hoped to be able to go inside and talk to the housemaids detained there. Usually, one needs written approval from the forces in charge (General Security) to be able to do that. That day must have been my lucky day since the guards simply let me by, as I was carrying food and following Sister Angela. I describe, later in this chapter, the details of this visit and how it affected my work. It was also agreed as a kind of a 'trade-off' (Lofland & Lofland 1984: 40) that I teach Achini to drive (they had a car but no driver) and that I take Achini on her monthly visits to a few of the female prisons in Lebanon. I took her twice to the Tripoli prison (in northern Lebanon) and once to Baabda (in the outskirts of Beirut). Since we did a lot of 'road' together, Achini and I became somehow close. Her input was very interesting and the talks we exchanged in the car were quite enlightening. Sister Angela managed to get me, on all three occasions, an authorisation to go inside the premises of the prisons, stating that I was volunteering within the centre.

My first visit to the Tripoli prison was very interesting. Four Sri Lankan housemaids were there at the time, one sentenced to ten years in jail for poisoning her Lebanese female employer. I managed to talk to her and took some notes. We couldn't stay long so I decided to come back a second time with a tape recorder and get more details from the housemaid. When I did, again taking Achini and her provisions, I was not allowed in. Prison guards who search us before allowing us in found the tape recorder in my purse. I had no idea that these items were not allowed inside the prison premises (I should have been more vigilant) and, despite my pleading with the guards, I had to remain in the car, waiting for Achini to come out. This, again, taught me a lesson; in the future I would be more attentive to the existing regulations. Luck cannot be always on my side. The visit to the women's prison in Baabda went without pitfalls. Seven Sri Lankans were held there at the time. I observed the conditions of imprisonment, which seemed fair in comparison to the detention centre. My contact with Laksehta ended soon after, for no particular reason.

Trying to set up field bases

As I mentioned before, I needed to find a way to interview Sri Lankan housemaids following the three categories I had defined: freelancers, live-ins and 'runaways'. To remind the reader, a live-in resides within her employer's household for the length of her contract, usually three years. A freelancer lives on her own (either renting or staying in a room in exchange for services rendered) and works on an hourly basis for different employers. A 'runaway' is a live-in worker who has decided for various reasons (mainly abuse and withholding of payments) to leave the house of her employer. She usually takes refuge at the embassy, NGOs and sometimes with her compatriots, or simply turns into a freelancer. These are not mutually exclusive categories, since all 'runaways' and most freelancers were live-ins at one point in time.

I had no idea initially where and how to get my sample. I thought I could start interviewing runaways at either of the centres (Sister Amelia's or Sister Angela's). Freelancers should be easy to meet as they are 'free' with their time and movement. I planned on using a snowball sample, as I did with the pilot study, by seeking the help of the freelancer who was working at our place at the time; she would refer me to her relatives and friends working in the neighbourhood. I also hoped that I could interview live-ins at their place of work, starting with acquaintances who would allow me to enter their homes and talk to their housemaids. As both attempts at the centres failed, I decided to turn to live-ins and figure out later how to access 'runaways'. In fact, it proved difficult to enter homes to interview live-in housemaids. Permission from the employer is required in the first instance. When I did manage to interview live-in housemaids at their employers' house (three in all), I realised that the results were not conclusive. Despite reassurances of confidentiality, they were afraid to make any negative comments about their employer or their employment conditions. Therefore, I came to the conclusion that interviews with live-in Sri Lankan housemaids at their place of work were unreliable. The example below gives a vivid picture of the above issue.

> Interview with Komari: I contacted a Lebanese female employer by phone. I did not know her personally; the contact was set up through an acquaintance of mine. Upon learning that the interview with her housemaid might take one hour or more, she expressed surprise over the phone – 'She is going to stop work for an hour?' but agreed to it. When I got there, I asked to interview the housemaid privately. The employer seemed upset; she had assumed she would be present throughout the interview. My guess is that she might not have agreed to the interview if she had known this previously. I suggested that the interview be cancelled and motioned to leave but she somewhat reluctantly insisted that I go ahead with it. She then wanted to know what questions I was going to ask her housemaid. I gave her a rapid overview of my study but insisted upon the importance of confidentiality. At that point she replied: 'I know, I have a psychology degree' and stepped out of the living room, leaving me with the housemaid. Just as the

interview started, the employer's husband entered. Ignoring me, he addressed the housemaid, 'Komari, if there are any questions you don't want to answer, just don't'. I responded that this had already been explained to the interviewee. I was finally alone with Komari. She seemed scared, uptight, answering briefly while looking down at the floor. It occurred to me that the employer accepted the interview on her behalf. But did Komari want to talk to me? Of course, in the beginning, I asked her whether she wanted to go ahead with the interview and assured her that it would be quite alright if she refused. But how could she, since the employer (and I) had decided for her? Was I, under the pretext of DPhil research, 'imposing' myself upon these women? Did I manoeuvre in a way that left them no choice, just as some Lebanese employers do?

I carried on with the interview and got timid answers, sad smiles and blurry eyes. Obviously, I was not getting to the truth. I reassured Komari that I was not going to relate any of the things she was telling me to her employers or anybody else for that matter. I still couldn't get through. She had no problems, her employers were great, everything was fine. I had a feeling the picture wasn't as bright as she led me to believe. I got small hints from her (apart from her sad smiles) that confirmed my doubts: when I asked her if she called her family from time to time she said: 'No, I can't call, I didn't ask but I know I can't'. I inquired about the 'I know I can't' and she replied: 'Before the previous housemaid left, she told me everything, she was happy to leave'. When asked if she was free to eat whenever she wanted she said yes. When pushed, she admitted she had to wait for them to eat first; she eats their leftovers but the quantity is sufficient. When asked if she liked Lebanese food she replied yes. Again, when pushed she said, 'Not really, but I got used to it'. When asked how much longer she wanted to stay in Lebanon, she said she wanted to go back home: 'The contract is finished, I am so tired, physically and mentally tired'. When asked why mentally, she replied with a smile that she meant physically tired, 'It's good here but I am so tired, I want to go'.

The interview was over. The Lebanese employer stepped into the living room and dismissed the housemaid. She then asked me: 'What did she tell you, she is happy here right?' I hesitated for a moment and replied: 'Yes, she is happy here but she needs to go back to her family'. In a way, I wasn't lying; this was what Komari kept repeating. But more importantly, I did not want to jeopardise the remainder of her stay with her employers. Despite my inability to get to 'the truth', this experience

was extremely revealing: it confirmed to me some of the complex dynamics existing in the employer-housemaid setting that I will be developing in my account.

I left the employer's household that day having doubts about my
fieldwork method; I had to find yet another way to reach live-ins, but
how? The answer came from the Sri Lankan embassy, another contact
that turned out to be the most important one for my research.

In the embassy

In an interview with the Sri Lankan ambassador in Lebanon, he expressed a genuine interest in my study and offered his collaboration.
The embassy provided various services to its nationals and women with
different needs were present there: women who were 'runaways', those
who were just renewing their passports, those who were facing problems and needed diplomatic advice, or those who were just accompanying their friends. It was therefore agreed that the embassy offices
would be used as a centre for my fieldwork and interviews with all
three categories ('runaways', live-ins and freelancers) would take place
there. The embassy afforded in particular a more conducive environment in which to interview those still living with their employers.

Thus it was that I conducted interviews in 2000-2001 with 70 Sri
Lankan housemaids: 33 'runaways', seventeen live-ins and twenty freelancers, within the premises of the Sri Lankan embassy in Beirut. I
went there virtually on a daily basis for almost four months and managed to obtain not only interviews with housemaids, but invaluable information using participant observation. The Sri Lankan ambassador,
who trusted me, was very cooperative and let me sit in on most of the
cases he was dealing with. Alongside the interviews, I observed other
activities going on within the embassy, as Lebanese employers and
agents came in on a regular basis to 'claim' their housemaids. I noted
how the Sri Lankan ambassador dealt with them, as well as the way
they reacted to him.

I also watched housemaids face the employers from whom they had
'run away'. I observed the attitude of deference housemaids displayed
in front of their ambassador. I did not just observe and take notes but
helped at times (I simply could not refuse when asked to do so). I often
sat with the ambassador as he received Lebanese employers or persons
in charge of recruitment agencies, and I acted as a translator when necessary. I called Lebanese employers when asked to do so by embassy
staff or the ambassador himself and tried to get information on particular cases dealt with at the time. I never claimed to be an embassy
staff member, only specifying that I was calling *from* the Sri Lankan
embassy. What people assumed at the other end of the line was up to

them, I thought. Was that unethical? Probably not. I only listened to 'the other side of the story' and reported back to the embassy staff, who decided on what to do next.

Below are some of my fieldwork notes characterising the variety of information I gathered at the embassy alongside my interviews. The notes refer to two cases I observed and, to a limited extent, participated in. The selection represents just a small part of the total data collected in this locale.

A case of 'runaway': present at the meeting is the Sri Lankan consul, an embassy staff member (Lebanese female), the housemaid (who took refuge at the embassy two days ago), and the sponsor[1] called in by the embassy staff. Later on in the meeting, the recruitment agency director (also called by the embassy staff) responsible for bringing the housemaid from Sri Lanka joins us. The housemaid has been working in Lebanon for the same sponsor for the past twenty months. The problem is as follows: the contract of the housemaid is for two and a half years. She tried to 'run away' four times; the first time only three days after arrival. She claimed she thought she was coming to care for an old woman and found herself, instead, with a family with six children. She tried going down from the balcony twice (they live on the first floor) using a bed sheet. She was caught every time, either right away or later on by the police, who brought her back to her sponsor. She succeeded at the fifth attempt.

The meeting is set to decide whether to send the housemaid back to her employers or keep her at the embassy until she travels back to Sri Lanka. The sponsor wants her to work for him for another two months and promises to let her go home then. The housemaid wants to leave now for Sri Lanka and doesn't wish to go and work for him anymore. The housemaid is standing by the wall throughout the meeting. She has bruises on her arms and face and is very skinny. The Lebanese female staff member at the embassy addresses the sponsor, agent and myself in Arabic then translates to the consul in English (he does not understand Arabic). The housemaid relates her story to the consul: she does not know how much money has been sent to Sri Lanka. She has no address of a bank in Sri Lanka. She has three children, living now with her mother. She is 35 years old. Her husband left with another woman. The last time she ran away (this time), she escaped via the balcony, took a taxi to a Sri Lankan place where they kept her for a day then brought her to the embassy. She had worked in Kuwait for two years. She was happy there. While in Kuwait, she sent money to her husband who gambled and took another wife.

Then she went back to Sri Lanka and from there to Saudi Arabia where she worked for eight months and then ran away. The house was good, the food good, but there was no money. That's why she ran away. While in Sri Lanka (after Saudi) she was working in a rice mill. An agent came to her village and recruited people for Lebanon. She paid him 3,000 rupees to come.

Sponsor: She says 'No clothes, no food, no money'. We are used to that. This is what they are taught to say. She also says that I am 'thinking of doing something' with her (sexual hint). We will repatriate her at two years, not two and a half.

Me: Do you hit her?

Sponsor: We do not make hitting our business. I get angry with her sometimes but I don't hit her. My wife sometimes, maybe. But it's not because of that. Yes, Madame hits her. Maybe just once a month. But it is only because she upsets my wife. She dropped herself from the balcony. We live on the first floor. She ran away from our house two days ago. She was not like that. She changed these two days [looking at her, hinting that the state she is in, bruises, weak and in tears, is not their doing]. We brought her to help us not to hit her. I take her off her [meaning the wife]. Ask her. There is no problem between us. The only problem is that she runs away.

The housemaid tells the consul that she hasn't been paid nor fed and that Madame beats her.

Consul: A woman cannot change in two days. She is obviously not fed properly, beaten...

The housemaid pulls up her shirt showing her stomach to the consul. I see it too. It looks shrunk, the skin is layered. [I saw the housemaid do the same with the ambassador, except that she pulled the shirt too high and her breasts appeared. Neither she, nor the ambassador, seemed to be disturbed by that.]

Embassy staff member: Was the housemaid paid?

Sponsor: We paid her over $1,000. She asked us to keep the money to take with her. She didn't want to send any more to her husband. I will not let her leave without paying her. She is lying.

Embassy staff member: No use to try to understand the way they think. We have to step down to their level. She needs to see the money.

Housemaid: Mister good.

Sponsor: My wife is the one who deals with her. That's why. She does things on purpose to upset my wife. Let me give you an example. We had a new mop. My wife asked her: 'Where is the new mop?' She said she doesn't know. The mop was in the toilet, inside.

Embassy staff member: Maybe it is just stupidity. She must have emptied the whole bucket inside the toilet and the mop fell in too. [Whispering to me: 'What do you think of the house-maid? She is lying, right?']

Me: I don't know.

Sponsor: Residency papers, we made them the first year. The second year, no, we'll do them when she leaves. We did not know about the embassy before. We won't upset you. We upset her but not you. We were nice with her at first. First three days, she runs away. Why? Her papers are with us. She must be stu-pid to leave. Where does she want to go? Her papers are with us. Then she started being hypocrite, doing things on purpose to upset my wife.

Consul: She doesn't want to go back with you.

Sponsor: You cannot let her do as she pleases.

Me: Why not?

Sponsor: Because I paid to bring her for two and a half years. Now, I'm willing to let her go at two years. But not before. After three days, she ran away. When caught, she said that there is no food, no money. How does she know there is no money? After three days only?

Housemaid: There is no food. I never saw any money here.

When asked how much money was sent to Sri Lanka and if he had kept any receipts:

Sponsor: I don't go to the bank. My wife sends money, not me.

Consul: This housemaid has three children. She left them to come here and gain some money. It is inhumane. She is not prepared to go back with you. You neither paid her nor renewed her visa.

Embassy staff member to me [in Arabic, the consul cannot understand what she is saying]: We should not encourage them to stay here. When we did, there were 120 runaways here. They were laughing in the corridors. When they see me, they start crying. Some cases are bad, really. But most of them run away and start saying: 'He raped me', et cetera.

The housemaid claims that she eats once every three days.

Sponsor: No. She would have died. Ask her how come every time she sees me, she says she wants to leave. Not 'I want to eat'. Ask her.

The housemaid talks to the sponsor in Arabic: She calls him '*baba*', meaning dad and she refers to his wife as '*mama*', mother. She says: '*Baba* doesn't know. You go to work. *Mama* doesn't feed me, hits me. You don't know. *Baba* good, but *baba* goes to work'. She says she is locked in her room.

Sponsor: We lock her in her room. My wife closes the door on her so that she doesn't run away again. She takes her out in the house for two or three hours to work then locks her in her room again. [Looking at me]: Don't think that she is a comfort to my wife... It is true that my wife has a temper.

The recruitment agency director steps in. He was at the time the president of the committee of recruitment agencies in Lebanon.

Agent: She came from there (Sri Lanka) having in mind one thing. She knows somebody here. When she ran away, I went to her and told her: 'There is a contract, these people paid money. I fixed things'. The family is big so what? Six kids, so what? The house is not big. If every girl coming from Sri Lanka wants to work at her convenience...

Embassy staff member: You should have changed her household when the girl ran away first.

Agent: At that time, transferring sponsors was not possible. The sponsor who brings a girl on his name becomes obliged to keep her. She becomes like glue.

Sponsor: Once we slaughtered a sheep. She got upset [note: the sponsor is Muslim].

Agent: I am very careful that the money is paid. But I also ask the housemaid to do her work. [Addressing the housemaid]: Why didn't you call the office and tell me there is no food? I would have gone myself to check.

Embassy staff member [to sponsor]: Don't take her back. Send her to Sri Lanka now, not in two months. If she ran away so many times, she might do it again, or even kill herself. You don't need this kind of problem.

Sponsor: I will tell you why she is speaking like this. The neighbour's housemaid jumped from the balcony. She broke her legs and arms. Then our housemaid started threatening that she wants to jump too. One time, my wife let her. She told her, 'OK, if you want to jump, go ahead'. She went out to the balcony and then came back.

Agent [addressing the housemaid]: The first day you came you were acting, and you are still acting.

Housemaid: Madame cut my hair [a practice very common by Lebanese employers towards their housemaids].

In the end, the sponsor insisted that the housemaid go back with him, as his children had exams and she was needed. The consul refused.

The agent [to the sponsor]: No, don't take her back. Let her go. She might give you problems, run away again, et cetera.

Embassy staff member: She might even kill herself. Why do you need this hassle?

It was finally agreed (written on paper and signed by the sponsor and the consul) that the housemaid would stay at the embassy, the sponsor would go and legalise her papers, buy her a ticket to Sri Lanka, bring her full fees and come back when all this is done to the embassy (in a few days' time). The sponsor left angry. The meeting was over. End of the first case.

Another case of a 'runaway', with the ambassador, the employers (husband and wife), their son, the housemaid and myself: the sponsor does most of the talking [in English to the ambassador]; he seems very angry. The housemaid is present too, standing on the side. She looks scared, tired. The ambassador talks to her to find out why she left.

Ambassador to sponsor: It takes time, they are not too fast ... She left because she thought she wasn't paid. She's ready to go with you if you want to take her. She's stupid. She's not a bad girl.

Housemaid: I have many problems in my country.

Another sponsor sitting in the ambassador's office waiting for his turn to discuss his case with the ambassador intervenes: 'We brought them to give them Air Conditioning? They came as housemaids. All this population is stupid.'

The sponsor tells the ambassador that they are, of course, sending money to Sri Lanka. Every three months they transfer money to an account the housemaid had given them.

Ambassador: She doesn't know that. Why didn't you tell her?

Sponsor: We are not thieves. Why didn't she ask me? Why did she run away? She is a liar. I saw her speak to a man from the balcony. All I could hear is the word passport. I don't understand Sri Lanki but I understand the word passport. She was planning on going away. It is not about money. I asked her who this man was. She said there was nobody.

The ambassador confronted the housemaid with the employer's claims.

Ambassador: She denies it.

Sponsor: She is a liar.

The wife of the sponsor kept repeating on and off throughout the meeting: 'She is stupid. I knew there was something wrong with her. She is not normal'. The sponsor says that he doesn't allow her to go out on her own, always with someone from the family.

Ambassador: Do you want to take her back with you? She wants to apologise to you.

The housemaid approaches her employers and says: 'Sorry, Mister, sorry, Madame'.

The sponsor [talking to me]: She will see. She was treated very well. She couldn't ask for better. But now, it's all going to change. She will see.

They leave with the housemaid. End of case.

Emotionality and the dilemma of (non-)intervention

I witnessed numerous cases such as the ones described above. I watched and took notes but, actually, I was in a sort of dilemma. Should I have intervened more often? Should I have lectured some Lebanese employers on how to deal with their housemaids? Should I have told them that it was *not* OK to lock housemaids inside the house, to hold on to their passports, to refuse to give them one day off per week, even if the recruitment agencies told them they not only *could* but *should* refuse this ('Do not let them out on their own, do not give them a day off...')? Should I have asked some housemaids to stop lying and admit to the real reasons behind their 'running away'? Sometimes, *a posteriori*, the ambassador would ask for my opinion regarding this or that case, wondering whether I agreed with the decisions he took. What could I say? Better yet, what should I say? I decided, early on, to remain neutral. I did not agree or disagree; it was not my place to do so. I told him that he knew best, that it was not easy to decide who was wrong and who was not. One has to keep in mind that all cases were 'urgent' ones, that people (employers, agents, embassy staff, housemaids) were constantly in and out of his office, that the issues at stake involved human suffering, anger, frustration and were not easy to deal with. Did I believe he was mistaken at times by wrongfully taking the housemaids' side, that his occasional bias did not serve the Sri Lankan cause but, on the contrary, led Lebanese employers, General Security officers and agents to work against him instead of with him? For sure. Could I, should I, have said all those things? I don't think so. I was there to observe and that is what I restricted myself to doing, most of the time. I hinted to him on a few occasions that maybe, just maybe, housemaids, too, could be at fault, that things were more complex than that. But, ethically speaking, I simply could not take sides, not with (or against) him nor with (or against) Lebanese employers. Many Lebanese employers expected me to agree with them as they complained about their housemaids, denying any mistreatment on their part. They often looked at me with an air of complicity as if to say: 'You know, you must understand, you're one of us'. I discounted those calculations. Just as when, at the embassy, a Lebanese lawyer accused of sexual advances to his housemaid dismissed the allegation while looking at me in conni-vance: 'You must know (since you are Lebanese) I would never touch a Sri Lankan woman'. I pretended not to understand the hint and looked away.

Was I acting, pretending to be neutral while I was just dying inside to be able to react? The answer is no. Actually, as I said at the begin-ning, my aim was never to condemn but simply to understand what was really happening and why. Others – NGOs, human rights activists, journalists, nuns or priests – followed (probably rightfully so) another approach. Not only could I not take sides as a researcher, but I truly be-lieved (and still do) that there were no sides to take, that all sides – em-ployers, housemaids and governments of host as well as home coun-tries – were responsible. My hypothesis was that, within this complex social dynamic, roles were not fixed; they not only changed depending on circumstances but more importantly, they fed on one another, act-ing and reacting depending on how the other behaved (or should I add, was expected to behave), how the other was perceived or was made to perceive. Newspaper stories, international organisation reports, etc., were more than clear. The ones to blame were the Lebanese employers, and those to sympathise with, help and empower were housemaids. Are they mistaken? No, of course not. There are plenty of facts to sus-tain such an attitude. But should one choose to dig deeper and avoid simplifying matters into guilty and innocent parties, one might find something that is indeed more complex, more frightening and perhaps harder to solve. Power, as I said before, is not the monopoly of one group. Power, dependence and resistance sustain one another. When I started this research, my premises were not based on a moral judg-ment but simply on questions that needed to be answered. And for me to do that, I needed to observe all sides with the same eyes and write down what I saw as honestly as I could. I had opinions, of course, about particular cases. But even when I noted wrongdoings, my aim was never to condemn but to understand why and perhaps, just per-haps, be able to answer one day: 'How can this be stopped?' Because unless we do this, unless we explain the process instead of simply pin-pointing the guilty party (or parties), help and money will keep flow-ing, and various NGOs and international organisations will keep healing the symptoms instead of identifying the 'sickness' and treating it from its roots.

I shouldn't have been, but I was, at times, overwhelmed by the emotions I was bound to feel in view of the delicate issues I was researching and the often painful events I was witnessing. On one particular occasion, early on in my fieldwork, I intervened in what could be qualified as a 'non-academic' way. The incident took place on the second floor of the embassy where 'runaways' often spent the day (the embassy includes two floors in the same building). I was there, as on any regular fieldwork day, talking to housemaids. A Lebanese woman, the director of a recruitment agency, rushed into the room we were in and tried to take by force a housemaid who had 'run away' from her employers. She wanted to take her back there. The housemaid was crying, holding onto my arm, asking me to help her. I did not think, I just acted: I pushed the Lebanese woman away. She shouted: 'Who gave [you] the right to interfere?' I answered (lying): 'I work at the embassy'. I then rushed down the stairs to the ambassador's office, holding the housemaid tightly by the hand. We were followed by the Lebanese woman as well as by other housemaids there. In retrospect, the scene resembled one in a movie. We all went in and I explained to the ambassador what was happening. He dismissed the agency director stating that: 'No one takes by force a housemaid from here'. After the agent left, the housemaid started thanking me and kissing me; actually, most women there saw me as a 'heroine' and wanted to hug me. That day affected the rest of my fieldwork; I had gained, in a very unexpected and unplanned manner, the trust of Sri Lankan women there. The word got out: 'Nayla is good, you can talk to her, you should help her with her interviews'. That day, I let my emotions guide me; I was no longer, or perhaps not only, a researcher observing and taking notes, I was also a human being witnessing the unacceptable, and I did something about it.

This incident reminded me of another (previous) one that took place in the detention centre where migrant women are held (and guarded by a male guard), supposedly awaiting deportation. Not that it was a similar situation in which I personally intervened, but it was one where I got emotionally overwhelmed as well.

More than 150 women were there when I visited (many had been there for months), all in one big overcrowded room. I recalled the words of the General Security director when I interviewed him: 'The temporary detention centre in Furn El Chebback can receive 200. You have 600. I asked the army not to send me any more'. The number included both men and women of course, but I could only check the women's room: he was right to ask for a 'halt' in the arrests. I was about to enter the room when the male guard asked me whether I was really certain I wanted to step in (hinting that it was too dirty). He had just brought back a woman from 'questioning' and confided to me with a smile: 'I gave her a good beating'. I did not respond but my eyes must have betrayed me because he hastily added: 'No, no, I mean I just threatened her'. I stepped into the room. I will not go into many details; I'll just say that, in order to cross from one end to the other, I had to literally step on the women's bodies and that the sanitary conditions were appalling (one bathroom for all in an indescribable state). As soon as I got in, women started pleading with me to help them get out, giving me contact numbers of friends, agents or employers I could call. I took the numbers but did not promise them anything. I was overwhelmed by it all and tried explaining to them that I was 'just' a researcher, that they should not count on me for help, that I would try but... Words suddenly had no meaning, my role as a researcher had faded and I found myself in the middle of the crowded room, completely lost. I meant to go there and ask questions about the way they were being treated, the conditions of their arrest and the length of their stay; I ended up listening to them talking at the same time, smiling at them, nodding my head and returning hugs and kisses. I left the room, and the women in it, feeling helpless and sad, and wondering whether or not I was fit to be a researcher.

These two incidents affected me personally (as did many others but these two were key moments in my research) and probably changed the course of my fieldwork, as they might its outcome. On both occasions, I put down my researcher's hat and acted impulsively. In both instances, paradoxically, I got closer than I ever did to understanding the reasons that drove me to be a researcher in the first place. On both counts, 'subjects' were no longer 'cases' but merely, and more importantly, human beings. By allowing myself to let go, I took control of my research. It is true that 'data collection' involves 'very real human contact, which may be troublesome and confusing and can be quite disturbing' (Williamson 1996: 29). As much as sufficient (or convenient?) distance is important in all research, one should not forget, or better yet, should always make it a point to remember, that 'closeness' can also be utterly enlightening. After all: 'The best possible methodological and empirical rigour is not incompatible with sensitivity and perhaps even sentimentality towards social research subjects' (Williamson 1996: 39).

Interviewing housemaids: trust and 'truth'

Despite having found the 'ideal' locale (the Sri Lankan embassy), interviewing housemaids was not an easy task. I needed to improvise at all times, probe at practically every account, try to understand and make myself understood, build a rapport of confidence and trust. On many occasions I felt that I was not told the truth. I never appeared to doubt what was related to me but I allowed myself to probe in an attempt to get, again and always, to the bottom of things. I was sometimes (maybe more often than I thought) deceived and lied to. I was, on one particular occasion. Puspa was one of many Sri Lankan housemaids I met and interviewed at the embassy. She was particularly outspoken and seemed at ease with me. To one of my questions relating to savings, she claimed that she had no money with her and that she had sent everything to Sri Lanka except for US $700[2] deposited in a bank in Lebanon. I insisted: 'Do you have money now with you?' Puspa: 'Euh... yes. Only $50. Because I have luggage I keep the money'. Later on, and as I followed her case with General Security, I found out from Puspa herself that she had $1,900 in cash with her at the time of the interview (other than the $700 in the bank in Lebanon and the money in Sri Lanka: 'In my bank, for me $2,000'). Why hide from me the fact that she had succeeded in a way by saving some money? I recalled what Gamburd (2000) pointed out in her book on Sri Lankan housemaids who went back home: some returnees did in fact dress differently and wore jewellery, but most did not show any external sign of wealth, fearing their neighbours' jealousy. Instead, they stressed the difficult conditions they had to face abroad: hard work, little food, confinement in the employers' household, limited freedom, etc. They were supposed to have 'sacrificed' themselves in order to improve the livelihood of the families they left behind and could not admit to any positive experience encountered abroad. Was Puspa following this 'victim' trend with me? Maybe she thought that, in order to receive help, she should appear helpless and penniless. Or maybe she was simply cautious. I will return to Puspa's case later on in this chapter. Hers was a breakthrough with regards to my work, and I do not mean it all in positive terms.

How was I to trust what I was told? I remember asking Sister Amelia, in one of our meetings, whether or not she had doubts about the stories Filipinas told her when they came to her for help. She replied: 'Of course, but at the centre, we choose to believe every story'. I am not a sister; I cannot choose to believe my interviewees, even those in need of help. Moreover, the story often changed depending on the narrator: employer, housemaid or agent. Gamburd (2000) heard, during her fieldwork in Sri Lanka, three versions of the same story regarding the death of a housemaid in the Middle East. The first one came from a group of returnees: the housemaid stole from her employers and was killed by them; her poor father died six months later from the shock. The second version came from the sister-in-law of the deceased housemaid: the employers claimed that their children pushed the housemaid from the balcony; compensation money was subsequently paid to the father. The third version was related by the older sister of the housemaid: this was not a murder, the housemaid fell by accident while leaning on a balcony railing; the employers not only gave the family some compensation money, but paid for the funeral as well. Whom to believe? There is no straightforward answer. Length of the research, experience, familiarisation with the issues at stake, variation of sources and of data-gathering tools; all are necessary (yet sometimes insufficient) conditions in which to attain a somewhat realistic and truthful account of the subject studied.

With regards to interviews, probing was crucial. For example, when I asked: 'Are you being locked in?' the answer was initially no. The next question was: 'Could you leave the house as you wished?' The answer was again no. I understood then that, even if they were not locked in, i. e. the key was not turned from the outside, they were still 'locked in', meaning, unable to go out. Following this, I always asked whether or not they could leave the house *even* if the door was unlocked.

Another example was the question of age. I would usually ask for the respondent's age and write down the answer. It is only when one housemaid answered 'Do you want my real age or my passport's?', that I realised that I was sometimes writing down false information. I then had to add the question: 'Is this your true age or did you change it to be able to come here?' Other questions relating to violence within the family (whether they were beaten as children by their parents, the father was violent with the mother, their husbands were violent with them or they were violent with their own children) were problematic. Most did not admit to any violence and I knew, from the way they shied away from the answer, that this was not necessarily the true reflection of reality.

Another potential problem I had to deal with while interviewing Sri Lankan housemaids was the language barrier. I do not speak Sinhalese or Tamil. When I faced communication problems with my interviewees I relied on the help of Sri Lankans present at the embassy whom I knew spoke good English or Arabic. Most of the time, however, I managed on my own (and I favoured by far being alone with my interviewee), using Arabic and English interchangeably. I also learned to use simple words and sentences and repeated the questions many times to make sure they understood me. Again, here, time and experience were essential. As I progressed in the field, I became confident that the language gap was somehow bridged.

I decided one day to conduct a focus group at the embassy but had to end it soon after it began, mainly because of the language barrier. It was difficult to follow a spontaneous discussion using the mediation of a translator (the language gap could be bridged on a one-to-one basis but not with a group). Moreover, housemaids were shy to speak out in front of each other. The attempt was dropped and one-to-one interviews rescheduled.

Because of the communication problems just mentioned, the length of the questionnaire (100 questions) and the repetitive probing, the interviews lasted between one and two hours. The interviewees got restless (as did I). After spending a day or even half a day at the embassy, I went home drained because of the energy, time and effort I put in. I was often discouraged, wanting to simply forget about this whole project, but I didn't. I am thankful now for that.

Other interviews, other fieldwork

As for interviews with Lebanese female employers, I chose to tape them as I felt that I needed to relate, through the transcriptions, every nuance given within the answers. I used a snowball sample but it did not grow as I had hoped. The employers became concerned that they were being judged as people, based upon the treatment of their housemaids. They all knew about others who were abusive employers; however, when asked, they were unwilling to refer me to them. I did manage, however, to interview ten employers during my first spell of fieldwork. Most employers portrayed themselves as 'ideal employers' often claiming 'I treat her like my own daughter'. Again, probing was an important tool I used to get beyond the 'perfect employment scenario'. Moreover, staying on neutral ground and being objective was not easy (especially after hearing one employer justifying the tight control she exercised over her housemaid: 'Do not buy a slave except with a stick in your hand') but I learned to do so and to try to understand why such attitudes were more common than unique.

I also researched in detail the legal and administrative arrangements pertaining to the migratory process of Sri Lankans into Lebanon, to try to give an overview of the policies and practices applied and to provide an account of typical setups detailing the legal and customary arrangements on entry and exit (including repatriation), as well as the procedures and costs involved in the renewal of work permits. This was done through contacts with General Security, lawyers, recruitment agencies, sponsors and the Sri Lankan embassy, as well as the housemaids themselves.

Moreover, I gathered many newspaper articles that dealt with the subject of housemaids in Lebanon. I came across many on my own through my daily readings, but I also used the paid services of an institution called Middle East Research Studies (MERS) whose data consist of all Lebanese newspaper archives entered onto computer. These data, however, were not of prime importance to me. They only highlighted the sensational character of the news coverage of this subject.

For an ILO project (see Jureidini 2004) at the end of 2000 and early 2001, I interviewed consuls and labour attachés from the diplomatic missions of the Philippines, Ethiopia and Nigeria. I also constructed ten case studies from housemaid interviews I conducted with four Filipinas, four Sri Lankans, one Ethiopian and one Ghanaian. Although I never intended to enter into a comparative analysis within my research, the fact that I widened my scope (even if in a limited way) to other nationalities was helpful in my assessment of the general picture of migrant housemaids in Lebanon.

Finally, I observed Sri Lankans in their informal meeting places. I went to mass with them, went to public areas where they usually meet on Sundays (notably Dora, an area on the edge of the Armenian district on the outskirts of Beirut that has become their meeting place *par excellence*), attended a musical concert performed by a Sri Lankan band flown in specifically for the Sri Lankan community in Lebanon, and engaged with the community in other ways too.

I went many times to Dora (actually this is where the Laksehta centre is also located), on weekdays as well as Sundays. But Sundays are special days for housemaids who meet there to shop, talk, dress up, eat, call their home country and transfer money to their families through the Western Union branch there. Some attend Sunday mass at Laksehta and then join the crowd on the Dora streets. The area is filled with cheap Sri Lankan restaurants and shops that display big signs in Sinhalese on the front windows. Shops, normally run by Sri Lankan males, sell Sri Lankan dry goods, tea, curry and other foodstuffs. Dressed-up, smiling women form a nice crowd, in contrast to the sad and lost women I met at Laksehta (or elsewhere). This, more than anything else, portrays the two-sided stories and multiple (often contradictory) experiences of this community living in Lebanon. Since most live-ins are not allowed out even on Sundays, the Dora crowd is mainly composed of freelancers. Men are also there (although outnumbered by women) mingling with the crowd. These happy moments are perhaps parts of the migratory experience returnees choose to leave out when they relate their stories to friends and relatives back in Sri Lanka (Gamburd 2000).

I would wander around the Dora streets, taking pictures, talking to women there, eating lunch in small Sri Lankan restaurants, entering shops and chatting with their owners. I learned from my numerous interactions with these women that they do not mind the attention, especially if they do not feel threatened or judged. I did not think twice about taking pictures without their previous authorisation. Actually when some noticed that I was taking their photos, they posed for me with big smiling faces.

Sunday is also the day when informal meetings may take place before and after church services at the Catholic churches in Hamra (Beirut) – one in which Filipinas congregate – and the other nearby for Sri Lankans. I went to both, though my main focus was to be able to interview Sri Lankan women present at the latter church. This attempt, however, was not successful; it was a time for them to relax rather than answer the questions of a researcher. This was prior to my visits to Dora and to my interviews at the embassy. This taught me never to ask for formal interviews when I met women in public places but, rather, to simply chat with them.

I also went more than once to a beach resort north of Beirut and chatted with many Sri Lankan housemaids living in a deserted building there. Its construction was interrupted a long time ago and was now the 'home' of many men and women from different nationalities who were employed by the beach resort administration and some who also worked for private employers (inside and outside the resort). Despite the harsh living conditions, they managed to make a suitable and quite warm place to stay. Each room had a TV, a fridge, a heater... I noticed many pictures of saints on the wall as well as candles scattered around the rooms. This group, for the most part, held legal papers and seemed content. They were not abused, they were free to move as they pleased and earned up to $400 to 500 per month (a live-in earns $100 a month). Many had been in Lebanon for more than a decade.

The first part of my fieldwork, lasting over a year, therefore ended successfully. I had managed to interview 70 Sri Lankan housemaids. From those 70 semi-structured narratives, I could extract straightforward answers to be coded and presented as numerical findings. This would allow me to draw conclusions based on simple statistical data. I could also qualitatively analyse the same questionnaires (using the housemaids' answers to my open-ended questions) and derive numerous case studies as well as insightful information. Moreover, I had completed ten interviews with Lebanese female employers (all taped and transcribed later on) to be analysed qualitatively. I also had an impressive file of notes I took using participant observation, whether in daily life or at the embassy. Added to this were my 30 interviews with the multiple actors involved in this field and my visits to prisons and detention centres, meeting places and gatherings.

Back to the field: second stage

During the year 2002-2003, I began the second part of my fieldwork. Needless to say, the second part proceeded with fewer ambushes as I already knew my field. I more or less repeated the whole process again.

The first thing I did was contact the Sri Lankan ambassador who was still in post. He showed an equal readiness to complete cooperation as he had in the past: I could resume my fieldwork just as if I hadn't left. Yet things had changed. Two Lebanese members of the staff were dismissed on the assumption that they were accepting bribes from agents and employers and working against embassy policies. The cooperation between General Security and the embassy was reduced to a minimum. No staff member from the embassy was allowed inside the detention centre, except for – on rare occasions – the ambassador or the labour attaché themselves. General Security officials demanded that every undocumented housemaid who went to the embassy for help be sent to their headquarters with a personal file detailing her employment and residence status in Lebanon. I heard rumours about the ambassador; he, supposedly, was not going to be allowed to renew his mandate (which ended in August 2002) and was severely reprimanded by the Sri Lankan authorities regarding allegations of corruption. The tension, already existent, between the Sri Lankan embassy on one side and Caritas, Sister Angela and General Security on the other side, had worsened.

The ambassador related to me that Sister Angela tried to discredit him and asked for his removal in March, but he 'made a strong case with the Sri Lankan government'. He managed to convince them to let him stay in office until the end of his term (August 2002) and was then hoping for a renewal of it. In fact the ambassador's contract was in the end renewed, as he had predicted, for over a year.

He said that Sister Angela takes money from the girls ($50 per person) who go to her for help and that the presence of the embassy means that less money goes in her pocket. General Security closed the embassy's safe house on the charge that it was illegal (the flat was not in the embassy's grounds). The ambassador asks: 'How come Sister Angela kept her safe house in Dora? Is it not illegal? But in the end, it was a good thing that the safe house was closed and the women deported. It saved me work and the women time. Now, women running away to the embassy are less numerous. They no longer have the luxury of staying in a house all day, eating and resting'. He was also critical of Caritas, as it cooperates closely with Sister Angela and General Security. He added that there was corruption within General Security itself, not necessarily at the top but with people who were handling Sri

Lankan housemaids. 'They have no heart', he says, and Sister Angela also talks badly about him, which worsens things.

There seemed to be two clans forming. Each clan accused the other of corruption. Whom was I to believe? Some housemaids seemed unhappy with both clans, as one told me in a conversation we were having:

> The embassy here is useless anyway. Sister Angela is doing also like the embassy, calling the police right away and sending them to General Security. She takes their money before that. *Mish haram?* (Isn't it a shame?). The money, you scrub I don't know how many toilets to get it, *haram* (it's a shame)... And it's gone. They have no God. We don't want an embassy here, what for? It's better if it closes.

I chose to put aside these delicate issues and carried on with my fieldwork at the embassy. The idea that the people involved with helping housemaids were, in fact, taking advantage of their vulnerability was indeed disturbing. Moreover, the core of my study was the complex relationship between Sri Lankan housemaids and their employers. Any form of exploitation by government, embassy officials or various NGOs was indeed relevant (and I did tackle these issues whenever they came to my attention), but this was not the prime purpose of my study. I could not – nor did I wish to – investigate in depth this aspect of the migratory experience of Sri Lankan housemaids in Lebanon. Later on, and following an incident I describe below, I had an opportunity to directly confront those controversies.

Things had indeed changed but not only on the levels described above. In fact, coming back to the field after a significant break turned out to be beneficial. First, it gave me time to 'step back' and reflect; second, it allowed me to notice small changes in the behaviour and attitude of housemaids that I might not have seen if I had stayed in the field continuously. The further I advanced in the second part of my fieldwork, the more I came to realise that housemaids seemed much more assertive and less defenceless. I saw many stand up to their employers in a way I never imagined possible in the very beginning of my research. One housemaid told her employer in front of me in Arabic: 'Madame, *ana mish lailik*' (Madame, I am not yours – I do not belong to you). Another one told her employer: 'I am poor, I am not like you'.

Another example of a change in the attitude of housemaids I witnessed at the embassy: a Sri Lankan live-in came to the embassy claiming that the sponsor wanted her to pay for her own papers, even though she only gets $100 per month. The embassy staff member called the sponsor. He explained that he could no longer afford to keep her. He was ready to send her back to Sri Lanka. Her papers are valid until tomorrow, but she needed to leave by then. The housemaid wants to be paid $1,000, she says it is her due.

> Housemaid [to the embassy staff]: 'Mister is engineer. He is good, Madame no good. I want my salary. And I want them to pay for my ticket. I will go to Sri Lanka but they have to pay for my ticket. I don't want to work outside [meaning as a freelancer]. Too much danger. I worked outside one month, they did not pay. One family, rich. They did not pay. I worked for a poor family, one day, they gave me $20. Why it's like this?'

The housemaid is 34 years old. She is married, a mother of two: a ten-year-old daughter and a five-year-old boy.

> Housemaid [talking to her sponsor on the phone]: 'I tell Mister, not my hobby for you houseworking. I work five months in your house... You not value my salary, only your salary value'.

The sponsor claims he has no money, he can only give the housemaid $300 plus the ticket.

> Housemaid [to sponsor]: 'You don't have too much problem. I have too much problem. I don't want anybody's problem. I want my problem... I am Lani, not Ousama Khatib (the agent). Madame *mehtale* (hypocrite). I will stay with you, I make *ikamé* (residency papers) but you pay me $150 a month. Plus the $300 now that you owe me'.

In the beginning, I viewed them more as victims than as women standing up for their rights and managing to 'resist' the various forms of exploitation they were facing. But I had since grown into the subject and so had they.

As I was conducting my second round of interviews at the Sri Lankan embassy and going through the usual witnessing of cases, taking notes, etc., the ambassador proposed to employ me officially as his assistant. I gently turned down the offer. I needed to be 'ties-free', not just physically to be able to come and go as I pleased, but also mentally. As mentioned earlier, the pressure at times was too strong and I found myself needing intervals to stay home, away from the embassy and the stressful issues I was researching. There was yet another reason: in view of the tensions between the embassy and the other parties involved with housemaids, and in order not to be alienated by them, I could not be labelled as an embassy employee. Moreover, being officially employed at the embassy might have meant doing things I did not approve of or stopping myself from taking steps I believed needed to be taken.

I kept going to the embassy a few days a week throughout the summer of 2002. I was even given my own desk in a room I shared with an embassy staff member. She was in charge of receiving 'runaways' and of organising their individual files for General Security. As usual, I watched, took notes, asked questions, interviewed housemaids and sat with the ambassador and embassy staff as they received employers, agents, etc. I used the same questionnaire design as before. I could then code and enter data from my second-phase interviews with twenty housemaids (ten 'runaways', seven live-ins and three freelancers). With these, I had a total of 90 cases to be analysed, plus the rich qualitative information gathered from those same questionnaires as well as from my daily notes taken at the embassy and elsewhere.

I also interviewed another ten female Lebanese employers, using, again, the same questionnaire design as before, as well as the same method for accessing these women, i.e. snowball sampling. I contacted and met with many of my previous contacts (lawyers, human rights activists, NGO representatives) to 'update' the information I had gathered throughout the years.

Another dilemma

There was one thing I still needed to do: visit the new detention centre, a parking lot under a bridge transformed into cells and financed by Caritas. I was sceptical about this project as it somehow gave General Security the 'legitimacy' to hold – for longer periods of time (often months) – a greater number of people, mostly women, awaiting deportation. When I met the General Security director during the first part of my fieldwork, he invited me on a tour of the site, which was still under construction: 'I rented a parking, turned it into the new detention house. Huge. The government couldn't help. Nobody did anything. I had the idea to turn this parking over. It can welcome up to 1,000. We also put TVs for them. After all, they are human beings'.

I promised myself then to come back once the new centre was built and ready to receive housemaids. A few years later, I needed to keep my promise, but how? A former Lebanese staff member of the Sri Lankan embassy[3] had warned me: 'You should go to the detention centre but do not do it through the embassy, use the intermediary of someone who knows X (the General Security director at the time) or someone who has a contact with General Security'. I no longer had a contact within General Security and, in any case, I wanted to be able to go there rather 'anonymously'. I did not care for a 'guided tour' especially designed for academics or human rights activists. I did go on one of those in January 2004, when I joined a group of foreign academics on a visit to Lebanon. We visited the detention centre and passed through the cells where women and men were held separately. We were kindly advised not to address the detainees 'because the visit would simply take too long, each detainee wanting to tell you his or her story'. We met with officials there and asked them questions about the number of detainees, the conditions of detention, the legal aspect pertaining to both the detention and release, etc. To one comment made about the detention centre being underground beneath a bridge and the difficult conditions of detention, a General Security officer replied: 'We are also here in the detention centre, as if we were in prison too. But we did it as a five-star hotel. Some of the foreigners who come here do not want to go anymore like Somalis, Africans... In their country their lives are much harder'.

I had an opportunity more than once to visit this 'five-star hotel' in the summer of 2002. My visits were not 'guided', therefore I was able to get inside information I could not have accessed as a researcher (and definitely did not when I went there two years later with the group of academics). The opportunity came through the Sri Lankan embassy. Despite the previous warnings of the embassy staff member, I accepted the ambassador's proposal to accompany a Sri Lankan housemaid (Puspa) to General Security's detention centre. Puspa was not a 'runaway' coming to the embassy for help. She was sent to work in Syria by the Lebanese agency in charge of her. This was totally illegal since her port of entry was Beirut and her original three-month visa was given to her by the Lebanese authorities. When her contract finished, Puspa decided to come back to Lebanon and went straight to the Sri Lankan embassy for advice on what to do next. She did not have a working visa and her passport was forged (the agent gave it to her after confiscating her original passport). As was the habit at that time, embassy staff followed General Security instructions to the letter: Puspa was to be sent to the General Security detention centre. The ambassador proposed that I accompany her and I accepted. I was doing them a favour since, as noted above, embassy staff members were not allowed inside the detention centre, but I was also seizing an opportunity to finally enter the new detention centre. So on that day, Puspa and I were driven there. I carried with me a letter from the embassy that went as follows:

Director General of General Security,

The embassy of the Democratic Socialist Republic of Sri Lanka has the honour to inform you that Mrs. Nayla Moukarbel is officially authorised to accompany the Sri Lankan ... (the full name of Puspa) to the General Security offices.

[Signed the ambassador at the time]

The letter was conveniently vague, I was not an embassy employee (on this, the note was truthful) yet no details were given about who I was and why I was chosen to represent the embassy that day.

Puspa and I entered a room where she was to be interrogated by a General Security officer. The interrogation lasted over an hour, during which I never intervened; I knew I had to let Puspa act on her own. She was then taken by other officers who took a few of her belongings from her (watch, money, etc.) and put them inside an envelope that was sealed in front of her. She was then asked to sign a paper that included a list of those items and was taken away. But before she disappeared inside one of the cells, she came to me in tears and hugged me. I told her not to worry, that soon she'd be home with her family, that she will be waking up before long from this nightmare... She didn't want to let go and nor did I, but we had to eventually. It was a very powerful moment for me, as a human being but also as a researcher. I was witnessing a housemaid being put behind bars for something she not only did not commit, but over which she had no control. Housemaids cannot choose their employers, they cannot apply for their working papers nor renew them, and yet they are the ones who are detained when their papers are not in order (an order for which sponsors and agents alone are responsible and should be accountable for).

I went back to see the officer who interrogated Puspa. He had guessed that I was an embassy 'outsider' and wondered what I was really here for. I remained vague and started asking him about his work. He admitted to occasionally hitting housemaids to get them to tell the truth: 'One slap and they tell you everything'. He also confided to me that housemaids were sometimes tied in a room: 'One hour and they are ready to talk. We might mistreat them, but we never steal their money, the General Security director is very strict on this; if he finds out you stole money, he automatically dismisses you from your job, and we cannot afford to lose our jobs'. He then added that embassy people tell housemaids that General Security officers are thieves and that they should leave all their valuables at the embassy before going to the detention centre. But housemaids, he noted, are taken to the airport straight from the detention centre and if, by any chance, they are driven to the embassy beforehand to claim their belongings, embassy staff systematically come up with pretexts: we can't find the key, the ambassador is not here, etc. 'They promise to send the belongings to the housemaids' addresses in Sri Lanka but never do', he said.

I didn't know who or what to believe anymore and went back home totally demoralised. I never believed previous rumours about corruption at the embassy or maybe I didn't want to believe and managed to turn a deaf ear under the pretence that a researcher should remain neutral and that this was not the subject of my study. But I could no longer ignore this lead as I was, this time, directly confronted with it. Consciously deciding not to investigate a subject is one thing, but refusing to follow through an incident one encounters is another.

A few days later, Puspa called me from the detention centre. The officer in charge (the same one who confided in me) allowed her to call me from his office as soon as he finished asking her a few questions. She wanted to see me. In answer to my queries she reassured me: she was not mistreated but just wanted to go home. She then handed the phone to the officer who explained to me that Puspa's case of the forged passport might take some time to be resolved. They needed her to stay to be able to build a case against the agent, who was illegally taking housemaids to work in Syria. I agreed with the officer that I would come the next day. He was, of course, doing me a favour by allowing me in as 'his' visitor. The embassy note had applied to that one day only; I had lost any official justification for going back there and I definitely did not want the embassy to know about any of my subsequent visits to the detention centre. I went there the next day and met with Puspa, who was brought into the officer's room. I found out that, following her demand, the officer arranged for a patrol to drive her to the bank in Tripoli (northern Lebanon) to withdraw her money ($700). This was quite an unusual measure, the officer told me, but he felt sorry for her. Puspa was happy and seemed quite at ease with the officer: 'He is nice'. I asked Puspa whether or not she had left money at the embassy before coming here. She hesitated before answering yes: she did indeed, $1,900 in cash as well as jewellery (gold earrings, bracelets, chains...). The ambassador advised her to do so, claiming that General Security officers might steal them from her. Did he give you anything in return, some type of receipt? 'No', said Puspa, 'nothing'. I did not know what to say; should I warn her that she might never see her money again? But what if the General Security officer was doing all this to, in fact, embezzle the money from her? I asked Puspa whether she wanted her money or preferred to leave it at the embassy. Her answer surprised me: she had been talking to women inside the cell, some are sometimes a little beaten (not her) but nobody talked about General Security stealing anything from them or from any Sri Lankan they know of. Puspa wanted her money. On my third visit, I found out the following: Puspa was taken to the embassy; staff there told her that they did not have the key to the safe where her things were held and that the ambassador was absent. Puspa asked for a receipt and was driven back to the detention centre. She showed me the receipt: a torn piece of paper with a name and address in Sri Lanka she was supposed to get in touch with once there, no signature, no embassy stamp, no mention of her belongings (amount of money, pieces of jewellery). That was the last time I saw Puspa. She called me on her day of departure from the detention centre (two months after her arrest). She was very happy, she was handed back her money ($700 they had withdrawn from the Tripoli bank) and was to be driven straight to the airport.

Between my first and second visit to the detention centre I kept going to the embassy, doing what I usually do there, interviewing, taking notes, etc. I never mentioned anything about my visits to anyone at the embassy, including the ambassador. I stopped going there after my second visit. I had completed my 90 interviews. I could have added another ten to reach my target of 100 interviews but I decided to stop there. I had enough interviews, enough information... and perhaps enough dilemmas. I only saw the ambassador once right after my first visit to tell him how things went with Puspa. The other times, I went straight to the room I shared with the Lebanese embassy staff member. I recalled the words of the officer: 'How do you think X got a brand new car soon after she started working at the embassy?' I found out in a meeting with the new ambassador in 2004 that X was dismissed from the embassy on charges of corruption more than a year later.

I hesitated a long time before writing this down; actually, this section was the last one written in this chapter and I kept postponing it for days and days. At one point, I simply had to make up my mind, and I decided to include it. I am not making any allegations, I am simply noting down what I saw and heard and explaining how this affected not only me (the personal level might be irrelevant) but my work. It is not my place to draw conclusions, but it is definitely my duty as a researcher to relate any detail that affected, whether directly or indirectly, my study.

Closure of fieldwork

In January 2004, a new ambassador took charge of the Sri Lankan embassy in Lebanon. The 'campaign' undertaken by General Security against the previous ambassador turned out to be true. In a 'Migrant Domestic Workers in the Middle East' seminar I attended at the American University of Beirut in 2004, a General Security officer who was also present there told me: 'We got rid of the previous ambassador'.

In May of 2004, I had an informal lunch with the new ambassador. He said that he was called to Lebanon following the urgent 'dismissal' of the previous ambassador and one member of the embassy staff (the

Lebanese woman with whom I shared a room at the embassy during the second part of my fieldwork). He updated me on his relationship with General Security: it was improving, but 'X (General Security director at the time) is a very direct man, tough... who did not really care about the human aspect of migrants, only about the economic issues involved. He told us when we met with him: "I hold the keys to this country"'. The ambassador added that he does not collaborate with the NGOs present in Lebanon like Sister Angela or Caritas... 'because of political reasons: they are converting Buddhists to Christianity'. We also went through various issues regarding Sri Lankan housemaids in Lebanon. The ambassador seemed anxious to improve things for his nationals present in Lebanon. Things seem to be changing for the better; as I was told by Ramia (the Sri Lankan freelancer who worked for me at the time): 'The new ambassador is very good. He said that every Sri Lankan should have legal papers. He is Tamil, Tamils are good. Not Muslims, Muslims not good (the previous ambassador was Muslim), Tamils like Hindus, Buddha.... But he is still new, this ambassador, yes, Leila?'[4] Ramia's hope (though topped with a tinge of scepticism) touched me. Did things change? With the replacement of the General Security director in 2005 (for political reasons that had nothing to do with the way he dealt with migrant workers in Lebanon), one could hope for the better. But somehow, as much as I wished for this to happen, just as Ramia did, I remained sceptical. After all, what happens behind closed doors remains to be seen. For this research, I had seen enough. My fieldwork had ended. Perhaps others will take things up where I left them and add to my contribution. As for me, I had to stop somewhere, and I did. All I can add is that from what I (still) notice around me, things are almost the same. Did the attitudes of Lebanese employers change? The Israeli-Lebanese war in the summer of 2006 proved the contrary. Accounts of employers forbidding their housemaids to join their embassies so that they could be evacuated outside the country were numerous. Housemaids were 'locked in' the house; some died trying to flee from balconies. A friend told me about his housemaid's friend (a live-in working in northern Lebanon) who keeps calling her, complaining about her employers: they left her alone in the house and fled. Lata (the Sri Lankan freelancer who currently works for my mother) revealed the following to me: 'I want to go, but my sponsor has my passport and working permit and he left for the mountain. Sri Lankans are going to Syria. The embassy is taking them by bus and there they fly directly to Sri Lanka. It is the Indian government who flies them for free. You know Indians are rich'. At my sister's workplace, a woman was warning another: 'You have to be careful now, housemaids are running away, because of the war, to reach their embassies. You have to lock them in'. I will come back to this in more detail in a later chapter and explain the reasons for such a tight control, but I had enough material (not just from incidents during the war) to be dubious about any forthcoming change.

Final observations on ethics and bias

I was once asked if I thought my sample was representative of the whole female Sri Lankan community working as housemaids in Lebanon. My answer was: of course not. All 90 interviews I conducted with housemaids were held at the Sri Lankan embassy in Beirut. I simply talked to whomever was available at the time and agreed to be interviewed. My sample might not be representative of this entire community, but it is an honest account of the problems that my interviewees confided to me. Moreover, by complementing these accounts with other tools of research, such as participant observation and case studies, I was able to draw more general lines of the real issues at stake.

The same goes for my snowball sample of Lebanese employers.[5] In fact, a representative sample needed logistics, time, expertise and money that I did not have (I received no funding whatsoever throughout my research). It would need hundreds of interviews (performed by a number of interviewers and not just one) – a random sample that represented Lebanese employers geographically, religiously and following a class and education divide. All I did, on my own, was to interview as many people as I could, and relate things as objectively as possible. It was also my opinion that the rather exploitative employer-housemaid relationship went beyond class, education, religious divides, etc., and was not specific to particular groups or even nationalities (as I noted in Chapter 1, the literature does uncover similar living and working conditions for housemaids throughout the world). It is indeed true that my choice of particular samples does affect the results of my study, but I made it consciously and am aware of its limitations.

Throughout my fieldwork, I did act in a fair and respectful way so as not to jeopardise anybody involved in my work. I never tried to mislead or deceive the people I interviewed. I always introduced myself to my interviewees as a researcher, stating the purpose of my study. People I interviewed were free to talk to me (and many refused to do so) and to withhold their answers whenever they wished. I also always asked for their consent whenever I used a tape recorder.

There were, however, other ethical issues I needed to resolve. I did, as I said earlier, specify to all my interviewees that I was researching the subject of Sri Lankan housemaids working in Lebanon. But I did not 'volunteer' those details wherever I went; whether to detention centres, prisons or even while talking to people, in general, during any of my social outings. Did I have to? I do not believe I did. I noted down conversations, events, opinions I witnessed throughout my years of fieldwork, but I never revealed details that could lead to the incrimination or identification of any of my 'informal' sources. I did the same with regard to friends who, of course, knew what I was doing, but perhaps did not realise that what they were telling me was ultimately going to be included in my book. I simply could not ignore such invaluable information, some of the most valuable data of my whole research.

Moreover – and in view of the sensitive information I was gathering – confidentiality was extremely important. Many of the housemaids were staying in Lebanon illegally and they risked prison or deportation if the police were notified. I tried building with them a relationship based on trust, assuring them that I would not divulge to anyone the information they confided in me. I could not risk housemaids' complaints reaching their employers as this might jeopardise their living and working conditions in Lebanon. When needed, I disguised the personal identity of my interviewees.

In 2006, I attended the screening of a film shot on location in Sri Lanka and Lebanon on migrant domestic workers, mainly from Sri Lanka, funded by Caritas, the Netherlands Embassy and the International Labour Organization, with the support of the United Nations Office of the High Commissioner for Human Rights. After the show, I introduced myself (and my work) to the director and editor of the documentary. She asked me what I thought about the film. My answer was that it was good but perhaps a little 'dramatic'; it portrayed, unrealistically in my opinion, the migratory experience as being mainly totally grim. She answered: 'Yes, I know. Actually, almost all the Sri Lankan women I talked to wanted to stay in Lebanon or come back. But I cannot say this in a documentary funded by Caritas'. I hesitated a while before I decided to use her statement. After all, she knew what I was doing, she did not tell me this 'in confidence', and it was too important to ignore. Moreover, it was in accordance with one of my research hypotheses: Sri Lankan housemaids in Lebanon, in general, are not simply victims (even if some are) of unscrupulous Lebanese employers. The dramatisation of reality is common amongst NGOs, human activists, etc., perhaps for funding purposes. This is another issue I will not go into here, but prefer to deal with in my conclusion.

Being a woman, I assumed at first that Sri Lankan housemaids would find it easier to confide in me. But there was a counterpart involved, as the 'abuser' was usually the Madame of the household. All housemaids I interviewed started addressing me as 'Madame' until I asked them to call me by my first name (as I did with them). This put them at ease from the beginning and as the interview progressed I felt that I was no longer labelled as a potential 'Madame'.

Being a woman also opened doors for me, in prisons, detention centres, etc. It allowed me to bend the rules a little and access places and information that were somewhat inaccessible. Yes, I admit to, at times, smiling to male guards or officials to be able to go into places I was not supposed to enter. I also used some of my father's 'connections' to contact and meet numerous persons (lawyers, economists) who were useful for my study.

Being Lebanese also meant that I belong to a different culture from the Sri Lankans. As I was conducting my research with a community from a different national, ethnic and, most of the time, religious background, I was aware of the need to be particularly sensitive to cultural and individual differences. I tried, as much as I could, to get closer to them and understand their cultural background. By asking them about their lives in Sri Lanka, their families, employment, education, etc., I was able to get to know them better. Moreover, and as I mentioned earlier, being in contact on a daily basis (for the past ten years or so) with the Sri Lankan housemaids employed by my mother provided me with a closer insight of Sri Lankan culture in general – not to mention the almost seven years now researching this subject.

Does being Lebanese hinder me from understanding particular issues relating to the migratory experience of Sri Lankan housemaids in Lebanon? Does being of Mexican descent give Romero (1992) more insight into the Chicana community she was investigating in the US? Maybe so, but there are numerous limitations (if one wishes to call different perspectives limitations) pertaining to every study. Being a female Lebanese probably gave me a different 'perspective' of (and into) the communities of female Lebanese employers and Sri Lankan housemaids I interviewed and observed than, let's say, a French male researcher. Would my views be more accurate and 'better' than his? Of course not. It just means that he will probably see things from a different angle than mine. It does also mean that the unique and specific 'baggage' I carry into my own research affects it one way or another, as does his.

I could have visited Sri Lanka on numerous occasions (the Sri Lankan ambassador offered to organise the trip for me) but I deliberately chose not to, as my primary focus was Lebanon. I decided to remain in Lebanon and to tell my story about Sri Lankan housemaids working here. One could look at things from so many different angles but, for one to get really embedded in a particular subject, one has to demarcate the angles and admit, in so doing, to the limitation of one's own research and method used. I hereby acknowledge the limited scope of my research as well as its distinct print.

Sample characteristics

In the final part of this chapter, I present a brief overview of my 'sample' of 90 interviewed housemaids. I do this here as a background and a bridge to the four chapters that follow, which are theoretically and empirically grounded. Mirroring the structure of the interview schedule, this section will be divided into four subsections: *general information* about the employment and legal status of the housemaids, their ethnicity, religion, length of stay, visits home, etc.; *pre-migration stage* regarding the decision to migrate, contracts, reasons for choosing Lebanon, etc.; *migration stage* dealing with the administrative aspects of their stay in Lebanon, wages earned, etc.; and finally, the *information housemaids had regarding their Lebanese employers.*

General information

My interviewees were in three categories: live-ins (24; 26.7 per cent), freelancers (23; 23.6 per cent) and runaways (43; 47.8 per cent). This distribution does not necessarily represent the 'true' distribution of housemaid categories in Lebanon, but, as mentioned before, these are not watertight categories; in particular, runaways had all previously been live-ins. Of the 90 housemaids interviewed, 62 per cent were 'illegal' compared to 38 per cent who were legal; the high proportion of 'illegals' is probably due to the large number of runaways in my sample, plus the choice of locale for my interviewing, the Sri Lankan embassy.

As for ethnicity, 90 per cent were Sinhalese and 10 per cent Tamil. The Lebanese are unlikely to be aware of the existence of ethnic differences (just as I wasn't, prior to starting this research). Regarding religion, 69 per cent were Buddhist, 22 per cent Christian, 7 per cent Hindu and 2 per cent Muslim. These percentages broadly match the religious distribution in Sri Lanka, except that my sample shows a higher percentage of Christians (22 per cent versus 8 per cent). The difference might be accounted for by the fact that many housemaids claim to be Christian in order to please the employer or the interviewer. Religion is very important to Lebanese in general, and I have heard many employers relating with pride how their housemaids were fervent believers who insisted on going to church on Sundays. It is also true that many see church as the only outing allowed to them. Moreover, there is a natural tendency for those who are receiving assistance from a Christian organisation to seek to identify with the religious order. Finally, Lebanon, with the highest proportion of Christians in the Middle East and a rather Westernised mode of life, can be considered an attractive location by Sri Lankan Christians.

Most housemaids (73 per cent) had not worked in any other country. Those who had (27 per cent) had been in other Arab countries (Kuwait, Dubai, Oman, Saudi Arabia, Qatar, Bahrain); one had worked in Singapore. The average length of stay was 4.2 years, ranging from a maximum of fifteen years to those who were fairly recent arrivals. But, of course, these figures are not 'true' averages of full lengths of stay, because I was interviewing housemaids before their stay had ended. I did, however, note a tendency for single, i.e. never-married, women to stay for shorter periods of time in Lebanon, since they go home faster to, among other things, get married.

Three-quarters of my sample, approximately, had never been home for a visit since their arrival in Lebanon. Even for those who had been in Lebanon for many years, many had never been back to see their children, parents, relatives or friends. It is worth noting here that live-ins cannot go back home, even for a visit, unless their contract is over and/or their employers agree to let them go. When the contract is over, housemaids either go back home for good or come back to the same (or another employer) after spending three to four weeks with their family. How often the contract is renewed and for how long is to be agreed by both parties: the employer and the housemaid. There is another important component that hinders housemaids from going to Sri Lanka for a visit and that is the legal aspect. Many of these women do not have legal documentation and are therefore unable to leave the country. When asked whether they intended to stay in Lebanon or leave, a little more than half said they would leave; the rest wanted to stay. The large proportion of runaways (43) in my sample might explain the high percentage of those who want to leave (30 runaways said they did).

Pre-migration

When asked for the reasons that led them to come to Lebanon to work as housemaids, all mentioned economic reasons behind their migration: no money and no work in Sri Lanka. Some mentioned problems with their husbands and their added need for money, others (especially those who were married) wanted to build a house and live on their own with their husband and children. The fact that agency fees to come to Lebanon were cheaper than for other destinations was also taken into account. A few also answered: 'because Lebanon is not a Muslim country' (when asked about the religion of their employers, 51 per cent of housemaids said Muslim; 46 per cent worked for Christians).

I often wondered why Sri Lankan housemaids came to Lebanon. Did they know about the country beforehand? Did anyone advise them to come here? When I asked them 'Why Lebanon?', they answered in two

main ways: 53 per cent mentioned networking (friends or relatives
working in Lebanon, or just hearsay); 47 per cent talked about the role
of recruitment agencies (many answered: 'Agency said Lebanon was
good'). However, it is the nature of interview data that answers are
mixed, and it is in the nature of migration decision-making that motives, too, are multiple. Here, to illustrate this, are a few examples from
my interview notes. It is worth pointing out here that many of my interview clips with the housemaids are in very simple, stilted English.
As I said before, language was, to a greater or lesser extent, an issue in
these interviews. So my quotations from the interviews reflect the linguistic level (in Arabic or English) of the interviewee.

> For money, I wanted to come. Agency said Lebanon good. Didn't
> know anybody here before. I worked in Dubai before. In 1995.
> Three years. Good Dubai. Paid agency 14,000 rupees. To Lebanon
> I paid 9,000 rupees. I borrowed from a man in Sri Lanka. I paid
> him back since. The money gained from Dubai I spent all on
> house.

> Went to agency in Sri Lanka. I wanted to go to any country. They
> sent me to Lebanon. Didn't know anybody here.

> Came to Lebanon first time in 1994. Friend was here, she said Le-
> banon good. No money in Sri Lanka. After school did nothing. I
> didn't find work there. So I came to Lebanon.

> Divorced my husband nineteen years ago when my little girl was
> one. Drunk, hits. Married at sixteen. No work in Sri Lanka after
> school. No money, no husband. Friend here, she told me come Le-
> banon.

> Money. Problem with husband. Friend sent me ticket. She was in
> Jordan, Madame was in Jordan, I was supposed to go there then
> Madame came to Beirut. That's how I came to Lebanon.

> After my husband died, friend in Kuwait said only $100, Lebanon,
> Christians, more money. She said Kuwait Muslims, not a lot of
> money. Lebanon good, Christians.

Usually, Sri Lankan housemaids' entry to Lebanon is by one of two
routes: either through a Sri Lankan agency (64.4 per cent of my sample) or through networks – i.e. friends or relatives in Lebanon who re-
commend a particular Lebanese sponsor (36 per cent). Those who do
not have recourse to agencies in Sri Lanka do not pay agency fees

there. The same applies to Lebanese employers who act as direct sponsors. A few specific examples:

> My mother-in-law was here. She found sponsor for me. Madame
> sent my papers and a ticket.

> No agency to come here. A friend in Lebanon sent a ticket for me
> [meaning finding a sponsor who will then send a ticket].

> Aunt here, she gave me ticket, I come.

In principle, all those who used the services of an agency should have
signed a contract in Sri Lanka prior to migration. The notion of a contract, however, is not really understood by some housemaids, who
might sign a paper but do not know it is a contract: 'I sign something
at agency, I don't know what it is'. My results show that only one-third
of my interviewees had signed a contract. Sister Angela of the Laksehta
centre commented as follows:

> They [Sri Lankan housemaids] don't have a proper contract. They
> sign something. Now the government, two years ago, we have had
> a contract which is signed, which has to be signed over here also.
> You see, they don't have a copy of their contract paper. Sometimes
> in Sri Lanka they are told that it's for two years. And they come
> here, the agency says, 'It's two and a half years', when they are
> put in the house, they say three years. They get them to sign
> things which they don't know. And you have to sign.

It has only been since early 2002 that migrant employment contracts
have become mandatory for Sri Lankans who are required to register
with the Sri Lankan Bureau of Foreign Employment and sign a contract prior to departure – 'Contract of Employment for Domestic Help-
ers from Sri Lanka in the Middle East Countries'. The extent to which
the conditions of these contracts are adhered to, and are enforceable, is
questionable. Many Sri Lankan agencies avoid paying registration fees
to the government (a registration is necessary for the issuing of contracts). Moreover, control at the airport regarding the 'mandatory' registration of housemaids is not systematic. The Sri Lankan ambassador
confided to me the following:

> Sri Lankan agencies are registered with the Ministry of Labour.
> They find migrant workers for agents in Lebanon. The Sri Lankan
> agencies are the suppliers. It's like a business transaction. Some
> avoid commissions. I know a few. I don't want to disturb them.

All I want is for my people to come here and work under good masters [employers].

Of those who said they did sign a contract, 17 per cent had no idea about the conditions stipulated in it. The rest talked about the salary and the duration of the contract. Usually, they are told in Sri Lanka that they are going to stay for two and a half years in Lebanon for a monthly salary of $100 (sometimes $150). Housemaids stated:

I came as $150 a month as a salary. The agency here said $100.

I cannot read Sri Lankan. I could not understand the *contrat* I signed in Sri Lanka.

They say $100, two and a half years. Here, Madame say three years.

The employment conditions, according to Lebanese agencies, are as follows: a two-and-a-half- to three-year stay for a salary of $100 per month. Most Sri Lankans end up staying for three years even if they wish to return. Cases, however, where employers have pressurised their housemaids at the end of the three-year contract to stay longer are numerous. For the employer, in general, it is convenient to keep the same housemaid. The Madame feels she spent a lot of time and energy 'training' her housemaid and does not want to go through this whole process again. Moreover, re-employing the same housemaid means not having to pay agency fees to get a new one. There might also be a human aspect involved as everybody, including the children, have become used to and maybe attached to the housemaid.

Housemaids interviewed paid on average $113 to the Sri Lankan agency to be able to come to Lebanon. Many did not pay the agency directly but had their first two months' salary withheld, meaning $200. Sometimes, agency fees are paid twice by housemaids (once in Sri Lanka and the second by having their first month's salary withheld). One Lebanese employer told me that the Lebanese agency she dealt with asked her (and not the housemaid) to pay them the equivalence of her first two months' wages. That amount was, they claimed, to be sent to the Sri Lankan agency. The employer inquired with her housemaid who said she did pay the Sri Lankan agency. The employer then called the Lebanese agency and told them that what they were doing was 'immoral, trying to take money twice from these poor women'. The Lebanese agency did not ask for the money again. According to the Sri Lankan ambassador, agents in Sri Lanka are paid between 5,200 and 7,200 rupees ($70 to $97). Only a small number of interviewees (12 per cent) had the amount available (mostly by working previously abroad); others (35 per cent) borrowed the money while many (27 per cent) agreed to have their first two months' salary in Lebanon used as payment for the agency fees. The rest sold whatever they had (mainly jewellery) to be able to come. This makes the pressure to 'succeed' in Lebanon even more crucial. Here are two responses, the second rather atypical:

> My sister sold her things and gave me money to pay agency to come.

> I sold a cow to pay agency.

Sri Lankan agencies require that housemaids undertake a medical test before leaving the country. Almost two-thirds of my interviewees said they took the test. However, Lebanese agencies dealing with their Sri Lankan counterparts do not consider these tests to be reliable. In the words of one director of a Lebanese recruitment agency:

> When she [housemaid] comes, the sponsor must go to the airport to collect the girl and take her to his house. The second day, they take her to the medical check-up. The Lebanese government doesn't accept the Sri Lankan medical check-up. Maybe the girl is sick. The children [employers' children] then get sick. We don't even see the papers of the medical check-up in Sri Lanka. Many times we return girls because they are sick. With the Sri Lankans, a lot are mentally sick.

Sri Lankan women may send a 'healthy' friend or relative instead of undertaking the test themselves. Moreover, some Sri Lankan medical laboratories have been known (as one Lebanese agency director told me) to give fake test results providing a certain amount of money is paid. The Sri Lankan ambassador in Lebanon, trying to limit such actions, recommended the use of one particular laboratory in Sri Lanka which he claimed was quite professional. I have seen him hand out the laboratory's address to Lebanese recruitment agencies as well as to Sri Lankan housemaids themselves.

According to the Sri Lankan ambassador, agents in Sri Lanka have to pay for a medical insurance for these women (following the medical test):

> It is true that they are insured in Lebanon by their employers. But in case problems occur with the employer, at least these women would have the Sri Lankan insurance. Some Sri Lankan agents,

however, try to avoid paying for the insurance. There are not enough immigration officers at the airport to check for the insurance on the passports.

The Sri Lankan ambassador also told me that the Sri Lankan Bureau for Employment has opened 35 to 40 centres for migrant workers. These centres offer twelve-day training sessions for women wishing to migrate. Potential migrants are taught various basic skills such as the use of electrical appliances and other household tips (including a few words in Arabic). The effect of such programmes cannot be precisely defined. It is my opinion, however, that it is helpful to a very limited extent. Participating in one of these sessions is, in principle, a compulsory pre-migratory condition. The reality, again, is different. The Sri Lankan ambassador explains: 'Agents have to pay for the insurance. To avoid the insurance money, some agents don't send them to training'. Only ten housemaids from my sample attended training sessions. These sessions are not of much use, according to Sister Angela: 'They are supposed to have some sort of training. And what is given in this training is a few words of Arabic and how to use electrical gadgets. This is not training'.

Migration in Lebanon

All told, three-quarters of the women interviewed either did not sign a contract or did not understand what a contract was. In reality, in order for work and residency permits to be issued for the housemaid, both the employer and the housemaid must sign a contract drawn up by a Lebanese notary public. However, this contract is only in Arabic. Housemaids are unlikely to understand the details even if it is translated (which is usually in English and not in their native language): 'Don't understand, only sign'. It is clear that they often do not know they are signing a contract at all. These 'work contracts' do not specify the obligations and responsibilities of the employer. Rather, they detail the need of the housemaid to be faithful, honest and dutiful.

For a housemaid to be eligible for the work and residency permit, she has – within three months of her date of entry – to present to the Ministry of labour the results of a 'clean' laboratory test as well as medical insurance coverage. The Lebanese laboratory test includes: AIDS, hepatitis, STD, tuberculosis and pregnancy. The sponsor or agency usually pays for the medical test. From my sample, 77 per cent said they did take a medical test soon after arrival, while the others (22 per cent) claimed they didn't and one did not know.

According to the General Security director: 'If the housemaid is found to have the AIDS virus, she is automatically sent home. As for other sicknesses like hepatitis, she is allowed to stay in Lebanon and be treated. But of course, in most cases, the employer doesn't want to use her services anymore'. Even if the housemaid gets sick later in her stay, she is almost automatically sent home. A doctor, a colleague of my sister (she is a pathologist), asked her to check the slides of his housemaid's biopsy. It turned out to be cancer. When my sister phoned him with the news, his immediate reaction was one of annoyance: 'Now I have to send her back to Sri Lanka'.

Medical insurance is mandatory for the issuing and renewal of Sri Lankan housemaids' work and residency papers. From my sample, 57 per cent of housemaids interviewed said they had medical insurance in Lebanon, against 38 per cent who did not, while the remainder did not know. Those who are 'illegal' are not medically covered (my sample had 62 per cent 'illegals'); runaways who become 'illegal' the moment they leave their employers can hold proper documentation (including medical coverage) prior to that.

The medical insurance Lebanese employers usually pay for does not cover regular check-ups and visits to the doctor, nor the cost of medicine. As one Lebanese employer related to me:

> Once she had an earache. I took her to do like an echo for the ear. And it was something she had from before. Chronic from before. Not something she contracted while she stayed with me, that I was responsible for. No. But still, I took her to the doctor. And most of them come with teeth problems. Their teeth need fixing. So, I take them to the dentist. All this is extra. I have to pay for this. The insurance does not cover this. Insurance is medical. Not for these things. These, I pay for them.

Given that the primary motive for the migration of Sri Lankan house-maids is economic, it was important to collect some data on the financial 'pay-off' of such moves. Above, I noted that most contracts for live-ins specified a monthly wage of $100, sometimes more. From my respondents, the average was $149, with a maximum of $400. Most live-ins got $100; the higher average being due to the extra wages available to freelancers – who, however, have to pay for their own accommodation and food as well as for their work and residency papers. Given that the average monthly wage in Sri Lanka is $24, the economic incentive to migrate is obvious: the wage differential is important.

Housemaids' information regarding employers

Constable (1997) claims that the Filipina housemaids she interviewed in Hong Kong had little knowledge of their employers' details such as the household composition, their jobs, etc. I wanted to know how much Sri Lankan housemaids knew about their Lebanese employers, and discovered (unlike Constable) that most were aware of basic details. However, some had only vague knowledge. I asked housemaids whether they knew where their 'contract house' (employers' house) was, since I came across a few runaways who did not have any idea where they were working. This meant that embassy staff members could not get in touch with the housemaids' employers. As one agency director remarked, on this issue: 'Many girls now in prison don't know the sponsor. She runs away without the sponsor's name. They say George. Where do they live? Beirut'. This is mainly why the General Security director decided in 1998 to introduce a computerised data system at Beirut airport to be able to enter information regarding housemaids and their employers.

Of the 90 housemaids interviewed, 84 per cent knew where their employers lived, while only 16 per cent did not. Usually, those who do not have only been in Lebanon for one or two months. The average stay of my sample is 4.2 years. The average number of residents in the employers' house (excluding the housemaid) is 3.2, according to housemaids. The maximum number of residents noted was eight.

Regarding knowledge about employment, more than half (53 per cent) do not know what 'Mister' did for a living, 24 per cent said 'Business'. Other more specific answers were scattered: 'In bank', 'In school', 'In airport', 'Doctor' or 'Mister away' (in Saudi Arabia, Egypt, France...). The majority of Madames (two-thirds) do not have paid employment according to their housemaids. This is interesting (if true) for two reasons. First, it reveals that many Lebanese households appear to be organised on rather 'traditional' lines: the husband works, the wife 'stays at home' (these traditional gender roles will be discussed at length in the following chapter). Second, the home-based nature of the Madame's life means that she and the housemaid are in the house or flat a lot of the time 'together'.

Regarding religion, half of housemaids interviewed worked for Muslim employers while 46 per cent worked for Christians; the remainder did not know. As predicted, religion is not representative of who is more likely to employ a housemaid in the Lebanese context.

Some have argued that Madame lets her frustration out on her housemaid partly because of an unhappy marital relationship (Young 1999). The argument made is the following: the husband is violent towards his wife, she in turn lets her anger out on helpless housemaids. This argument does not stand (as I will explain in more detail later). Moreover, and according to the housemaids I interviewed, violence does not seem to be that common within their employers' households:

almost two-thirds said there is no violence between the couple. In the words of housemaids:

> Relationship between couple? Not good. They fight because of me. I work son house, daughter house. Arguing. Mister very good. Madame too much problem with me. No real violence in the house.

> Violence in the house? No. Only with me. When Madame shout at me Mister tell her don't shout. And he tell me not to speak to Madame [answer back].

3 Gender and domestic work in migration

Introduction

This chapter explores issues of gender and power in relation to female labour migration, specifically women who migrate to work as housemaids. As mentioned earlier in Chapter 1, domestic work has been receiving a lot of attention lately, especially in studies relating to international migration. Domestic labour in many countries has become almost restricted to migrant and ethnic minority women, although in earlier historical periods such labour was supplied by poor, rural girls who were internal migrants. Within this type of labour, gender issues as well as power struggles and acquisitions are highlighted. Moreover, the employment of migrant domestic workers can be reflective of the gender division of labour in countries of both origin and destination.

This chapter is divided into two parts: the first introduces gender as an important social and cultural issue that affects migration patterns and needs to be more seriously addressed in studies pertaining to migration. The second, much longer, part includes a more detailed description of gender issues and power struggles associated with domestic work in general and migrant domestic workers in particular. It unfolds in ten subsections, mixing my reading and interpretation of the literature with my own data from my fieldwork in Lebanon. I start by posing the question: Is domestic work 'real work'? I continue by examining the unequal gendered division of labour and domestic work, and the 'need' and demand for domestic workers. Then I look at the dynamics within the household: women as 'managers', conflicts of interest between women, and power struggles. My attention then shifts more directly to the housemaids – their 'power acquisition' through migration and their empowerment through the earning of wages and sending of remittances. Finally, I focus on 'transnational' motherhood.

An overview of gender issues in migration

Gender, a term that refers to 'socially constructed differences between the sexes and to the social relationships between women and men'

(IOM 2005a: 5), is an important relational element in understanding human activity and thought. Social relations and practices affect gender relations and they, in turn, are affected by them. Gender-ascribed or 'gender-appropriate' roles are different for men and women (IOM 2005a: 7). Men typically have productive roles, while women's roles are of a reproductive and domestic nature. These roles are reflective of societal norms and are subject to change. Challenging gender roles or, on the contrary, adhering to them is important in understanding social relationships in a particular time and place.

As gender is socially and culturally constructed, its dimensions change over time and space. Gender issues are particularly relevant to migration processes, as migrants face various cultural and spatial changes (Boyd & Grieco 2003). Migration affects men and women differently, mainly because of the unequal expectations that societies have on each of them. Migration experiences also bring a reassessment of the cultural and individual beliefs that are inherent to gender constructions. These moves often involve power struggles or acquisitions. Moreover, men and women migrate for different reasons using different channels: 'Gender is deeply embedded in determining who moves, how those moves take place...' (Boyd & Grieco 2003: 6). Just as the ways in which women are participating in the migration phenomenon and the reasons behind migration are changing (what I referred to in Chapter 1 as the 'new' feminisation of migration), roles and relationships between men and women are affected by migration in new and different ways, whether in the countries of origin or of destination. Gender, a concept deemed essential when looking at any subject in general, is unavoidable in migration studies.

Early anthropological studies of migration saw the migratory process as automatically leading to the breakdown of local cultures and the 'modernisation' of traditional institutions. Others, by contrast, assume that this process – especially when economic needs are met and migrants then return – helps to maintain the traditional structures of a particular culture (Gmelch 1980). The reproduction of notions of identity and belonging is inherent to migratory processes. 'The balancing of forces of modernity', plus the maintenance or even production of 'traditionalism', are two of the constant themes in migration studies (Gardner 1995: 5). Migration is, in fact, an ongoing process involving different stages and processes. It is, therefore, almost impossible to have clear-cut images of the cultural dynamics at stake within the migratory experience. Rather than presenting migrants as caught between two cultures (cf. Watson 1977), it would be more appropriate to view them as part of two worlds relating to one another: '... whilst all journeys are physical, they are also "acts of the imagination", in which home and destination are continually re-imagined, and thus forever changed' (Gardner 1995: 35).

Buijs asserts that migrant women generally hoped to preserve in the 'host' country 'the essentials of the culture and lifestyles which were theirs at home' (1993: 2). As migrants, they were forced to question their preconceptions and rebuild their identities in an attempt to adjust to their new situation. They were faced with many losses, having to re-construct their everyday life away from the familiar patterns they were accustomed to at home. Culture becomes a symbol of these losses as these women try to reconstruct their collective identity through signs pertaining to their culture, such as poetry, music, and song.

As part of what can be called a 'cultural preservation', Sri Lankan housemaids in Lebanon (mainly freelancers, as live-ins are generally not allowed out) attend concerts (performed by Sri Lankan bands and sing-ers flown in especially for such events), walk on the streets of Dora (an area I described in detail in Chapter 2), eat in Sri Lankan food places and meet friends. Sri Lankans usually meet up on Sundays, attend Christian masses (even those who are Buddhists), then socialise for the rest of the day. In the grounds outside one Catholic Church in the Hamra district of Beirut a shrine has been established that resembles what must have been used for a nativity scene, but which is now used by Sri Lankans who prefer to sit or stand in front of it as a sacred area for prayer. How-ever, there are no Buddhist images in the scene, only symbolic figurines of saints and others formerly used by the church. As the priest present at the church said, smiling: 'They [Sri Lankans] like to come here and pray. It reminds them of the way they prayed in Sri Lanka'.

Live-ins have a harder time holding onto their cultural identities. They are dressed and fed by their employers. One Lebanese employer said about her 60-year-old housemaid: 'I buy her her clothes, I know her size'. Another employer gave me a diatribe about her housemaid's food habits, which she would not tolerate:

> In the morning, she wanted to have something with curry. In the morning, for breakfast! We don't eat breakfast like this. We eat a sandwich for example. Curry for them [Sri Lankans] is anything with sauce and onions and hot spices... I can't accept this... They have no timing: for example, in the morning I eat light. At noon I eat more. No, she can wake up in the morning and eat a sheep.

Live-in housemaids are usually not allowed out nor are they authorised to speak to others. Some have their hair cut short by their Madames. In short, they are 'guided' – every step of the way – away from their culture and into an appropriate mould set by their Lebanese employers.

Gender in migration research

Traditional migration theory was either gender-blind or totally sexist, privileging the male perspective. 'Women were invisible in studies on migration and when they did emerge tended to do so within the category of dependants on men' (Buijs 1993: 1). The social role of women in the migratory process was, therefore, underestimated. The traditional absence of women in migration studies could be accounted for by the fact that almost all early migration researchers were men (King, Thomson, Fielding & Warnes 2005: 32). Another reason, according to Campani (1995), could be the predominance of the temporary migration model in Europe in the 1950s and 1960s. In this model, state policies were set to provide for the needs of industry, leading to various demands for temporary foreign labour migrants – mainly males. Women were either to stay in their own countries or join their husbands at a later point under the new family reunification laws. They were considered as secondary players, entering the host country only as migrants' partners. State laws and policies, Campani argues, 'expressed and still express (not having been changed in the majority of countries) a patriarchal conception of gender relations' (Campani 1995: 546).

Only recently have researchers started looking more closely at the role of women in the new composition of migrant populations across the world. The development of feminist theory in the 1980s and 1990s further contributed to the use of gender as an important variable in migration. However, the difference between men's and women's migratory experiences, in most cases, is still merely reduced to a classification of men and women as separate categories. Gender does not just equate with women (Carling 2005; GCIM 2005; Indra 1999; IOM 2005a) and cannot, therefore, be limited to studies relating to women. In fact, within most studies relating to women in migration, 'There has been a tendency to treat gender as additive and to reduce it to looking at women migrants' (Anthias 2000: 15). The problem, according to Carling (2005: 19), 'is not that a lot of research documents the particular experiences and vulnerabilities of migrant women, but rather that it is labeled as research on gender when this is not the case'. Boyd & Grieco (2003: 3) fear that this new 'gender sensitivity' will lead to a new focus on women while ignoring men in accounts of migration experiences and that 'this would inadvertently undermine the gendered view of migration that helps explain the experiences of both males and females'. Researching female migrants is indeed important, yet the key aspect of gender as a relational term should not be undermined. Men should also be focused upon, and a comprehensive approach to femininities and masculinities is needed. Furthermore, gender is not a dimension to be studied on its own but in relation to other social divisions such as age, race, ethnicity and class (GCIM 2005).

Most research within the field of migration, and especially of refugee studies, has concentrated on the oppression of women migrants, who are almost inevitably labelled as victims (GCIM 2005). Western feminists – even though this might be changing – still tend to implicitly regard women as virtuous and oppressed. 'There is an underlying assumption in much gender research that women-in-general are everywhere oppressed by men-in-general' (Carling 2005: 3). This assumption is misleading. First, some men do feel vulnerable and rejected, especially if they do not fit into the 'breadwinner' role assigned to them by society. Second, gender relations also encompass relations between mothers and sons, brothers and sisters, work colleagues, etc., and are not just relevant to 'a model relationship which is invariably oppressive and heterosexual' (Carling 2005: 3). By contrast, most studies on migrant domestic work (including mine) show how women (employers) are the principal oppressors of other women (housemaids). This introduces a new perspective on gender dynamics in migration; although, of course, such women-on-women oppression is set within wider gender relations, both in the society of destination and that of origin of the migrants.

There is a danger of beclouding the diversity of migration experiences among women, casting them as invisible – because homogenous – as they were in migration research until the 1980s. The visibility of women cannot afford to be only stereotypical. 'In short, gender stereotyping is not much better than gender-blindness' (Carling 2005: 20).

Gender influences behind migration

The economic push-pull model sees migration as a mere rational choice. 'Whilst giving a central role to human agency, that agency was treated in the light of the ideal rational economic action' (Anthias 2000: 18). This model did not account for other social pressures affecting the choice to migrate. Gendering migration has indeed often meant portraying migrant women as passive victims of particular junctures. But if these women were in fact 'forced' into migration, 'Why did some individuals migrate when others did not in similar circumstances?' Anthias (2000: 18) asks. It is true that economic and labour-market issues are crucial in deciding whether or not to migrate. Other factors, however, need to be considered as well, such as independence, adventure, upward social mobility and the wish to escape from patriarchal forms of social control and broken marriages. As Momsen (1999: 302) observes: 'It is often the most adventurous who migrate, and for many such women the search for personal freedom and the accompanying rejection of traditional gender roles is as important as economic reasons'.

Therefore, and as Gamburd (2000) notes, less socially acceptable motivations to migrate should be acknowledged. The Sri Lankan women she interviewed asserted that they pursued employment abroad in order to help their families, but some also wanted to get away from their families, especially those who had to face physical abuse and/or unfaithful husbands. Others were abandoned by their husbands who left to go off with other women. In the absence of governmental help, migration was the only solution. 'Frequently... patterns of drinking, wasteful spending, and failure to prosper predate, and even prompt, female migration' (Gamburd 2002: 193). In the words of one Lebanese employer I interviewed:

> They [Sri Lankan housemaids] are mistreated by their husbands there. They beat them. Most of them. Men stay at home, and make their wives work... So they run away from their husbands and come here [to Lebanon]. I know one. The husband was drunk, too much, she said: 'I don't want to go again. I prefer to stay here.'

For female migrants, especially those who have unhappy marriages, who are widows or have been deserted by their husbands, migration might have been a means of escape from difficulties in their home countries. 'In some cases where unions disintegrated, migrant women have found the end of their marriages a relief, not a tragedy.... Official pronouncements and national news items that lament the adverse effect of migration on matrimony rarely take into account the pre-migration quality of many of the failed relationships in question' (Gamburd 2000: 146). As one woman admitted, 'In the plane... I felt like a bird whose cage had been locked for many years... I felt free. Deep inside, I felt homesick for my children but I also felt free for being able to escape the most dire problem that was slowly killing me' (quoted in Hochschild 2000: 4).

Even though Sri Lankan women working in Lebanon can earn maybe ten times the income level available in Sri Lanka, it is important to note that many are also motivated to migrate for other reasons. For example, the Sri Lankan Government Bureau of Foreign Employment has noted that:

> Twenty-five per cent of the women who travelled for work [outside Sri Lanka] were pushed by the poor lifestyle at home and the abuse of a drunken husband... The motive to travel, in most cases,

is to get out of Sri Lanka to a safe place away from abuse and mistreatment and have new relations abroad (quoted in Tawk 1998).

Sister Angela, the nun who led the Laksehta centre in Lebanon, related
to me some of the reasons that, in her opinion, drove Sri Lankan women to migrate:

> Yes, it's a male-dominated society [Sri Lanka]. Yes, they [Sri Lan-
> kan women] are mistreated. And also, in certain areas, the think-
> ing is limited; you know, the vision is narrow. Some people think
> you have to live in this way, you know, some stereotyped regula-
> tions. Whereas here [in Lebanon], they can go with another man,
> speak to another man, nobody says anything. Nobody suspects.
> But if they do that there, somebody will complain... There is a
> sense of closeness in the village, togetherness which has its posi-
> tive aspects but also negative aspects. But now, little by little, wo-
> men are becoming conscious of their dignity, their rights... Some
> Tamils can't go home because of ethnic problems. And they came
> because if they remain maybe their life was at stake. So, for those
> reasons some have come. But I wouldn't say that's the large ma-
> jority. There are a few also who because of the family situation,
> husbands harass them, beat them. And so to get rid of that pro-
> blem they have come here. There is one here expecting repatria-
> tion now. She says 'I should have not come. I could have managed
> there, with great difficulty but we could have managed together'.
> But her husband wasted all her money. So, there are reasons. Also
> some of them, they don't feel free. They need freedom. So they
> come here and experience a certain amount of freedom. They say
> 'We can't go back and live in the prevailing conditions there. We
> are not free'. But the main reason is economic...

Referring to a survey of migrant workers in the Gulf carried out in Colombo, Sri Lanka, Zlotnik (2000) analyses the effects of temporary labour migration on marital stability. She notes that marriages do not
usually collapse when men migrate, while female migrants' chances of
separation increase upon return. However, the conclusion that female
migration increases marital instability cannot be drawn. In reality, female migration and divorces are linked because those who are separated or are facing difficulties within their marriage are more likely to
migrate than those who are in stable unions. Divorce and separation
are more likely to occur with returnees not only because of pressures
related to migration, but also because women, having gained more
self-confidence whilst away, are more likely to break up problematic
marriages.

It can be easier to challenge patriarchal roles through migration where these control forms are absent. Getting employed as a housemaid abroad might be the only means a migrant woman has to challenge the gender-role constraints within her own country. Especially if these constraints are very important, as they are, for example, for Sri Lankan women whose culturally ascribed norms and virtues are 'chastity, docility, passivity, obedience and subservience in a life guided by demands of the household...' and who suffer from 'the restricted freedom of movement, both physically and socially; the extreme emphasis on motherhood as the sole approved role; the limited range of activities considered appropriate for women...' (Brochmann 1993: 88).

The researchers' inability to grasp in full the experiences of domestic workers and account for the ways in which these women challenge societal constraints when they migrate is common, Pappas DeLuca notes (1999).

Migrant domestic workers and gender issues

Is domestic work 'real' work?

Family and work are still separated into different spheres. The dichotomy work/home or public/private still holds. Housework is performed in an affective environment, where women are wives, mothers and often both. It is not included in the economic sphere of activity and cannot – the traditional argument goes – be exchanged in the marketplace. It is the responsibility of wives and mothers and is generally linked to the affection they hold towards the family, and receive in return. 'Housework has further been disqualified as "real" work by referring to it as "labor of love"' (Romero 1992: 21). Moreover, housework cannot be regarded as 'real' work as it is unpaid. Domestic work is 'work' at home and is, therefore, difficult to be considered as 'just another job' (Anderson 2000: 11).

Housework, however, continues to be devalued work even after it is sold in the marketplace (Romero 1992). Domestic work has entered the global market, with more and more migrant women applying for it, but, at the same time, employers are still seeking 'the "soft" and personal qualities of affectionate care' generally advertised by employment agencies (Carling 2005: 14). There is a combination of the affectionate and the commercial within domestic work. It is indeed a business in terms of economics but also (and above all) it is a business of care. 'In the advertisements, images of smiling nannies and children are coupled with commercial catch-phrases such as "money back guarantee", "special package", "free replacement" and "excellent after-sales service"' (Carling 2005: 14). In Lebanon, pamphlets are distributed on the streets: 'Tweety's Agency for Services. Housemaids from Sri Lanka, the Philippines, Ethiopia, Madagascar, Bangladesh, India. Special offer: contract for a Sri Lankan maid $950. We also have maids who speak French and are also experienced in cleaning houses. For your comfort and to save you time in traffic, our delegates are at your service wherever you are in Lebanon'. The extensive tasks given to maids who live with their employers and become in a way 'part of the family' demonstrate how the subordinate role of women as unpaid family workers is extended to paid family workers. 'The expectations that families have on the wife and mother now are placed onto the domestic maid but without the potential emotional and other rewards as well as the reciprocities involved in family structures' (Anthias 2000: 27).

Unequal gendered division of labour and domestic work

The international migration of domestic workers can be described as part of a 'global care chain' (Hochschild 2000) that starts with women migrants from poor developing countries and ends with women from rich developed countries. This approach 'highlights the way in which gender relations at origin and destination are linked in the migration process' (Carling 2005: 14). In the past, the 'breadwinner' was the professional male while wives dealt with domestic chores. Today – and despite the fact that some men contribute to household tasks – women (whether they have joined the public sphere or not) delegate household responsibilities to women employed as paid carers. This (unequal) gendered division of labour, according to Hochschild (2000), is at the core of the problem. If men and fathers participated equitably in household chores and childcare, women would not need to resort to other lower-class women from the global chain for help. Carling spells out the issues more explicitly and in more detail: 'The problems created by the gender division of labour in industrialized countries are not solved, but passed on to other women. The hiring of a full-time domestic worker means that patriarchal household and work structures can go unquestioned, women pursuing a career and a family need not "rock the boat" and any guilt over exploitation is assuaged by the knowledge that a less fortunate woman is being provided with work' (Carling 2005: 14-15). As one of my own interviewees, a Lebanese employer, said about her 'less fortunate' housemaid: 'Why is she complaining anyway? With the money I give her, she is building a house in Sri Lanka. Do you know how they live there, in total misery? She's lucky to have me as an employer...'

Stating the obvious, as she says, Hondagneu-Sotelo (2001) notes that women employers are almost exclusively responsible for hiring domestic workers. This proves that feminist egalitarian aims to share household chores and responsibilities are far from being achieved. Hondag-neu-Sotelo (2001: 22-23) sees women employers as contractors: 'By subcontracting to private domestic workers, these women purchase release from their gender subordination in the home, effectively transferring their domestic responsibilities to other women who are distinct and subordinate by race and class'. Male privileges, therefore, are yet to be contested, while new inequalities are formed (between women employers and those 'less fortunate').

The 'need' for domestic work

As Anderson (2000) notes, humanity could not go on without the performance of such domestic tasks. A basic level of cleanliness and order are needed. '[W]ithout domestic work we would, literally, be living "like animals"' (Anderson 2000: 14). Having a big apartment and a busy schedule can create the 'need' for domestic work but the domestic worker is there also to confirm the status and class of the household owners, specifically the efficiency and merit of the person (usually the housewife) responsible for the household. Employers often speak of their domestic workers as their 'substitutes'. But this reference is only symbolic, as tasks carried out by workers are not tasks employers are prepared to do. Anderson gives the example of a maid complaining about her work. She is employed in a big house with a white carpet and three dogs with long hair. Anderson (2000: 16) asks: 'Would her employers have both white carpet and dogs if they (or, most likely, the female employer) had to clean the house themselves?' Probably not. As Romero notes, '[d]etailed descriptions of actual housework performed by domestics indicate that, while some women hire to replace their own labor, others hire women to do much more demanding household labor' (Romero 1992: 100).

This is also true of Lebanese Madames who are obsessed with cleanliness. Lebanese employers have their 'system' as this one notes:

> For example, my sister. My sister is like me, she is obsessive, clean. We have a problem, we are obsessive with cleanliness (*msar-sabeen*). As long as one [the housemaid] comes and understands that we need everything in its place and clean... I no longer tell her a word. That's it, if she's done everything. My sister, her maid didn't understand her system. One year and a half. In the end, before her contract was over, she shipped her back (*chahanita*)... They need to understand our system, if not, I cannot live with them.

This 'obsession' becomes a luxury with the presence of a housemaid (who gets the 'system') to carry out household tasks. The Lebanese Madame wants the bathrooms cleaned, the house dusted, the floors mopped (and the list goes on) every day. She needs the sheets (even sometimes the underwear) ironed. Her exigencies are never-ending when a housemaid is there to carry out orders. In the absence of a housemaid, one wonders if the housewife would still consider those tasks as absolute necessities or choose instead to turn a myopic eye to the dust in the living room. Domestic work allows the employer to maintain these demanding lifestyles and housemaids are asked to do tasks that employers would never envisage performing. 'The employment of domestic workers meant women could negotiate the contradiction between domesticity, requiring physical labour and dirtiness, and the cleanliness and spirituality of feminine virtue. "Ladies" need servants' (Anderson 2000: 18). In Lebanon, the 'need' is even more pressing, as men generally never participate in household tasks. As one Lebanese employer told me: 'I want one who lives in because my husband is very demanding and he doesn't do anything or move anything. Take this from me, bring me this, feed me.... Like this. So I can't stay all the time serving him'.

Demand for domestic workers

The demand for this form of paid labour in developed countries has increased over the last fifteen to twenty years. This was caused mainly by the fact that more women (many of whom are mothers) from the middle class were seeking employment outside the home. American women today make up 45 per cent of the US work force. A huge increase in the number of women in paid work was witnessed in the past half-century, from 15 per cent of mothers of children aged six and under in 1950 to 65 per cent today (Hochschild 2000). Earlier generations of American women relied on their mothers, grandmothers or other female relatives for childcare. Today, these women are also working. The story is much the same in developed countries in other parts of the world.

Most European states' increasing inability to provide care for the young and the elderly has led to a significant increase in the demand for domestic workers (Anderson 2000; Anthias 2000; Lutz 2008). Changing family structures implies that families, more specifically women, find it harder to ensure that the basic reproductive work of the family is met. Moreover, extended families' support and caring networks have declined, leaving the nuclear family in need of outside care. Domestic help is there to replace (or add to) the help previously managed by the state or the extended family.

Help provided by extended family members in Lebanon is less important than before. The previous head of General Security was complaining to me about this issue when I interviewed him: 'Before, in my mother's generation, they used to help each other. If the neighbour had a baby, my mother would go there to help, to cook, to wash clothes... And the same if my mother was sick. I prefer my mother's generation. When I was eight, I used to know how to make coffee. Now my daughter who is eighteen, I get scared if she comes near a stove'.

Women who enter the labour market can do it at the expense of migrant women, who 'also often bear the responsibility for supporting their families back home and are an important familial resource' (Anthias 2000: 27). The 'burden of reproduction' is carried by both women: the employer and the maid. Female employers were able to look after husband and children while '[m]ale employers proved *their* superiority by never having to consider domestic drudgery, while enjoying the home as a refuge, a well-deserved rest from the stresses and strains of productive work' (Anderson 2000: 18; emphasis in original).

As women migrate to get away from their own gender constraints, among other things, female employers employ maids to avoid renegotiating their own gender roles (Anderson 2000; Momsen 1999; Pappas DeLuca 1999; Zlotnik 2000). Women build careers and try to minimise family obligations by relying on someone else to deal with household chores. Despite their employment, women are still expected to take responsibility for household chores traditionally identified with women's role in the private sphere. It is easier to employ somebody to do them than to renegotiate gender roles and relationships with their partners. Rather than 'nag' or 'rock the boat', women will do it themselves or employ someone to do it.

A nuance here is worth mentioning with regard to Lebanese women's expectations in this area. Lebanese housewives do not expect their husbands to share in household chores nor do they try renegotiating traditional gender roles. How many times have I heard my mother kick my father out the kitchen when he offered to help: 'Get out, a man does not belong in the kitchen'. However, they expect their husbands to provide help for them since it is available and quite affordable. The 'nagging' here takes different proportions, as the following interview quote by a Lebanese employer reveals:

> I remained four months without a maid. I did not have a life for myself. Cleaning the house, cooking... I was constantly complaining about it to my husband. I lost my body to have kids and I had no life of my own anymore. He told me: 'Get two maids but stop nagging'. Lebanese are lucky to have such husbands. What for-

eigner buys his wife a very expensive piece of jewellery? We are very spoiled'.

When men do help with household chores in Europe, they tend to do it by task and are supervised by women who manage the process. This renders men's insertion into the domestic labour of the household even more difficult (Anderson 2000). 'In the past, the professional was a man and the "someone else to deal with [chores]" was a wife...Today, men take on much more of the child care and housework at home, but they still base their identity on demanding careers in the context of which children are beloved impediments; hence men resist sharing care equally at home' (Hochschild 2000: 5-6). Domestic workers become the 'new solution' (Anderson 2000: 40) for problems encountered with the advent of economic and social changes. So, domestic work can be seen as essential in freeing women to do more 'productive' work. 'In effect, employing a cleaner enables middle-class women to take on the feminine role of moral and spiritual support to the family, while freeing her of the feminine role of servicer, doer of dirty work' (Anderson 2002: 106). They can do that at the expense of other women, those who migrate. Employing a maid, therefore, allowed the female employer to 'escape the "dual" or "triple" burden of being a worker outside the home, and a housewife and/or mother in the private sphere' (Narula 1999: 149).

Women's employment in the public sphere does not fully explain the rising demand for domestic workers. As Anderson (2002: 104-105) notes: 'The demand for domestic workers has been steadily rising in Europe, and although one can point to many economic and demographic forces that may have contributed to this trend – the retrenchment of the welfare state, the rise in the ratio of older to younger people, the feminization of the workforce, the rise in divorce, and the decline of the extended family – they leave a good deal unexplained'. In fact, many Lebanese employers do not work in the public sphere. Of the twenty Lebanese employers I interviewed, only six held paid employment.

Referring to Cock's (1989) South African study, Anderson notes that only a quarter of the married female employers held jobs outside the home, 'while for the majority the employment of a domestic worker facilitated leisure activities and a high-status life-style' (Anderson 2000: 17). This is also the case for most Lebanese women who employ Sri Lankan housemaids. In the words of the General Security director: 'Now Lebanese women bring maids to have fun, drink coffee... I prefer women if they don't have to work for economic reason, to stay home and take care of the house'. Seventy per cent of the Sri Lankan housemaids I interviewed said that their Madames did not work outside the home.

Charbel Nahas, a Lebanese economist, observes that, in all countries, women work less than men, though the difference in Lebanon is more tangible. Lebanese women between fifteen and 64 years of age represent 21 per cent of the Lebanese workforce as against 77 per cent of men of the same age frame. The rate is, therefore, as follows: one Lebanese woman is employed for every four men (Nahas 2001). Another characteristic concerns the unemployment of Lebanese women: the rate of employment diminishes as the woman grows older. In the age range 25-29 years, 34 per cent of women are employed; at age 30-34 years the employment rate is 30 per cent. At 35-45 it falls to 27 per cent, and at 60-64 it is only 8 per cent. Nahas goes on to describe more specifics of the Lebanese situation:

> Some women think that they don't need to work. Others work awaiting marriage. After marriage or the first child, they often terminate their employment. The cost that families bear with regards to the education and training of women is money thrown out the window. The rate of domesticity (employing domestics) in Lebanon is very high. One might be led to believe that women, liberated from household chores might look for a job. Yet this is not the case. Salary is not a sufficient criterion for employment. In a period of economic crisis, a second source of income is necessary, but this is not the case in Lebanon. A part of the active population is unproductive. This leads to a higher demand for foreign labour (Nahas 2001).

In summary, employing a maid cannot be merely explained by a woman's desire to take on a career or avoid conflictive subjects with her husband. A maid is also a sign of status and class available in the new (Lebanese) economy.

In Lebanon this kind of help, nowadays, is no longer restricted to the high and middle classes (just as it is not restricted to 'career' women). This is partly explained by the low cost of this service (a Sri Lankan housemaid is paid $100 a month). Employing two Filipina housemaids rather than one is a sign of status, as it is almost exclusive to the high social classes. Lower and middle classes employ Sri Lankans or Ethiopians. As the General Security director claimed over lunch (he kindly asked me, as soon as the interview was over, to stay and share this meal with him. I accepted): 'Everybody has a maid now. It is a matter of prestige. Even this guy who is serving us, if I ask him he might have a maid'. Or as the Sri Lankan ambassador said: 'If a Lebanese has a maid, the neighbour wants one too. The Lebanese are like this. People who cannot afford to maintain a maid want one anyway. Anyone can apply for a maid, be a sponsor. The man selling vegetables, the taxi driver wants a maid'.

Women 'managers'

Domestic work falls in the category of 'reproductive' work (that was and still is assigned to women). It is culturally determined and necessary for social reproduction. As Anderson (2000) notes, washing clothes is not crucial for survival, though most people agree, as social beings, on the cultural necessity of wearing clothes that do not smell. 'How a house is ordered, what food is cooked, how children are brought up and the elderly cared for are in part a personal expression of the household, and particularly of the (female) household manager' (Anderson 2000: 13). In Lebanon, the responsibility of an ordered, clean and shining household rests solely on the Lebanese housewife. I asked one Lebanese employer to tell me who the decision-maker was within her household. She answered:

> It is my husband. The big, important things, buying a house... he decides on his own. Even without asking me. But other things, simple things, I decide them. It bothers me sometimes because it is nice to take the other's opinion even if by the end he'll do what he wants. As a couple, it is nice to talk about things. As for the maid and the household, it's my prime responsibility. My husband doesn't interfere, he just pays [for the housemaid].

Despite the efforts of young couples to break away from traditional gender roles and embrace Western norms, Lebanon remains a patriarchal society whereby the reproductive sphere is women's domain (or place). As one Lebanese employer related to me:

> I am in charge of household issues. My husband will not move a chair from its place because it's my house. The house is for the woman, this is what he says. The house is for the wife, for the woman. Because she lives most of her time in the apartment more than the man. For example, if I ask him, 'Do you like this, shall I put it like this?', he says 'You put it the way you like it because, in the end, it's your place...'

The credit of the good work of the maid goes to the 'managerial' skills of her employer. Maybe that is partly why Lebanese employers do not like their orders questioned by their housemaids. They are the managers: if the house is well kept, it is because they have everything under control, but if the house is not, it is the housemaid's fault (she did not follow orders, or is too stupid to understand them). Lebanese husbands, in general, do not deal directly with housemaids. They ask their wives to transfer orders on their behalf should they need a glass of water or something to eat. Criticisms towards the housemaids also take indirect paths: 'Tell Candy that my shirt this morning was not well ironed. What do I pay her for?' When I asked one Lebanese employer if her husband interacted directly with the housemaid, she answered, laughing:

> No, he has no patience (nor interest) for these things (*ma oulou jleideh*). My husband never asks anything from them [housemaids]. He tells me: 'Tell her...' And her, if he wants to have dinner she doesn't tell him for instance: 'Mister, you want to eat now?' She tells me: 'Now Mister want to eat?' Meaning, 'Ask him if he is hungry'.

Husbands, it is true, do not usually interfere in the details relating to the daily management of the household (and housemaid); instead, they leave this 'power' to their wives. But, as one looks closely into the matter, are women given complete freedom of action within the private sphere? It is my belief that, even if the wife is granted the privilege of running the household, her managerial skills do not go unquestioned and decisions relating to the housemaid are not left entirely to her. Thus, some husbands keep a watchful and at times critical eye over general household matters (and wives). The housemaid can become an issue and a conflictual subject between the couple. As one Lebanese employer declared:

> We [my husband and I] had fights about it [the housemaid issue] [laughter]. Yes because I used to deal with her. Sometimes he used to come and say things, what he didn't like... I said: 'You pay her, I deal with her, that's it' [laughter].

The wife is sometimes blamed for failing to properly manage the household, showing signs of weakness and good-heartedness towards her housemaid. As for the housemaid, she is accused of laziness and opportunism. A man I know did not like the way his wife was 'spoiling' their housemaid. And since he decided that the housemaid was taking advantage of his wife, he stepped in and fired the housemaid. At the wake following my grandmother's funeral, the subject of housemaids (a common 'salon' subject, no matter what the circumstances of the gathering are) was triggered; not by me, I hasten to add. A female relative, X, was complaining about the problems she had to go through because of her Sri Lankan housemaid: 'She came through an agency, Y [the husband] paid $1,400. She was supposed to have worked before, speak Arabic, et cetera. It turned out she knew nothing, did not speak Arabic, did not even know what a mop was... Y wanted to send her back to the agency who accepted to replace her (the three months' guarantee was still there). But I refused and felt pity for the woman. I said: "I'll keep her and train her"'. The husband intervened at that point: 'My wife treated her too nicely'. Another male relative present there replied: 'You cannot be too nice with these people [Sri Lankan housemaids], ours was giving problems to my wife, we took her to the agency, one slap and she was OK afterwards'. X carried on with her story: 'The maid wanted to leave after only a few months. She claimed that her mother was sick. My husband was upset with me because I was too nice with the maid. I was telling her: "If you are not happy here you can go back to Sri Lanka"'. Y interrupted his wife: 'She's [the housemaid] a liar, her mother had nothing. I did not want to let her go back because of the money I paid, $1,400! But my wife insisted so we sent her back. But I told my wife: "That's it, no more [live-in] maids then"'. X has since been employing freelancers.

Despite appearances, women cannot always take independent decisions when it comes to their housemaids. A Madame I know could not take her housemaid with her on vacation to Europe. Her husband was categoric: 'She will run away there'. So the Madame had to manage differently and look for help elsewhere. At times, women decide it is best to 'leave out' their husbands when doing things their way. One Lebanese employer told me: 'I give my maid bonuses from time to time but I do not let my husband know'. Or as another female employer said: 'When my husband is away on a business trip, I give my maid Sunday off; when he's here he does not allow me to do so, he says we need her on Sundays'. At the Sri Lankan embassy, I witnessed many couples coming in together to speak with the ambassador about their 'runaway' housemaid. I observed that it is always men who, in the end, decided on the future course of action.

Conflict of interests

Tensions are at the core of this type of employment. According to Romero (1992: 68), 'relations between middle-class employers and household workers replicated class tensions and structured contradictions between capitalist and proletarian'. Conflicts of interest are also present between 'household managers and household workers, as the manager seeks to extract maximum hours and minimum wages – thereby having an interest, in her capacity as household manager, in devaluing household work' (Anderson 2000: 20-21). Various studies on domestic

work have described the inhumane working conditions of these women, who work sometimes up to fifteen hours a day with no day off
per week. 'The hired reproductive worker is reproducing social beings
and sets of relationships that are not merely not her own but also
deeply antagonistic to her own interests' (Anderson 2000: 19). Lebanese employers try to make the most of the housemaid's presence.
'Madame is never satisfied', Sri Lankan housemaids confide. There is a
saying in Lebanon that goes like this: '*Biddi missoulah dammah*', meaning 'I want to suck out her blood'. The saying is representative of Lebanese employers' will to 'take their money's worth' till the last cent... or
drop of blood.

The employer/housemaid conflict can further be explained as follows. Housework carries with it an emotional dimension by which women demonstrate their value as good wives and mothers. Housework
becomes a vital tool which is non-dissociable from women's identities.
A homemaker who has her identity tied up in home and family cannot
simply hire another woman to care for her family's needs without
threatening her self-image. Thus, when private household workers are
hired to maintain a particular lifestyle, many homemakers feel obli-
gated to retain control even though they do not actually perform the
work. 'By the act of supervision, the homemaker's home becomes a
showpiece, a symbol of *her* womanhood as well as of her husband's
success' (Romero 1992: 69). In Lebanon, the 'control game' is obvious.
The Madame not only supervises every aspect of the housemaid's work,
but also all aspects of her private life. This 'symbolic violence' will be
the subject of a later chapter.

State processes also play an important role 'in the facilitation of subordination within the employer/employee relationship' (Anthias 2000:
27). The migration status of these workers is dependent on their work
status upon entering the country as maids. Employers act as sponsors
and are responsible for the renewal of the work and residency permits
of their maids on a yearly basis. In other words, employers decide
whether or not the status of their maid's residency in the host country
is legal or not. A domestic worker cannot renew her own papers even
if she can afford to.

The hidden place of these women within the private economies
further opens the door for exploitation and abuse (Anderson 2000; Jureidini & Moukarbel 2004). 'Many occupations place women in informal work situations with little access to networks and social support,
leaving them vulnerable to discrimination and abuse' (IOM 2005a: 18).
This abuse cannot be controlled, as the lack of formal regulations within host countries allows for basic human rights infringements to go
unsanctioned.

Power struggles

As migration opens the door for women's empowerment through physical and financial independence, another form of power is witnessed; yet this type is at the expense of migrants. Domestic work becomes more and more racialised (dominated by immigrant women of colour), bringing together under the same roof women from different class and race backgrounds. Race relations add to class relations and result in many conflictual situations. 'The struggle between women that was once based on different class interests now has the added dimension of race and ethnic conflict' (Romero 1992: 69). The common belief, therefore, that women's main oppressors are men, no longer stands. Control and power relations exist between men and women but also amongst women themselves. Moreover, in the words of Anderson (2000: 19), 'The issue is often one of gender relations: unwilling or unable to argue with a male partner and children over sharing domestic chores, and unable to manage the house to everybody's satisfaction, the woman employs a domestic worker. So gender and generational conflict over domestic work is averted (or often transferred to relations between female employer and female worker)'. It is interesting to note here that women who might have migrated to get away from patriarchal pressures in search for greater independence fall under the control of their female employers who direct every aspect of their lives (food, sleep, outings, sexuality, contact with family and friends, dress codes, etc). If they hoped to gain freedom by migrating, they instead get entrapped in a very constraining situation where the employer's household becomes a prison (in the symbolic but also literal sense: employers often lock their housemaids inside the house when they go out). The only way to escape from this entrapment is usually by fleeing the employer's house. As soon as they do, housemaids become illegal and can be arrested by the police and detained in real prisons.

Power 'acquisitions' through migration

Many scholars have tackled the issue of the empowerment of women as a result of migration. It has been argued that independent wage labour attained through migration can empower women within the domestic sphere, enhancing women's authority and independence within their families and affecting traditional gender roles (Brettell 2000). Buijs notes, however, that 'Assumptions that change leads towards a more egalitarian relationship as a result of Westernisation must be treated with caution' (Buijs 1993: 5). Despite the power gained, cultural pressures remain strong.

'The multi-faceted and complex nature of women's position does not permit us to see migration in simple terms as either leading always to a loss, or always to a gain, in social status' (Anthias 2000: 36). According to Anthias, migration may empower women, earning them greater self-confidence, authority and sense of independence. Migrants' financial and physical independence and the fact that they have become their family's main providers allow them to become agents of change, renegotiating gender relations in their society. Yet one cannot assume that migration leads inevitably to greater egalitarianism. Remittances are generally perceived as part of the family's income and not the women's own possession. As Brochmann (1993: 179) notes, Sri Lankan maids working in the Gulf have little control over their remittances, 'a fact that underscores [their] subordinate position'. Migration can also reinforce traditional women's roles, as many husbands, feeling their male identity threatened, 'seem to reinforce the control of their wives in the wake of migration' (Brochmann 1993: 179). Some women's entry into the workforce leads to added pressure unless they find alternative means for childcare and housework in their homes whilst away. Migration can also open the door for new vulnerabilities as a result of precarious employment and legal status, exclusion and isolation. It can take women down roads of violence and abuse (whether verbal, physical or sexual), entrapping them in sex-segregated jobs with difficult working conditions (long hours and low wages). Migrant women might also have to deal with broken marriages and scattered families, poverty and illness upon return. Migration can result in 'success stories' but it can also lead to fragmented and even shattered lives (Jolly & Reeves 2005).

Pertinent to this subject are Gamburd's (2000) views on the effects of migration on gender roles and power relations in Naeaegama, a village in Sri Lanka. Many women from this village worked as domestic workers in the Middle East. Initially, Gamburd states, women are supposed to stay home and care for their husbands and children while men provide for their wives and children. High local unemployment for men and women in Sri Lanka and demand for female domestic servants in the Middle East often led women to leave their families and seek employment abroad while men stayed at home and managed with the remittances sent to them by their wives. Migration challenged common notions of motherhood, as married women (most of them with at least one child) were absent from their homes for long periods of time, and sometimes years (Gamburd 2002). As women adapted to their new identities as breadwinners, men also had to face new responsibilities, as their masculinity was somehow threatened. Some men felt a loss of self-respect when their wives took over the breadwinning role. Due to strong gender roles, men often refused to take over 'women's tasks' such as child-care and cooking; instead, they relied on female relatives for help. However, Gamburd notes, more men participated in child-care and household chores than people generally reported. Men were often accused of wasting their wives' earnings abroad and taking up drinking. When a migrant woman returns to Sri Lanka, her husband often claims her money and spends it on alcohol; mainly to increase his status by buying rounds for friends whose financial situation is lower than his. Alcohol is seen in Naeaegama as a sign of group bonding, masculinity and wealth. Although they enable their husbands' drinking by providing them with money earned through migration, or even by buying expensive bottles from duty-free shops on their way home, women try to limit this activity and press their husbands to spend money on family items rather than on alcohol. But women, whether abroad or at home, have little authority over their husbands. Women, in fact, are often blamed for the bad behaviour of their husbands (gambling, drinking or womanising), as their absence is thought to be driving men to act improperly. Images and representations diffused in television shows, newspapers and local gossip implied that men spent the money their wives earned abroad on alcohol to overcome their sadness at being left alone. 'Representations of delinquent, emasculated men appear in these stories in tandem with images of promiscuous, selfish, pleasure seeking women who neglect their husbands and children' (Gamburd 2002: 191). Negative stereotypes circulated in the village, portraying men as incompetent both as breadwinners and as lovers. Some of the women told Gamburd (2002) that Arabs consider Sri Lankan men as 'donkeys' since they are unable to provide for their wives and children.

In Lebanon (as in other Arab countries), a man is supposed to provide for his wife and family. It has become acceptable for women to be employed in the public sphere. The idea, however, that men sit at home while their wives provide for them is totally rejected. Lebanese employers often talk with disdain about Sri Lankan husbands who send their wives to work as housemaids while they lie drinking and spending their wives' money. Two quotes from my fieldwork:

> And they stay there, and they send the woman to work in an Arab country. Why don't they go to work, for example? Usually the man works to support the family, not the woman. She's 21 [the housemaid], she leaves her boy three years with her mother. She will be back for her boy in six years. And her husband stays at home. What does he do? I don't know. He's a driver, something like that. You want money, go yourself and make money. You don't send your wife to make money.

My Sri Lankan *concierge* sits there all day, doing nothing while his
wife works very hard.

Moreover, allusion is made in Naeaegama to the inability of men to
sexually satisfy their wives (Gamburd 2000). If they did, these women
would not leave their homes and perhaps sleep with Arab men. Popu-
lar stereotypes of migrant women are also spread. These women are
believed to travel in search of better economic gratification and a more
satisfying sex life. 'Female migration symbolizes a man's failure to provide adequate financial support for his family, and a woman's absence
deprives her husband of his legitimate sexual partner' (Gamburd
2000: 177).

'Horror-story-genre' accounts about women's sexual promiscuity and
sexual abuse were regularly published in the local press. In a letter to
The Island, a Sri Lankan newspaper published in English, the author
blames the government for allowing women to go and work abroad
and put them at risk of sexual assault and rape. Women, viewed as innocent victims, should not be allowed to migrate, 'for their own good'
he adds (quoted in Gamburd 2000). Ironically, Lebanese employers
use the same sentence to justify locking their housemaids inside the
household. Those women who tried to move away from traditional gender roles (through migration) were accused, upon return, of having
been badly influenced by their migratory experience.

Many women told Gamburd that employers used stories of promiscuous maids to forbid them to go outside. Most said that their sociali-
sation and mobility were restricted. Some women did not mind these
restrictions because employers treated them 'just like my daughter'.
Gamburd wondered why, then she realised that by being locked in,
maids were mainly saying that they could not have had any relationship with a man abroad, thus defending their 'own respectability and
chastity' (Gamburd 2000: 225).

'Empowerment' through wage earning and remittances

It has been suggested that wage earning from migration would increase women's power and consequently affect gender roles; or that, on
the contrary, returnees would passively re-embrace their roles as housewives. Gamburd (2000: 148) notes that 'gender roles that emerged
from the flux of individual lives in Naeaegama revealed a reality somewhere between these two extremes'. Women did gain in self-assurance
by working abroad but did not acquire new skills they could sell – once
back in Sri Lanka – to augment their earnings. They seem to easily
take back their roles as mothers and wives upon return, unable (or unwilling) to reject accepted customs. Gamburd argues that an important

sign of the change in women's images is the display of photographs within households. Prior to the migration 'boom', these photographs were snapshots taken at the wedding ceremony. In 1994, most migrants had photo albums filled with snapshots taken abroad, taking the same physical space as marriage photos did. According to Gamburd, this denotes the importance given to women's employment, portraying women as individuals rather than as halves of a couple. While the signs of prosperity might not be automatically visible to others, this does not mean that they do not exist. A poor family struggling with debts might need several years of steady earning before showing any signs of prosperity, such as buying a piece of land, building a house, etc. 'Similarly, women laboring under older gender hierarchies might need years of economic independence before they can overthrow cultural prejudices and sexist restrictions' (Gamburd 2000: 150). Long-term research on the subject can be enlightening.

Therefore, even though the optimistic gender revolution predicted by some scholars did not occur, the pessimistic one viewing women as passive and powerless is not a good portrayal of reality either. Renegotiations of gendered power structures do occur, even if not in a revolutionary manner (Gamburd 2000). The same could apply to Sri Lankan housemaids working in Lebanon.

Sri Lankan housemaids in Lebanon, in general, do not keep a record of how much money they send or have sent home. During my interviews, many answered: 'Everything', or 'Little', or 'Every few months I send $100 or so'. Remittances are usually sent to mothers (40 per cent) and husbands (30 per cent). Other answers included children, siblings (mainly sisters), father... Remittances can be a source of conflict back home. The son of a Lebanese employer I met at the Sri Lankan embassy told me: 'My mother [on behalf of her housemaid] sends money to Sri Lanka every three months. The maid's parents and husband fight over money there. Every time she gets a letter, she starts crying'.

To my question: 'How is the money spent at home?', all 90 housemaids answered 'Family expenses' (food, school); one-third mentioned building a house (on top of family costs of living). Building a house in Sri Lanka is very important for married women who want to live on their own with their husbands and children. Usually, married women share a house with their parents or parents-in-law. One Lebanese employer was telling me about what her housemaid was doing with the money earned working for her:

> She bought a plot of land. She is building a house with her money. Her husband injured himself at work, he used to be in construction. She showed me photos of her house, wonderful, co-

conut trees... Sri Lanka looks so pretty, they have a lot of green. I
imagine it is nicer than India.

Only 14.4 per cent mentioned saving money in a bank on top of other
uses (three of whom talked about a personal bank account: 'Bank in
my name in Sri Lanka, for me').
A general mismanagement of money is obvious, as one housemaid
told me: 'Too much spend money before, clothes, like this. I keep little
money on side'. Housemaids do not generally have long-term plans
and many, after going back to Sri Lanka and spending all their savings,
need to migrate again. Some keep postponing their return ('two or
three more years to make more money') and end up staying a long
time, partly because of their family's dependence on them. One housemaid in her eleventh year in Lebanon explained:

> And now I am work here too much, I don't have money, I help his
> family [husband], my family. Now more my family I help because
> my father die you know, and I don't have money, I don't have
> house. Eleven years. I help my all family, his all family, I don't
> have money now. Listen, Leila, me work, work, work. She [her sis-
> ter in Sri Lanka who used to work in Lebanon] calls every month
> she wants money. I send $200. Now this month Madame give me
> $250, I sent mama $100, Mali [sister] and her kids $75. I tell her
> 'I send you money little, little. You don't come, don't go another
> country'. My husband very poor, Leila. My husband, his parents do
> not help him at all. If he doesn't give them money they cannot eat.
> How do you want me to bring baby? If I bring baby here I cannot
> work. If I bring baby, I cannot work, they cannot eat. I think like
> this, I don't want children. I don't have a house, Leila.

However, the reason for endlessly postponing the moment of return can
be other than the need to make more money. As King et al. (2005: 38)
note:

> Like all aspects of the migration process, the dynamics of return are
> highly gendered. Often it is observed that... women are more reluc-
> tant to go back since it would mean giving up new-won freedoms...

This is something I observed during my research, especially with freelancers, some of whom have been in Lebanon for over a decade. They
were generally very happy in Lebanon, working, gaining money and,
more importantly, enjoying their independence away from familial and
cultural constraints – a viewpoint shared by Mozère (2005) following
her study of Filipina domestic workers in Paris. Mozère found that Fili-

pinas, who had somehow reversed traditional gender roles by becoming the ultimate 'breadwinners', were admired and respected by their families during their visits home. When asked whether they wanted to return to the Philippines for good, most said without hesitation that they could no longer adapt to the way of life there.

Wage earning and control of remittances can empower migrant women but the reality is usually not as bright. In general, the Sri Lankan women I interviewed did not seem to have much control over their remittances. Traditional gender roles and expectations seem to be very much anchored in women's minds despite the distance and the newly acquired 'freedom'. However, it has to be noted that things might be evolving: a few women I talked to stopped remitting to their husbands when they felt them to be wastefully spending the money. In the words of one housemaid:

> Money sent to Sri Lanka? $1,500 in four years to brother. Brother good. Not sure of husband. Sent first $200 to husband. He didn't do anything with it. So I stopped sending him.

Or of Lebanese employers:

> She sends a little bit for husband only. And the rest she wants to leave it and take all the money with her.

> I pay her $120 per month. I send the money via a bank every three months. My relative works in a bank. She sends the money to her mother. Not to her husband. I totally understand, she's right. What if he divorces her... The neighbour's maid warned her. It seems the other one, her husband took the money and cheated on her. Now she's saying: 'I want money in my hand, don't send anymore'. I told her, 'As you wish, but then you tell me when they need money'. Now, the last year, she tells me: 'Leave the money with you, when I leave for good to Sri Lanka I take the money with me cash'.

And yet many Sri Lankan housemaids I interviewed kept sending all their remittances to their husbands despite wasteful behaviour on their part. Some chose to send only parts of their wages, some none. Reactions to careless husbands are as multiple and complex as are the effects of migration on gender roles. But again things might be changing: 'lessons learned', as many said. Ramia, a freelancer who used to work for me, told me that her sister finally paid her back the $5,000 she owed her. She wanted to go to Sri Lanka to deposit the money in the bank. I asked her: 'Are you going to deposit the money in your hus-

band's name, in your name or both?' She said: 'No, Leila, in my name,
it is my money'.

Sometimes, Lebanese employers advise their housemaids to keep
their wages to themselves. One Lebanese employer told me:

> The previous ones [maids she employed in the past], when they
> come, at the very beginning, they used to send their money to
> their family. It happened that she is not married [her current
> maid]. But the previous ones were married. I used to get mad, you
> know. I used to tell them, 'You come here, you work like donkeys
> and you take your salary, the $100, and you send it to Sri Lanka.
> You're stupid, honestly. Poor things. Keep the money at least for
> you, take it with you when you go'. So, at the beginning they used
> to send. Then, when they start realising what you are telling them,
> and then, they hear stories and stories and stories, they leave the
> money with them here. Stories like their husband leaves them at
> the end, he takes the money, or the father spends the money...'

I remember my father advising Jamileh (our Syrian maid) to stop giving her money to her parents when she became an adult. We had
heard that Jamileh's brother had just got married and that he was
building a house using his sister's remittances. Not long after Jamileh,
following my father's advice, stopped sending them her wages, her parents came and took her away. She could have refused but, as I said before (in Chapter 1), she wanted to 'get a life' and get married. My sister
told me that her friend's Sri Lankan housemaid, Soma, had gone back
home with the money she had saved. As soon as she got down from
the plane, her father and brother took the money from her. The story
was that the brother wanted to get married and build a house for himself and his bride-to-be. Jamileh's brother built a house in Syria in the
mid-1970s. Soma's brother wanted to build a house in Sri Lanka in
2005. Different countries, different times, different women... same
story. When will we stop hearing similar stories?

'Transnational' motherhood

Within this 'transnational' existence, a new form of motherhood,
'transnational motherhood' (Hondagneu-Sotelo 2001), is created with
the migration of women working as domestics. Both employers (who
are themselves mothers) and employees rely on substitute mothering.
Domestic workers usually leave their children back home in their countries of origin, often limiting their mothering role to financial support.
Employers leave their children in the care of a foreigner. 'Both women
have removed themselves from the reproductive burden of their own

households, and both struggle with mothering from a distance. Both become totally dependent on the mother substitute in order to carry out their duties in the productive sphere, but at the same time resent her closeness to their own children' (Momsen 1999: 303). In the words of one Lebanese employer I interviewed:

> But listen, I read about 'soft medicine', they are all against a for-eign presence in the house. They tell you, it destroys the energy of the mother... Even for a couple the presence of a maid is no good. But what do I do? I have to. When they [her children] go to day-care till five, I take appointments till five then take them to my mother-in-law for a while then bring them home. I read a lot on *médecine douce* (soft medicine), macrobiotic. They tell you that the mother has energy, they encourage mothers to cook, even if she doesn't cook well, to prepare a salad, to put all the love in the salad for her children... The Sri Lankan prepares but she is tired... I pre-pare out of love. That's what I'm talking about. OK, they help us but the Sri Lankan takes away the mother's energy from the house.

This 'transnational motherhood' produces new inequalities. By provid-ing child care for their employers, domestic workers are denied the right to raise and care for their own children. Most domestics criticise their employers and view them as being neglectful parents. A form of discourse on 'comparative motherhood' follows, as domestic workers engage in a comparison between themselves, as poor parents highlight-ing the sacrifices they made for their children, and the privileged em-ployers who are perceived as neglectful. One Lebanese employer was telling me about her housemaid who was late getting her son ready for school one morning. The employer criticised the housemaid who then answered back: 'Why don't you take care of your own kid? Wash your face and take care of them'.

The economic aspect is the main focus of most writing on globalisa-tion. Studies of women migrants working as domestics include another indispensable aspect, the aspect of love and care. '[G]lobalization may be increasing inequities not simply in access to money – and those in-equities are important enough – but in access to care. The poor maid's child may be getting less motherly care than the first-world child' (Hochschild 2000: 7). Freudian psychology talks about the 'displace-ment' of emotions, meaning if one person is unavailable to receive one's love, one will turn to another person to love. For instance, a Sri Lankan housemaid working in Lebanon who is separated from her children might project/displace her affection onto her employer's chil-dren. Hochschild (2000) wonders if this 'surplus' love that a rich child is receiving is not 'borrowed' from someone else (i.e. a less fortunate child further down the care chain whose mother migrated to 'sell' her care elsewhere).

Within the 'globalisation of love', the housemaid is paid to care. Can it be true care? I have seen housemaids care for their children's employers with total love and giving. But I have also seen housemaids 'act' loving to please their employers. How does this affect the 'rich child' when his mother leaves him in the care of the housemaid? As the General Security director put it to me: 'The maid is taking care of the children. It is not the same. Maids prepare children to go to school, they make them sandwiches. Some children would run to their maids and not their mothers'. One Lebanese employer told me: 'She [the housemaid] is not me, but at certain moments she is replacing me [as a mother]. She is with my child, she is giving him lunch...' This 'substitute' care has become so widespread in Lebanon that it has alarmed the clergy: priests are now preaching on Lebanese television, urging Lebanese mothers to get more involved in their children's education instead of leaving them all the time with the housemaid.

This is indeed a very complex subject, as Lebanese mothers do want their housemaids to care for their children but not too much. Jealousy is at times felt by Lebanese employers, as expressed in one interview: 'You see, X (her five-month-old son) adores her; with me, he never laughs like this. I am going to kill her'. I have personally observed the satisfaction on the housemaids' side when this happens. One housemaid, when asked if she was allowed out, said:

> No, I don't want to go out. Because I don't go anywhere I look this baby like my baby. I see before come here, I see newspaper, every country baby fall down, die... like this, there is people jail, like this I am too much afraid and this baby sleep my bed night. He don't go her mother near. Mother give *biberon* (baby's bottle), he don't take... laughing... Only with me, everything me. Like my house I see this house.

Lebanese employers often doubt their housemaid's ability to care for their own children. In the words of one Lebanese employer:

> Two days ago, my daughter was crying. I told her [the housemaid]: 'For sure you did something to her. I know you did not hit her but maybe you harmed her, you made her do something'. 'No Madame, I like her'. They are scary in this regard, for sure she did something to her. Turned out that my daughter wanted me not her... For instance, we get in the car, I put my daughter in her car seat, I ask her to hold my son because he refuses to sit in his seat,

I see her bending on him. We cannot count on her. She says: 'Madame, I get carsick'. We come in the evening, the doctor told me to relax, so I ask her to put the kids to bed, I know that a maid cannot take the place of a mother, but I needed to rest, so I ask her to do it and I see her asleep in bed. You see? Things like that. You cannot rely on them'.

Where does work start and end, but more importantly where does love start and end? How much love is a housemaid 'allowed' to feel? But also, how much love does a housemaid allow herself to feel knowing that, one day, she will have to leave the children she is caring for to go back to her own (who, meanwhile, were cared for by someone else, another 'substitute mother')? Housemaids console themselves by reiterating the importance of their actions in assuring a brighter future for their children. In the words of one housemaid: 'I send money for education, food, house... They are well taken care of there anyway, it is better for them that I leave'. Does sacrifice alleviate bad conscience and is this why some housemaids refuse to admit to the positive side of their migration experience, concentrating instead on their 'victim' role? Is victimisation an easier way out for them (the only state they can admit to) since they cannot admit to being happy away from their families?

Hochschild (2000) points to the 'hidden costs' of migration. At times, children do not even recognise their mothers when they return home. Sri Lankan women sometimes stay in Lebanon for long periods of times (fifteen years or more with only two or three visits to Sri Lanka). Mothers who were not able to displace their love may suffer from phases of depression. They get into a 'mood' that Lebanese employers dislike and cannot comprehend. One Lebanese employer said about her Sri Lankan housemaid: 'She sits there all day long, with a face of an owl (*wij el boum*). I tell her, "Finish, stop crying, work!"'.

Despite the 'hidden costs', female emigration is still increasing and women are still leaving their families. Does this mean that positive gains surpass negative costs in migration?

There are no easy solutions for the human costs of global care. Perhaps one answer would be to raise the value of caring work, which has been so relatively low compared to other types of labour. 'The low value placed on caring work is due neither to an absence of demand for it (which is always high) nor to the simplicity of the work (successful caregiving is not easy) but rather to the cultural politics underlying this global exchange' (Hochschild 2000: 7). Care workers should be given more credit and higher wages. Fathers should contribute more to household chores. Care then, according to Hochschild (2000), would not need to be relegated down the social class ladder but would be shared equally by parents. The potential hidden losers of the global care chain are yet to be addressed. Long-term studies on children of migrants might be helpful in this matter. But also perhaps, the children of employers.

4 Power, resistance and racism in domestic work

'Tout pouvoir, parce que pouvoir, abuse et abusera'
'All power, because it is power, abuses and will abuse'
Alain (*Propos*)

Domestic work is a particular type of employment. It takes place in a unique setting within the privacy of households, where the space of work is the same as the space of life. The relationship between a housemaid and her employer is more intense than other types of worker/employer relationship. As Romero (1992: 119) notes, it is out of the ordinary in today's societies to witness women 'from different social-economic, racial and ethnic backgrounds interact(ing) in an informal and intimate setting'. This interaction generates hierarchies and matrices of domination and subordination which are perhaps typically characteristic of gender relations. And yet, in the case under study, they are between persons of the same sex. It also triggers various sets of reactions to counter-effect the domineering patterns. Moreover, the degrees of 'otherness' are somewhat intensified and highlighted in a context where different cultural worlds coexist (Momsen 1999).

This chapter attempts to show, by looking at various cases present in the literature and supplementing them with my own findings, how issues of power, resistance and racism are interplayed within this special type of employment held by migrant housemaids of colour.

Power

The employer-employee relationship

The living and working conditions of migrant workers depend largely on the relationship they have with their female employers. The dynamics created by the complex relationship between the two women constitute the core of studies relating to domestic work. The employer-employee personal relationship is often portrayed as one of exploitation and control (control over work but also the person). 'What makes domestic service an occupation more profoundly exploitive than other comparable occupations grows out of the precise element that makes it unique: the personal relationship between employer and employee' (Rollins 1985: 156). Figures from Kalayaan (a movement for the rights of overseas domestic workers) for 1996-1997 are characteristic of the difficult circumstances which domestic workers face. Of 195 workers registered at the centre in the UK, 84 per cent reported psychological abuse, 34 per cent physical abuse and 10 per cent sexual abuse. Physical and psychological abuse is usually carried out by female employers (unlike sexual abuse which is perpetrated by men). Indirect modes of control and power are more common than straightforward violence. That is not to say that direct abuse does not exist within this type of employment. 'There are certainly domestic workers who are being abused physically, mentally and sexually, as well as low-level abuse and exploitation' (Anderson 2000: 79). But the extent of the abuse is hard to measure, as women are ashamed or afraid to speak out. More importantly, Kalayaan figures indicate that 'women's experiences could not be passed off as simply due to a bad employer' (Anderson 2000: 97). This is an open invitation to scholars to try to uncover the intricate reasons and means of such abuse.

Domestic workers are deemed to be 'inferior' beings. As discussed in Chapter 3, employers have recourse to the services of domestics in order to avoid reassessing traditional gender roles. 'The battle that housewives have in convincing males and children that housework is real work is replayed in the conflict between domestics and housewives' (Romero 1992: 130). Paid housework is constructed following the model of the unpaid housework of the housewife, a model that reinforces women's inferiority. Female employers 'simply perpetuate the sexist division of labor by passing on the most devalued work in their lives to another woman – generally a woman of color' (Romero 1992: 131). The domestic is, in fact, an 'extension of the more menial part' of the employer; should the female employer identify with her, she does so negatively (Rollins 1985). As one domestic in Genet (1976: 100-101) said, impersonating her Madame: 'I hate domestics... Domestics do not belong to humanity... Your face of horror and remorse, your wrinkled elbows, your old-fashioned blouses, your bodies wearing our old clothes. You are our deformed mirror, our safety valve, our shame, our dreg'. This negative 'projection' and internalisation of domestic workers' inferior status might explain, in part, why domestic service is viewed not so much as formal employment, but more as an informal arrangement that is open to abuse.

Employers do not just want their house cleaned; 'They want their psychological needs to be fulfilled and their self-esteem and well-being enhanced' (Romero 1992: 130). By supervising and controlling their domestic workers, employers achieve a sense of power and authority. The more workers are pushed into demeaning work and are made to feel inferior, the more employers believe in their own superiority. The real subject of conflict is the person and not the labour. 'To this extent the employer must overcome their common gender and shared experiences as women. Violence may be one mechanism for doing so' (Anderson 2000: 143-144). Through control and power strategies, the employer asserts her own superiority over the domestic but, more importantly, her own difference.

Power over the person

The domestic worker or housemaid is not just accomplishing tasks but performing a role, and the employer is not just getting services but a whole person associated with these services. Therefore, one could assume that labour is not the only thing 'commoditised' within this particular form of employment. It is the worker's 'personhood' rather than her labour that the employer is trying to buy. Anderson (2000: 108) notes that the 'tension between "labour power" and "personhood" is particularly striking with reference to migrant domestic workers'. The employer is buying total control over the lives of the maids. It is, therefore, the 'slippage between labour power and personhood, and the employer's power to command the whole person of the domestic worker... that can help us begin to understand... how it is that some women exploit others within a general theory of care as women's work' (Anderson 2000: 125). As mentioned throughout this book, Lebanese employers usually control every aspect of their live-in housemaids' lives and personhoods. Anderson calls 'personalistic power' (power over person) the power exercised by employers over their domestic workers. By 'dehumanising' the domestic and choosing to view her as 'a human being who is yet not a real human being – with likes and hates, relations of her own, a history and ambitions of her own – but a human being who is socially dead' (Anderson 2000: 121), employers exercise an extreme form of power that is uncommon in other employer-employee relationships.

'Re-naming' housemaids can be seen as one aspect of this ongoing 'dehumanisation'. 'In Victorian England, servants were deliberately depersonalised and often called by standardized names, whatever their real name might be' (Cock 1989: 74). In a different setting (nineteenth-century France), Mirbeau (1983: 37) describes in his novel how the new maid meets her 'bourgeois' male employer for the first time:

> What is your name, my child?
> Celestine, Sir.
> Celestine... he said... Celestine? ... Damn... Beautiful name, I'm not saying the contrary... but too long, my child, much too long... I will call you Marie, if you don't mind... It is very nice too, and it is short... And also, I called all my maids Marie.
> Celestine [to herself]: They all have this odd habit of never calling you by your real name...

This 'practice' is also common in Lebanon. One Lebanese employer related to me in an interview:

> My grandmother had a maid. Her name was... I don't know, her name was very difficult to remember. And my grandmother was so lazy. She looked at her, she said: 'The other one was called Nada, I'm going to call you Nada'. And they [all the family members] called her Nada for ten years. You can hear it from many, many families. They always give her the name of the one who was before.

Another Lebanese woman I know used to call her neighbour's housemaid Rani. She had once employed a housemaid by the name of Rani and since then: 'They are all Rani to me'.

A domestic worker is hired not just for her physical labour but also (if not especially) for her emotional labour and personality traits (Anderson 2000; Constable 1997; Rollins 1985). Employers are looking for someone '"affectionate", "loving", "good with children"' (Anderson 2000: 119). The domestic worker has to be caring but not too caring; the emotional responsibility of caring for the children remains the prerogative of the mother-employer. Some want a clean, non-smelly person; others look for someone who is honest, trustworthy, not too attractive nor too smart, and unskilled (with the exception of skills relating to household chores). In short, employers want to safeguard their 'power to control' and choose housemaids accordingly.

In Lebanon, recruitment agencies prepare small dossiers that include various demographic data and a photograph of the housemaid for employers to choose from ('I chose her by catalogue, she had a scary picture in the catalogue'). Some Lebanese employers interviewed specifically asked for young women:

> At her age [nineteen], it's easier than if they were 40. Because she's new, you regulate her as you want. As if somebody you raise, educate. Not like with someone already grown up who has a lot of demands. So I brought her and told myself: 'I'll try her (bjarreba)'. This is what the agent said, he said: 'Try her for two months; if you don't like her, return her (reddiah), don't start her papers before two months'. But she turned out OK.

Others wanted older women, preferably ugly, who would have overcome or could control their sexual desires:

> I have a friend, she is the one who has the most experience with them [housemaids]. She told me once, 'I chose her, not beautiful

> and not young. A woman of 50 and ugly. I chose her at the agency, the ugliest woman in the contract'. Because it is less worrying, so that she does not go out, and starts asking: 'I want to go out with my friends, et cetera'.

Some wanted her to be married with children: 'If she's not married she might not be tender with children'. Others did not want her to be married: 'She will spend her time here missing her husband and children'. Preferences varied but all requirements had similar implications (naïve, inexperienced and not sexually promiscuous) that seek to maintain power and control over housemaids on a continuous 24 hours-a-day basis. In brief, employers wanted housemaids who could be 'moulded' according to their own needs.

Employers, Constable (1997) notes, also have ethnic and racial preferences; they prefer foreigners because they are cheaper, more docile and subservient. Employers in her study wanted to employ Filipinas who had little education and came from rural areas, as they were more docile and more accustomed to the kind of landowner/tenant relationship. Other studies have also documented how, in many countries, such as Taiwan, Italy and Spain, Filipinas are imbued with certain 'good' qualities as domestic workers and carers (Cheng 2004; Zontini 2002); they are the preferred nationality, but are also (as in Lebanon) more expensive to hire. Employers in my study preferred to employ Sri Lankans who often came from rural areas and were easy to 'manage'. In the words of one Lebanese employer I interviewed:

> Whenever I bring a maid, I bring a maid from a village from Sri Lanka. She doesn't know anything. I train her the way I want.... I tell him [the agent]: 'I want somebody *ma bayess temma ella emma* (whose lips have not been kissed other than by her mother)'. I don't know... And it happened that all the maids that I got, let's call them employees, I don't like to call them maids, I never have problems. At the end, of course they are after all human beings. They come to my house, they like me, and they don't want to go back.

Lebanese employers prefer foreign housemaids to Lebanese ones, as I noted earlier. It is true that, nowadays, very few Lebanese women wish to work as maids. When or if they do, they usually do not live in and they charge higher fees than foreign housemaids. When asked why they do not employ Lebanese maids, employers generally talked (again) about the issue of control. In short, foreigners are easier to control and ignore:

I prefer to bring somebody far from our country, not to worry. The problems are closer to them [Lebanese], the thinking... Foreigners feel that they are far. And abandoned. There's no permanent contact [with their family]. I think that those who understand your language and live a life close to yours they start to want to be like you in a way. There was a maid at my parents' house, Syrian, she used to say, when the phone rang and my parents were out, she used to answer and pretend she was the lady of the house... I don't know, I prefer a foreigner, someone who is 'distant'. If you're saying something in the house they [Lebanese] become more curious, want to know more. Their way of living is like yours, the habits and traditions are the same, everything is closer to them. She [Lebanese maid] might want to go out... they are more demanding maybe. I think they [Lebanese maids] become familiar faster (by-akhdo wij asrah), because they already are citizens... I remember from my mother, when she used to go out the maid would wear her clothes for example. As if she was like her. They had 'a kind of complex'. So, I think, I prefer foreigners as maids...

'Less-educated and poor domestics' (Rollins 1985: 195) showed more deference and docility and were, therefore, in 'demand'. Rollins relates how one employer had doubts about hiring her as she considered her to be 'too educated' (Rollins worked as a domestic worker as part of her fieldwork). Rollins (1985: 162) realised that she had gone to the interview 'somewhat carelessly relaxed: I carried myself and spoke in a natural way, without the deliberately subservient manner I had feigned during my first set of job interviews'. She went to see her employer-to-be the next day and made sure to 'perform' as expected. She did get the job after showing enough signs of deference. Deference is encouraged by employers. Through deferent demands, employers reassert their superiority. Rollins (1985: 180) notes that: 'The presence of the deference-giving inferior enhances the employer's self-esteem as an individual, neutralizes some of her resentment as a woman, and, where appropriate, strengthens her sense of self as a white person'. Acts of deference encompass gesture, clothing, speech but also an attitude toward the tasks assigned to her. A maid, for instance, is supposed to take pleasure while working. Filipinas interviewed by Parreñas (2001) complained about the 'emotional labour of smiling'.

Emotional power

Maternalism
Maternalism has been condemned by many (Anderson 2000; Parreñas 2001; Rollins 1985; Romero 1992) as the main disguised strategy of

power and exploitation used by employers. Maternalism is an indirect form of power; it advocates affection and care while, in fact, reinforcing the employer's superiority in opposition to the worker's inferiority. Rollins (1985) believes that maternalism is inherent to all female employer-domestic relationships. The female employer still holds a position of authority, a 'masculine role' according to Rollins, yet the fact that she is a woman employing another woman in the private sphere affects the way this role is applied. The historical and feudal basis for maternalism is paternalism: 'the employer's obligations of protection and guidance in return for the servant's work, loyalty and obedience' (Rollins 1985: 178-179). As both employers and employees are women, this authoritative relationship changes to a more nurturing role where feminine characteristics are implemented. The intimacy created between them, however, is not to be understood in positive terms. Maternalism presupposes a relationship of domination, and not just one of protection and care. The emphasis the female employer puts on the emotional aspect of the relationship is, in fact, a form of manipulation.

Both maternalism and paternalism are in fact 'the conceptualization of the domestic as childlike' (Rollins 1985: 187). Viewing maids as irresponsible beings just like children somehow justifies the maternalistic attitude. 'Maternalism is based on the superordinate-subordinate relationship, with the female employer caring for the worker as she would for a child or a pet, thereby expressing, in a feminised way, her lack of respect for the domestic worker as an adult worker. It is encapsulated in the use of the term "girl" to describe the adult woman. It is an over-personalisation of employment relations and a refusal to properly acknowledge the employment relation, but presenting this overpersonalisation as a benefit, as friendship' (Anderson 2000: 144). Hence, Lebanese employers call their housemaids *binit* (girl) even if she is 60 years old. The fact that maids accept such treatment encourages employers to carry on with the same attitude. But maids, according to Rollins, have to accept this type of treatment in order to survive in the job. After all, it is the employer who holds the ultimate authority.

Power is often disguised, according to Anderson (2000), and is, in the case of female employers, expressed insidiously through charity: '... through kindness and charity the powerful woman asserts her "feminine" (clean woman) qualities of morality and pity over the helpless recipient' (Anderson 2000: 144). Employers often complain about the ingratitude of their workers. They treat them kindly, pity them and offer them a job and, in return, workers are not grateful. Nina, an employer complaining to Anderson about her worker from Bulgaria, moaned:

I had a bright thought, 'She needs to see her friends'. Because I was tired of all the girls changing so many times I gave her Sunday off. Now, every morning, including Sundays, the girl wakes, helps grandmother to the toilet and changes her pamper... Then she goes, but she must be back for seven pm... Then, after all I do for her, the girl says every Sunday she would like to be back at midnight and not to do any work – that is not to change pamper in the morning' (Anderson 2000: 144).

Nina, according to Anderson, is an example of maternalism. Nina did not give her worker a day off because she was rightfully entitled to it, but because of Nina's compliance with the job. When the worker asked for more, Nina was upset and felt that her kindness was rejected and concluded that the worker was heartless and ungrateful. The domestic worker is pitied, sustained, always treated as an inferior and never as an equal. The real objective of maternalism, therefore, is not to 'lift up' the domestics, encourage and nurture; instead, it is deployed to confirm the inferiority of domestics.

Lebanese employers, too, often moan about their 'ungrateful' housemaids. As one employer complained to me:

The more you get them used to kindness, the worse they get. Other employers do not give days off and they are not so nice. In the contract it is forbidden that they go out. I give her Sundays out. I ask for take-out food for her when there's nothing to eat. Daily meals just as I do for me from take-out restaurants, good ones, you know... I give her clothes I don't wear anymore, I buy her deodorant, today I made her change her toothbrush... When my husband comes late from work let's say it's after eleven and she's in bed, I'm the one who prepares dinner for him. You know X [her husband], he would not hesitate to wake her up. But I don't let him... The second one [she asked for another housemaid], I will be careful, *je vais la dresser* (I am going to train her). You can't give them too many rights.

Maternalism is regularly conveyed and sustained through gifts (mostly not desired). When it comes to employers and domestic workers, gift exchange is representative of the power relations involved. A domestic worker interviewed by Rollins (1985: 190) said:

This woman was always giving me her old size five-and-a-half shoes. I wear an eight! But my mother always said, and she did domestic work for years, she said, 'No matter what they give you, you take it because one day they're going to give you something worth having'. And I dragged those damned five-and-a-half *double*

A shoes home! I'd give them to somebody else or throw them away.

Gift-giving is a form of maternalism used 'to "buy" and "bond" the domestic' (Romero 1992: 109). Gifts, in this particular setting, are often used as a substitute for wage raises or other benefits. Raises are rare, negotiating hours of work and or days off are difficult. One way for employers to compensate their domestic workers is by giving them gifts. 'Gifts from sponsors to housemaids provide an appropriate mode of symbolic and material compensation for services above and beyond any formal, contractual rights and obligations' (Gamburd 2000: 113).

Employers usually give old clothes to their domestics or other items they want to get rid of. 'This practice of giving old clothes within a work setting is unique to domestic service. It is almost inconceivable that the same woman would consider offering her old linen jacket to her secretary' (Romero 1992: 109). The employee has to show gratitude for such acts of generosity. Instead of refusing undesired objects, employees play the game and accept gifts with appreciation. The custom of gift-giving is, therefore, significant in highlighting the unequal relationship and class distinction between the employer and her domestic. Not only is the domestic unable to reciprocate but she has to accept the gift, even if unwanted, and praise the gift-giver for her benevolence.

'Part of the family'
Being constructed and admitted as 'part of the family' can be seen as another strategy to exercise power. Employers often say about their domestic worker: 'We treat her as a member of the family'. According to Anderson (2000: 123), 'the phrase suggests a special relationship beyond the simple bond of employment'. In the words of a Lebanese employer:

> I might speak with a temper a bit [to the housemaid]. Let me tell you how, once or twice I raised my voice. They have a lot of pride, if you give her an observation, she becomes cross with you. This I can't stand. That's why then my answer is a bit tough. For me she is a member of the house, I treat her with respect, just as I act she acts. That's why I can't accept from her anything wrong. I can't accept. It is not acceptable that she acts wrongly with me by acting just once impolitely. I am very good with her.

The clear advantage for the employer is that it weakens the position of the worker, making it harder for the latter to discuss wages and working conditions, to draw the line between her labour and life. Anderson

(2000: 123) cites a Filipina domestic worker in Paris: 'The problem is, they don't treat me as a slave or anything. The problem is they treat me as a family...' Trying to 'embellish' the exploitation by giving it a 'familial' context is typical of employers. In one interview, a Lebanese employer said about Syrian maids working in Lebanese households in the past:

> You know how old the Syrians used to start working? Nine years old. Me, I knew one who worked for one of my aunts, she was nine. I used to tell my aunt: 'How can you make her work?' She used to answer: 'I am not making her work, she is like my daughter (*mitil binti*)'.

The more the worker feels and cares for her employer, the more she is subject to exploitation. A joke told by Filipinas in Hong Kong (Constable 1997: 104-105) is quite representative:

> A Filipina domestic worker arrives in Hong Kong at the home of her new employer. The employer says to her, 'We want to treat you as a member of the family'. The domestic helper is very happy to hear this. On Sunday, the helper's day off, her employer says to her, 'You must work before you leave the house on Sundays because you are a member of the family'. And the employer adds, 'And you must come home in time to cook dinner for the family'. 'But Sir, ma'am, I would like to eat with my friends today, because it is my day off', says the helper. 'But you are a member of the family', says her employer, 'and because you are a member of the family, you must eat with us'.

According to Romero (1992: 130), '[e]mployers' references to domestics as "one of the family" concretizes these gender-specific characteristics, equating the work with homemaking'. The personal relationship between the employer and the employee makes it harder to distinguish between paid and unpaid housework. This relationship, which takes its roots from the feudalistic master-servant tradition, is inappropriate in the capitalistic model (Romero 1992). Housewives and domestics, unlike other workers, have to deal with the added pressure of having their work considered as 'non-work'. In fact, employers refuse to admit to the fact that their homes have become the workplace of the domestic workers. They do not consider the domestic to be a worker but an extension of themselves.

Within the household, a sort of intimacy (or emotional blackmail) is created on the part of the employer that hinders the objectivity of domestics and results in a rather accommodating and at times 'over-zealous' attitude. Quoting a domestic working on her day off, 'exceptionally today I will take C with me… for a birthday party – no one is available and for a child it's a pity to miss the party, his old friends – so I did it' (Anderson 2000: 124). The 'job' is no longer considered as such; instead, it carries with it an emotional involvement (or investment) that, at times, drives domestic workers to forget about their rights (in that instance, a day off).

The employer finds herself able to manipulate the situation for her own benefit; that is, asking for more work and paying less. 'It is by slipping between the two imagined domains of the public and the private that the employer consolidates much of her power: the worker may be treated as "part of the family" (governed by customary relations) when it is a matter of hours and flexibility, and as a worker (governed by civic relations) if she becomes too sick to work' (Anderson 2000: 5). When Rollins (1985: 216) asked a group of six domestics whether they considered themselves to be 'one of the family', they laughed and answered: 'No! Of course not! Employers just say that in order to get more work out of you'.

The pretence of belonging to her employer's family is also an attempt to dehumanise the domestic worker by almost eliminating her own family. 'While being part of the family may be perceived by the employer as a great favour, for the worker it may be experienced as a denial of their humanity, a deep depersonalization, as being perceived only in their occupational role, as a "domestic" rather than as a person with her own needs, her own life, and her own family outside of the employer's home' (Anderson 2000: 125). Moreover, while the worker is supposed to care for employers and be deeply involved emotionally in their lives, these feelings are not reciprocated. Employers in general did not want to know about their domestic workers' private lives (Lebanese employers, for example, had very little information about their housemaids: 'She is married, mother of two', or 'She comes from a village'). According to Rollins (1985), employers did, occasionally, treat their domestics as confidantes. However, employers only confide in their domestic workers because 'the domestic is so far from being socially and psychologically significant to the employer' (Rollins 1985: 167). In fact, Rollins believes that the employer does not care what the domestic thinks of her. The domestic is physically close but, in reality, she belongs to a totally different social setting. The employer does not even consider the possibility that the domestic might relate her secrets to anyone close to her milieu. It is, in fact, safe to confide in the domestic worker: she is invisible, insignificant and certainly not considered as a close friend (Constable 1997).

Legal power

The *kafala*, or sponsorship system, can be viewed as another 'control mechanism' (Longva 1997). On top of their own power as employers, sponsors held other powers: the one delegated to them by the state over the migrants and the one migrant workers had to assign to them for representation. According to Longva (1997: 101), '[b]efore the law... the sponsor represented not only himself but also the state (*vis-à-vis* the migrant worker) and the migrant worker (*vis-à-vis* the state)'.

In the United Kingdom, Kalayaan demonstrated how immigration laws reinforce the notion of the domestic workers being 'part of the employer's family', and not independent workers, by linking their visas to the name of the employer (Anderson 2000). This takes place in many other countries which 'import' domestic workers, as the various contributors in Lutz (2008) show. Romero (1992: 120) notes: 'house-hold-labour negotiations frequently occur within the underground economy; they involve few government regulations'. Employers, there-fore, benefit from great latitude of action and determine as they see fit the working conditions, wages, raises, etc., of their domestic workers. This added power, characterised by the legal and administrative condi-tions migrant women face in the host country, renders the workers 'at the mercy' of the employers (Chang 2000). First, the domestic worker enters the country with the employer's name stamped on her passport and cannot change employer whenever she wishes. Second, assuming that the migrant does negotiate a contract with her employer (it does happen even if it is not the common practice), 'she has no bargaining power or legal recourse if the employer violates it' (Chang 2000: 139). Moreover, it is common practice for the employer to hold on to the do-mestic worker's passport, strengthening the exploitative bond already existent. Employers can also report a worker should they become dissa-tisfied with her work. This might lead to her deportation. Finally, the minute housemaids 'run away' (usually without their passports) their status turns to illegal, with a risk of imprisonment and deportation. Undocumented migrants are trapped in the host country, 'running up ever-increasing fines as overstayers...' (Anderson 2000: 30).

> The fact that employers are citizens and the workers are not citi-zens formalizes their unequal power relations – even outside of the employment relationship, workers and their employers are not equal before the law. This facilitates the persistence of the master/mistress-servant role. (Anderson 2000: 193)

Thus, as many studies in different contexts have shown, immigration status reinforces the inequality within the employer-employee relationship and renders migrants more vulnerable to exploitation and abuse (Anderson 2000; Chang 2000; Longva 1997; Momsen 1999; Parreñas 2001; Romero 1992).

To summarise, control manoeuvres, whether 'personalistic power', 'maternalism', being 'part of the family' or 'legal dependence' all constitute indirect means used by employers to reassert the inferiority of the domestic and hence, their own superiority. All are used to keep the maid in 'her place' (Rollins 1985). Behind closed doors, female employers, encouraged by state regulations, assert their power by using 'smooth' methods of control founded mainly on emotional manipulation. More direct methods carry the risk of sullying their self-proclaimed reputation of 'ideal employers'.

Resistance

Despite the fact that it is the employer who holds the authority and defines the employer-employee relationship (which is one of inequality), most studies pertaining to the subject of migrant domestic workers agree that the power relationship within the household is not unidirectional. 'Nor do employers have a monopoly on power and workers a monopoly on resistance. Rather, power and resistance coexist and constantly reassert themselves against each other' (Constable 1997: 11). For sure, housemaids may be vulnerable, having to endure their employers' desires and demands. They can, however, attain a certain degree of power and independence through unofficial strategies of resistance. 'Although official hierarchies trumped informal insubordination, housemaids playing their cards correctly could achieve a significant degree of power and autonomy in the homes where they worked' (Gamburd 2000: 103). As direct confrontations with the employers are considered to be risky, 'anger could usually be expressed only in silence' (Romero 1992: 108). Strategies of resistance might be inaccessible to employers but not to certain scholars who have managed to interpret the more discrete signs of dissent sent by domestic workers.

Closeness and dependency

For most domestic workers, the only available way to improve their living and working conditions is by developing a long and close association with their employers. Within this form of employment, characterised by pervasive closeness, good interpersonal relations are very important. The entire household becomes more and more dependent on the migrant worker or the 'other' who holds a strategic role within it (Momsen 1999). By developing emotional ties with members of the household (especially children), domestic workers are somehow able to defy the clear-cut cultural and personal confines of the employer-employee relationship. According to Gamburd (2000), however, one cannot confirm the conscious manipulation of or by domestics, as they themselves become emotionally involved with their employers. 'Personal relationships obscure a straightforward narrative of resistance and critique' (Gamburd 2000: 104).

The indispensable nature of the work, added to the personal ties developed within the household, contribute to the access of domestic workers to 'informal power'. The domestic worker's 'centrality to smooth domestic functioning gives her a certain power to negotiate boundaries and resist her subordinate position' (Gamburd 2000: 109). As noted previously, the 'part of the family' strategy reinforces the authority of employers as they use emotions to control their domestic workers. However, workers, too, capitalise on the dependency and attachment of employers by using 'intimacy to de-emphasize servitude' (Parreñas 2001: 180). As one Filipina notes (in Parreñas 2001: 184): 'They treat me well because they need me'. In the words of two Lebanese employers:

> She changed my life. No housework, more quality time with my family. All that. I think, when she leaves, what am I going to do?

> I have to treat her well because I leave my son a lot with her.

However, Lebanese employers are careful to ensure that housemaids do not get *too* close, as one Lebanese employer told me:

> I don't know how to explain... Sometimes, you cannot be too nice to them [housemaids]... Sometimes they stop even doing things because they consider that they are now a part of the family. I don't mind as long as they do their job. That's it.

Inter-dependency is, in fact, inherent to the employer-employee relationship. Employers treat workers 'like one in the family' to encourage them to do a good job while workers do a good job to be treated as human beings or 'like one of the family'.

Other mechanisms help domestics cope with the fact that they are treated as 'non-persons' (Rollins 1985). Apart from a strong personal value-system based on an individual's worth and not on material gains, domestics gain strength based on the insight they construct by having access to their employers' lives. By working closely with their employers, domestics are able to observe and discover their weaknesses and fragility. As they get to know their employers – in some ways more than anybody else – they are able to disregard the disdain and maintain their self-respect. Domestics 'knew the importance of knowledge of the powerful to those without power' (Rollins 1985: 216). Below are two examples from Rollins (1985: 213-214):

> I used to feel envy of all the things they have. When I was younger, I did have a little envy. I wondered why they could have it all and we didn't have any. But I don't anymore because as I got older and took a good look at them, I realize material gains don't necessarily mean you're happy. And most of those women aren't happy, you know. I feel I've done a good job. All three of my children came here to me to Boston. They're doing well. I'm proud of what I've done. I don't have any regrets' (Ms Roy).

> Even today – and he's [her employer's son] a big doctor now – you know, when she wants to tell him something important, she calls me and asks me to call him. 'Cause he'll hang up on her! He hates her! When I was there [when the son was a teenager] he used to yell at her. He never yelled at me. Said then and he says now that I'm more of a mother to him than she is. I still get a birthday card and a Mother's Day card from him every year. Never sends her one. Now isn't that an awful way to live? (Ms Samuel).

The material dependence maids have on employers is faced by a psychological independence that helps them keep a mind and a value-system of their own. Domestics are proud of the courage they had to leave their country for a better life; they recognise the hardships and the efforts invested in order to keep a stable job. They realise above all that they cannot progress very far in life because of their class and race. 'This ability to assess their employers' and their own lives based on an understanding of social realities and on a distinct moral system is what gives domestics the strength to be able to accept what is beneficial to them in their employers' treatment while not being profoundly damaged by the negative conceptualizations on which such treatment is based' (Rollins 1985: 218-219).

Limiting the employers' intrusion into their private lives is another 'survival strategy', according to Rollins (1985). When asked personal questions about their lives, domestics cannot but answer. They are careful, however, about not giving away too many details. They also sometimes simply make up stories to satisfy their employers' curiosity. One Lebanese employer told me about how her housemaid lied about her marital status:

> The previous one, she was married and just before she left Lebanon, I found out that she was divorced, and she had a baby, a son,

beautiful son, green eyes and... Just before she left, I found out that she was divorced. She was not telling that she was divorced [laughter]. I don't know why they lie. They lie maybe because they are scared.

Coping strategies

Filipina domestic workers in Rome and Los Angeles studied by Parreñas (2001) do not passively accept the conditions of their downward class mobility (most of them had acquired a high level of education in the Philippines). 'They attempt to subvert the pain inflicted by their decline in social status in numerous ways, which include, surprisingly enough, accepting the racialization of domestics, embracing the setting of intimacy in the workplace, and, more expectedly, incorporating "immediate struggles" in the performance of domestic work' (Parreñas 2001: 172). While sticking to the script, they have recourse to various strategies to attain more material rewards and fewer emotional adversities. Frowning can be a tactic (especially when expressed on rare occasions) used to manipulate the employer and make them feel guilty. Subversive acts can also include working at a slow pace, crying (while still working) so that employers allow them to go out, banging things like pots, etc., to receive attention. Filipinas know that 'the smallest detour away from the script is noticeable to employers' (Parreñas 2001: 190). Emotional outbursts take the employers by surprise and lead them to accommodate their workers. 'Talking back' can be a last but effective resort, because it is generally unexpected. It can lead, however, to the worker being fired (while emotional display does not). Quitting is only applied as a last resort should all these 'immediate struggles' fail. Filipinas also stress the privilege they have as migrant women compared to poorer women who stayed in the Philippines, and the financial gains associated with the job that insures better lives for them and their families. Moreover, they take comfort in their job's temporary aspect. 'However, the central means by which they ease their pain do not question but instead maintain the relations of inequality established by employers in the organization of domestic work. For example, they wish to someday be just like their employers' (Parreñas 2001: 172). The 'fantasy of reversal' – employing domestics once back in the Philippines – is their ultimate consolation.

Attempts by household workers to improve their working conditions remain isolated and personalised, according to Romero (1992), since most workers are not unionised. Yet, despite the fact that acts of resistance remain limited to individual struggles, their goals 'have similarities with issues of collective action: raising wages; providing benefits such as paid vacations, holidays, sick leave, and workers' unemployment compensation; changing attitudes toward the occupation; and creating public awareness about the value of the labor' (Romero 1992: 161). Romero believes that strategies of resistance are, in fact, mainly aimed at preserving one's dignity and self-worth and not at revolutionising the existing order.

Romero (1992: 9) claims that Chicanas (Mexican maids in the US) use 'unaggressive aggressiveness' to lessen the degrading aspects of the job. One strategy of resistance is to try to minimise the supervision of the employer. Chicanas do that by carrying out only demanded tasks, not letting the employer know when the cleaning materials or the last vacuum bag has been used or refusing to assist the employer in fixing an appliance. Employers are then left with workers who take no initiative or interest in the job. This situation encourages the employer to lessen her control over the worker and give her more latitude in the job. Another example would be to refuse cooking Mexican for the employers. As one worker told Romero (1992: 158), 'I didn't want to share my culture with them...' Romero, however, studied live-out workers who are not totally under the control of employers. The live-out arrangement chosen by Chicanas limits the exposure to manipulation and abuse. 'The strategy to transform domestic service by selling labor services rather than labor power is also useful in eliminating potentially exploitative aspects of the domestic-mistress relationship' (Romero 1992: 161). Day workers choose different employers to remain independent and minimise the employer's control. They negotiate labour arrangements, refuse to do tasks that are not agreed upon in the verbal contract, charge a flat rate instead of hourly wages so that they are not rushed or given more work, threaten to quit or actually do quit to find another employer. They do their job well and claim to be 'experts' in the field. This expertise allows them to enter the negotiating stage with their employers with a more powerful stand (Romero 1992).

Romero (1992) stresses the element of choice. Chicanas, according to her, choose this type of employment despite harsh conditions because of the salary, independence and flexibility associated with the job. They choose to be day workers instead of live-ins, and are careful about working for 'good' employers. I find that Romero (1992) gives a rather optimistic picture of resistance and portrays Chicanas as almost totally in control of their situation.

Constable (1997), on the other hand, gives accounts of resistance without idealising its successes. She asserts that systems of power do not fail just because resistance exists. According to her, 'romanticising' resistance is inaccurate, as resistance can only teach us about the complexity of power. Direct forms of resistance such as negotiating with employers, participating in rallies or demonstrations, breaking contracts, etc., are rare. Constable analyses subtler 'everyday' forms of resistance.[1] For instance, if domestic workers are not given enough food, they will buy their own and make sure the employers see it and feel embarrassed. They refuse dress codes, pretend to be taking baths by just running water in the tub, put on a walkman while working to avoid hearing the nagging of employers, lie about train congestion when arriving late. Friends, family, religion, Sunday gatherings, future goals (whether business, land, house, marriage) help workers survive and alleviate the daily hardships.

Brochmann (1993: 113), studying Sri Lankan women who had worked as maids in the Gulf, talks about 'the striking creativity the women demonstrate when it comes to circumventing difficulties overseas'. Sri Lankans find ways or 'escape routes' aimed at avoiding the employers' control and surveillance. Housemaids who are not allowed out use the phone when the employer is away, pretend to be Catholics in order to be allowed to go to church on Sundays, ask their families in Sri Lanka to send them a letter urging them to go back home because someone in the family is dying, or give letters to acquaintances working in the area if they are not allowed to write to their families. Despite being constantly under control, therefore, housemaids manage, at times, to evade the rules of conduct set by employers.

The strategies used by housemaids to handle a problematic *kafala* (sponsorship) relationship, according to Longva (1997: 93), were 'necessarily informal; they ranged from placating the employers and appealing for their goodwill and compassion (compliance), through work boycott, sloppily performed tasks, and sullen silence (passive resistance), to open confrontations resulting in the work contract being rescinded and the worker being repatriated or, as a last resort, absconding (overt resistance)'.

Abiding by the rules

Deference demands are often used to emphasise the employers' superiority and degrade domestic workers, as we have just seen. Nevertheless, deference can also be a strategy of resistance applied by domestic workers. Abiding by the rules can be a means to bend them a little. According to Cock (1989), servants use survival strategies such as silence, mockery or stealing little things, etc. She adds, however, that the 'domestic worker's main mode of adaptation is the adoption of a mask of deference as a protective disguise' (Cock 1989: 103).

Rollins (1985) notes that deference is intentional, mainly aimed at safeguarding the domestics' sense of dignity. Domestics refute the assumption of inferiority and do not consider their employers to be superior beings. They deliberately abide by the rules of the game because they have no choice but to be in a subservient position. By complying with their employers' wishes and putting on an act of deference, domestics consciously adapt to a powerless situation. Yet, one should not forget, Rollins (1985) reminds us, that domestics perform only because employers want them to. They cannot express their feelings of anger, hatred or envy and can only submit to domination. They do, however, carry a strong sense of '*ressentiment*' towards their employers. 'The presence of such resentment attests to domestics' lack of belief in their own inferiority, their sense of injustice about their treatment and position, and their rejection of the legitimacy of their subordination' (Rollins 1985: 231). One way to resist, therefore, is to avoid problems by 'performing', following the script written by employers, but, more importantly, refusing to interiorise judgments over their persons made by employers. In other words, employers can control them materially but not psychologically (Rollins 1985).

In fact, deference acts performed by domestic workers are mainly aimed at safeguarding their self-esteem and not at changing the rules of the game. As Constable (1997: 205; emphasis in original) notes, 'Although an awareness of deference behaviors alters our understanding of the formulation of power, it does not alter the *apparent* structure of the relationship between employer and the worker'. The worker is still viewed as a subordinate by the employer who is comforted by the deferential attitude of the worker; even if the worker thinks he or she is fooling the employer and 'derives pleasure' from this performance (Constable 1997).

There is a class-consciousness among Filipinas who are aware of the general economic and social patterns involved; they criticise the Filipino government for the chronic job shortages at home but the fact remains that these women are 'in essence, struggling for the right to continue to do menial work under exploitative conditions' (Constable 1997: 209). Constable suggests that Filipinas' forms of resistance do not lead to the transformation of their working and living conditions. In fact, 'Filipinas try to live up to their employers' ideals, rather than to contest them' (Constable 1997: 206). They want to become 'ideal workers'. Filipinas engage in activities that are enjoyable (birthday parties, outings, etc.) instead of finding ways through unions and more politicised meetings to alleviate their working conditions. Their resistance is geared towards survival and not change. 'By and large resistance remains on a discursive level, expressed quietly and as a form of personal release' (Constable 1997: 210).

Informal networks

Sri Lankan returnees' narratives recounted to Gamburd challenged the image of these migrants as passive beings. None of the workers she spoke to portrayed themselves as helpless victims (unlike, she says, what is generally written in the national press and scholarly literature in Sri Lanka). Sri Lankan domestic workers had a minimal range for negotiation within regulated (by employers) frameworks. 'Women simultaneously resist and accommodate the dominant discourse' (Gamburd 2000: 121). For instance, and despite employers' attempts to limit their social lives, domestics still found ways to construct a social network of acquaintances and friends that was helpful, especially when a crisis emerged. Employers usually do not allow domestics to go out of the house unsupervised and restrict their contact with the outside world. Domestics managed to develop relationships with other house-maids in the neighbourhood by arranging to meet on the rare occasions they leave the house (on their way to the shops or when they take the rubbish out).

Just as bureaucracies (whether official or private) try to regulate migration, Sri Lankans challenge the governing system by avoiding traditional routes of employment (agencies, training, moneylenders, etc.) and creating their own routes through direct contact with sponsors in the Arab countries, based on efficient personal networking. Sri Lankan housemaids who live in a foreign country away from relatives and friends are disadvantaged should a conflict arise. The police, in general, side with nationals, the agency only intervenes during the first three months of the contract and the embassy has very little power of action. But despite all this, according to Gamburd (2000), maids resort to informal networks for help, save money and manage to improve their families' living conditions.

Within the employer's household and despite important constraints, domestic workers are able to negotiate, in their own manner, details regarding their working and living arrangements. By using 'regulated improvisations' (Gamburd 2000), 'immediate struggles' (Parreñas 2001), 'unaggressive aggressiveness' (Romero 1992), 'coping strategies' (Anderson 2000), 'survival strategies' (Cock 1989; Rollins 1985) or 'escape routes' (Brochman1993), migrant domestic workers are sometimes able to bend the rules a little by, paradoxically, abiding by them. As Constable (1997: 12) reminds us, Filipina workers in Hong Kong 'resist oppression in certain ways but also simultaneously participate in their own subordination'.

Domestic workers, however, have failed to change their employers' behaviours and the fundamental essence of the employer-employee relationship which is, of course, based on manipulation and power. In the end, it is employers who hold the ultimate power and control; domestic workers, who adhere neither to complete resistance nor to total compliance, are left with a very thin margin of action.

Racism

It is not my aim, in this section, to go into the classic debates on racism or deal with these issues in general and theoretical terms. My purpose, instead, is to narrow my analysis to the terms that were (according to me) relevant to my work. This section, therefore, in its limited scope, gives only a quick overview of issues relative to racism as discussed in the literature on domestic work and highlighted by me. It will also, needless to say, encompass my own views and findings on the subject.

Domestic work witnesses an 'occupational ghettoisation' (Rollins 1985) as it is increasingly held by migrant women of colour in many contexts, including the Lebanese. The degrees of 'otherness' are somewhat intensified and highlighted in a setting where different cultural worlds coexist (Momsen 1999). In an attempt to explain the dominant-compliant relationship between employers and housemaids, scholars have analysed the cultural oppositions at stake as yet another source of conflict.

Many writers compared the exploitative and abusive living and working conditions of migrant domestic workers to those of previous slaves. 'There is a surprising consensus that slavery continued despite its formal abolition – particularly for domestic workers' (Anderson 2000: 148). The personal dependence of the housemaid on her employer (whether through her immigration status or her inability to leave or change employers), and the power of the employer over all aspects of the domestic's life and personhood, can in fact resemble the conditions previously imposed on slaves. But, as Anderson (2000) notes, the use of the word 'slavery' is mainly to highlight the fact that these conditions are, nowadays, simply unacceptable.

What is of interest to me, beyond this comparison, is the issue of racism that is inherent to both. It is true that the relationship between an employer and her maid can be best described in terms of power and domination, a fact that brings back to mind the master/slave context. Nevertheless, 'There is another reference that underlies the headlines: racism. Slavery has for centuries been associated with foreignness, with being an outsider... so slavery and racism are intertwined in contemporary consciousness' (Anderson 2000: 146). The end of slavery, therefore, did not mean the end of racism, and the belief that black people are 'naturally suited' to specific types of labour, and black women, to domestic work, is still very much alive (Anderson 2000).

The 'innate' inferiority of maids

The issue of racism is undoubtedly difficult to avoid if one embarks on research into migrant women working as housemaids. According to Phizacklea (1983), throughout and underneath the colonisation process lay the presumption of the 'innate inferiority' of the dominated. This 'ideology of racism', however, survived the colonisation period and widened its margins: it is 'not only directed at ex-colonial migrant labour, but all foreign labour' (Phizacklea 1983: 5). Following racist stereotypes, it has become accepted that some women of particular skin colour, religion and nationality are more suitable (or 'naturally suited') to domestic work than others (Anderson 2000; Constable 1997). Filipina domestic workers in Hong Kong, for example, 'are increasingly seen as a group whose differences are not simply class-based, or even ethnic or cultural, but racially, biologically, and "naturally" constituted' (Constable 1997: 38). The term *banmui*, meaning 'Philippine girl', is used interchangeably with 'maid' (just like 'Sri Lankan' comes to mean 'housemaid' in Lebanon; a little boy was heard in school asking his friend 'Is your *Sri Lanki* a Filipina?').

Even the behaviour of the weak (such as performing acts of deference, lying, etc.) is attributed by dominant elites 'not to the effect of arbitrary power but rather to the inborn characteristics of the subordinate group itself' (Scott 1990: 35). 'They [Sri Lankans] are all liars' or 'I'm against [employing] Sri Lankans, I have a feeling they are dirty' or 'You should not be nice with these races' are sentences often repeated by Lebanese employers. Moreover, the lack of citizenship (i.e. their legal status as 'temporary' migrants) and state rules and regulations applicable to migrant workers (including sponsorship) corroborate such stereotypes and help to implement this 'ideology of racism': 'Harassment and arbitrary deportation remain a hallmark of immigration officials... racism is given legislative legitimation' (Phizacklea 1983: 5).

Racism involves the use of different powers (political, social, economic or legal) to legitimise exploitation (Castles & Miller 2003). One should not minimise, however, the effect of the emotional power used (such as maternalism) to 'keep the maid in her place', a place assigned to her by her employers and described best in racial rather than class and occupational terms, according to Rollins (1985). As noted before, maternalism is not about care; it is mainly aimed at reinforcing the inferiority of maids. 'Such inferiority cannot be "outgrown" or overcome with education; to allow for this would be to question the innateness of the inferiority' (Rollins 1985: 198). Alternatively, but still to confirm the importance of racial paradigms within this type of employment, maternalism (and the apparent kindness it involves) can also be a way for the employer to prove she is not a racist and show she 'can enjoy excellent human relations with her black domestic worker' (Anderson 2000: 146). One reason for hiring a foreigner to start with could be to affirm a non-racist image (Rollins 1985). Moreover, and as we have seen before, one form of resistance by maids is to use 'intimacy to de-emphasize servitude' (Parreñas 2001: 180). 'The additional assaults upon their personhood forces women of color to do more emotional labor than white women or men in order to keep their jobs' (Romero 1992: 133).

As Anderson (2000: 147) notes, 'in the manufacturing of difference between female employer and female worker "race" can be very important' even though it is not the only factor operating within this complex relationship. Parreñas studied Filipina domestic workers who left the Philippines and its gender-stratified system to enter into yet another system in industrialised countries (Italy and the US); she concluded as well that: 'Racial, class, and citizenship inequalities aggravate their positions in receiving nations' (2001: 69). The racial dimension might not be the only determinant within the Madame/housemaid relationship, but it is nonetheless very tangible through the attitudes and behaviours of employers: the 'overt fear of contamination from the bodies of these "Others"' is common amongst employers (Anderson 2000: 147). Maids are asked to undertake numerous medical tests (HIV, tuberculosis, pregnancy, etc.) before departure and upon arrival in their host country. Maids might not use the term 'racism', though they complain about not being able to watch television in the same room as their employers, of having to use their specially assigned cutlery or wash their clothes separately. In fact, most complain about a sort of 'disgust' that employers show towards them (Anderson 2000).

In Lebanon, the 'inferiority' of housemaids is further symbolised by the female employer buying them an inferior brand of sanitary pad or feeding them only leftovers. The racial assumption of Sri Lankan housemaids being 'dirty' is exemplified by Lebanese employers (with only one bathroom) insisting that they scrub the whole bathroom with anti-bacterial products after taking a shower or using the toilet. Or to give another example: instruction was given to the housemaid (as I witnessed at a friend's place) never to kiss the baby grandson on the cheek. She could stay with the little boy when his grandmother and mother were busy elsewhere. She could carry him, feed him, breathe in his face. She could and she did cook for the whole family. She was in charge of cleaning the bathrooms as well as the kitchen, but she could not kiss the baby on his cheeks.

The 'invisibility' of maids

Rollins (1985: 209) notes that, during her seven months of domestic work, the thing that bothered her most ('one of the strongest affronts to my dignity as a human being') was to be treated as if she was not there, as 'invisible'. The 'invisibility' of domestics, according to her, is an aspect of racism: coloured people are more easily ignored than white people. 'Being treated as though one is invisible is a complaint commonly voiced by domestic workers of color working for white employers', according to Hondagneu-Sotelo (2001: 197), who interviewed Elvira, a Mexicana, days after she fought with her employer and left. Elvira, despite her important financial need, did not regret her move, in part, because the 'almost completely nonverbal relationship that she had maintained for several years with the *patrona* had been so strained' (Hondagneu-Sotelo 2001: 198). There was very little interaction between the two, even though the employer did not work and was home a lot of the time. Elvira complained about the 'lack of verbal recognition': 'I would arrive [in the morning] and sometimes she wouldn't greet me until two in the afternoon... I'd be in the kitchen, and she'd walk in but wouldn't say anything... Sometimes she wouldn't speak to me the whole day... she'd act as if I was a chair, a table...' (Hondagneu-Sotelo 2001: 198). A Lebanese friend/employer, talking about her housemaid, told me: 'In the beginning I hated her, now I don't see her any more. When you treat them right, you feed them right, you don't see them anymore. I give her a bonus every month. She has what she wants and I too have what I want. I don't see her anymore. In the morning, I say "Good morning" without even looking at her'.

Is the 'invisibility' of maids merely a racist issue or is it also a part of the 'depersonalisation' mechanism employers use to control not just the labour of the maid but her 'personhood' as well? Are we dealing here with what Anderson (2000: 121) calls 'personalistic power' that renders the maid 'socially dead'? I believe it is both. Were Arab (white) maids employed in the past in Lebanon less 'invisible'? I do not think so. They were ignored as well and treated with the same disdain. As one Lebanese employer, when asked whether she had a maid taking care of her as a child, remembers: 'We had, I remember, a Lebanese maid, she was maybe nineteen, I was fifteen or sixteen. Yes, I remember that my mother used to tell me that I wasn't supposed to talk to her, be friends with her. Because she's working at home and she's not supposed to be my friend'.

I believe it is more a matter of ignoring the maid because she is looked upon as inferior, erasing her personality and limiting her being to her 'serving position'. In fact, what bothered Lebanese female employers I spoke to the most was when the housemaid stood up in front of them and 'answered back'. Housemaids in Lebanon are treated as 'invisibles' despite their obvious 'visibility' (which is mainly due to their skin colour). One cannot avoid 'seeing' housemaids everywhere. This vivid paradox characterising the experiences of housemaids in their host country is not the only one worth noting (others are being 'part of the family' yet isolated and exploited, indispensable yet easily replaceable, etc.), but it is perhaps the most 'apparent' one, and one that is solely based on looks (dark colour skin, dark hair, etc.). The point I wish to make is that housemaids are easily recognised because they 'look like' maids. Perhaps no other job is as easily identifiable as the one of housemaid occupied by migrant women of colour in Lebanon. This can, however, prove to be unfortunate for some: the wife of the Filipino ambassador was mistaken for a housemaid in a beach resort in Lebanon and asked to get out of the swimming pool. Or very fortunate for others: the Polish maid of my Lebanese friend, 'invisible' to the vigilant eyes of the beach resort guards, was able to swim undisturbed.

Racialised hierarchies and preferences

Sanjek and Colen (1990: 7) argue that 'ethnicity is often a central factor in differentiating household workers and employers'. According to them, where there are patterns of recruitment from particular ethnic groups (such as Filipinas in Hong Kong or Latinas in the US, etc.), 'will not notions of ethnic hierarchy be reinforced by the widespread employment of such household workers?' Anderson (2000) talks about 'racialised hierarchies' within domestic work in Europe, with Filipinas on top and black Africans at the bottom. Employers and agencies prefer certain nationalities over others but, according to Anderson (2000: 153), 'this often seemed to be code for the precise shade of skin colour... Broadly speaking... the lighter one's skin the better one's wages and the easier it is to find work'.

Talking about 'racial preferences' amongst employers in Los Angeles, Hondagneu-Sotelo (2001: 56) asserts that Latinas are preferred to African Americans and notes that '[t]he old stereotype of the bossy black maid is apparently alive and well, now joined by newer terrifying images associated with young black men...' As one employer told her (Hondagneu-Sotelo 2001: 56): 'Uhm, ah, I would never hire a black woman. I'd be too scared to, and I'd be especially scared if her boyfriend came around'. Employers, on the other hand, viewed Latinas as dedicated, hard-working, caring with children, trustworthy, etc. The same stereotypes are found in Chang's (2000) work on 'disposable domestics' working in the US: Latinas are viewed by American employers as ideal workers, available and controllable, whereas blacks are deemed unreliable and lazy.

In Lebanon, Sri Lankans are towards the bottom of the status hierarchy compared with women from the Philippines, who receive higher wages. Following racial and ethnic stereotypes, housemaids are shut away in categories: Filipinas are strong but heartless, Sri Lankans are stupid ('they are more clever, the Filipinas, then come the Ethiopians then these ones [Sri Lankans]... Those are completely out of it, *taltamis* (stupid) especially if they are not coming from the capital but the village. If they come from outside the capital they turn off the stove with their mouth, they blow on it'). Ethiopians are stubborn, they are good with babies, but they cannot be trusted because they are 'hot', etc. The employers' preferences, however, are not so much related to skin colour (all have dark skin) as they are to personality traits: Sri Lankans are considered to be more submissive and easier to 'mould': 'My sister is looking for a maid because her Ethiopian maid did not want to stay any longer and left. Anyway, my sister no longer wants an Ethiopian, they are arrogant. The Ethiopian maid once told her [the sister]: "Shut up!" She [the sister] is now looking for a Sri Lankan, they are easier to deal with, *maksoura chawkitoun* (they are broken inside)'. Filipinas, by comparison (who are 'more educated and less naïve'), command more respect and are more likely to stand up to abusive treatment. 'I prefer Sri Lankans, not Filipinos. Let's say, you can dominate them more than the Filipinos. Filipinos are much more educated. They are stronger in character. The Filipinos... well, for example, if she doesn't like it, she will open the door and go'. A very revealing 'slip of the tongue' by a Lebanese employer I was interviewing speaks for itself: '... Then we had a Sri Lanki, no, excuse me, she was a Filipino. No, no, she was a Sri Lanki. But she was very wild. That's why I thought she was a Filipino...'

Power based on race or class?

Whether racial issues are present and affect the employer-housemaid relationship leaves no doubt: they certainly are. The ongoing debate, however, is whether the exploitation and abuse of migrant housemaids are in fact the result of racism or simply the consequence of 'mere' class differences. To put it in simple terms, is the problem one of racism or class? Are these women being exploited because they are 'black' or because they are poor?

Following the claim that racism is indeed important in the determination of the degree of exploitation, Romero (1992) notes that the deferential behaviour performed by maids upon their employers' demand is not only based on class inequalities but also on racial and ethnic differences. Domestic service encompasses traditional racial stereotypes whereby women of colour are regarded as inferior beings. 'Employing white women or college students as household workers does not establish the same power differential as does hiring ethnic minority women and Third World immigrant women' (Romero 1992: 132). According to her, domestic service *is* actually different, whether performed by a white woman or a woman of colour. White women are probably never asked to use separate cutlery, or accept graciously discarded items as gifts; they are not exposed to racial reflections or degrading comments about their culture.

Taking an opposite stand, Bales (1999) develops the following argument: migrant women of colour (or 'new slaves') are easily deceived because they are economically vulnerable. He suggests that economic vulnerability is a key factor in the modern forms of slavery, asserting that race (or ethnicity) is not the determining variable in the choice of the 'new slaves': 'In the new slavery, race means little... The common denominator is poverty, not color. Behind every assertion of ethnic difference is the reality of economic disparity... Modern slaveholders are predators keenly aware of weakness... rapidly adapting an ancient practice to the new global economy... The question isn't "Are they the right color to be slaves?" but "Are they vulnerable enough to be enslaved?" The criteria of enslavement today do not concern color, tribe or religion; they focus on weakness, gullibility and deprivation' (Bales 1999: 10-11).

Constable (1997) follows this argument: the mistreatment of domestic workers is primarily the result of class differences. She compares Chinese *'muijai'* who worked in the past (young girls between eight and ten years old who were sent by their families to work as live-in domestic workers with wealthier Chinese families – a practice that supposedly ended after World War II) and Filipina domestic workers in Hong Kong today. She notes various similarities such as the particularly low status held by these women, the exhausting work demands and tough disciplining measures. While acknowledging the 'inexcusable atrocities' inflicted on many Filipina domestic workers by their Chinese employers, such as iron burns, starvation, etc., she adds: 'They do seem somewhat less inexplicable when we realize that such abuses are not new or directed solely toward *foreign* domestic workers. Although there is often an underlying – and sometimes overt – racial hostility toward foreign workers in Hong Kong, it is clear from the history of the muijai that these abuses did not originate as "racial incidents", as some have suggested. They may have evolved into expressions of racial and ethnic tension, but this is an acquired meaning, not the simple cause of abuse' (Constable 1997: 47; emphasis in original). The same could be said about Lebanese employers who also mistreated their Arab (and Lebanese) maids in the past. Mere racial tensions cannot, therefore, explain the abuse witnessed by Sri Lankan housemaids in Lebanon today. But what does?

In his report on migrant workers in Lebanon, Young (1999: 99) attempts to explain the reasons behind such abuse. He agrees with the statement that the mistreatment of migrant workers has little to do with their ethnicity: 'The accusation that most Lebanese are racists is not a satisfactory explanation for abuse'. According to him, both Lebanese and non-Lebanese who are low on the social hierarchy are mistreated. This, however, is a rather simplistic proposition. To compare low-wage, overworked Lebanese employees to the total vulnerability of Sri Lankan housemaids in Lebanese households is misleading. The complexity of the situation migrant housemaids face (the way every aspect of their lives – and not just their work – is controlled) is in no way comparable to the Lebanese case. But Young goes beyond the class factor and adds: 'If an employer beats a domestic worker, the chances are that he would not hesitate to beat his wife or children' (Young 1999: 99). This claim does not hold, I have seen throughout my research (and life) kind women who were not the least aggressive to others but were, indeed, abusive towards their maids. In the words of one Lebanese employer: 'I do let go my anger. But not on my maid. I let it on my daughter. Like my husband, if he shouts, it's on me not on her. She gets always the nice word'. Furthermore, according to him, 'The treatment an employee receives is, in the end, largely a function of the nature of his or her employer' (Young 1999: 99). Father Augustino (a Filipino priest I interviewed who helps migrant housemaids in Lebanon) seems to agree with Young on this issue: 'The Madames are abusive maybe because of marital problems they have at home. The Lebanese Madame gets back at her employee... It is in the character. They [Lebanese employers] would like to dominate the domestic helper and could not do it with Lebanese... It is natural to Lebanese [shouting]. There is nothing malicious from the part of the Lebanese'.

Are the problems encountered by migrant housemaids in Lebanon merely symptomatic of the 'nature' of Lebanese employers? Are some Lebanese employers 'naturally' fit to be abusers, and housemaids, as some claim, 'naturally' fit to be maids? I do not believe these types of (racial) generalisation stand up in a scientific debate. I do agree with the claim that class is a major factor in the determination of the exploitative experiences endured by maids. I also support the argument regarding the influence of ethnicity and race. Lebanese, in general, could be described as racists. As the Special Rapporteur noted (Huda 2005: 8), many of her Lebanese interlocutors, including senior government officials, 'acknowledged that discriminatory attitudes on the basis of race, colour and ethnicity continue to be held by significant parts of Lebanese society'. A Lebanese employer told me that her dentist refused to treat her Sri Lankan housemaid unless it was after hours so that no one could see her coming into his office. Many Lebanese still use the term *abd*, meaning 'slave', when referring to 'black' people. White skin is looked upon in positive terms; my grandmother, for example, would shout at me in the summer because of my suntan: 'You are going to become just like a Sri Lankan'. A commercial of a soap powder aired in Lebanon in 1987 used the following concept: you get perfect white results with the use of the product. Next scene: a Sri Lankan is seen turning inside a washing machine. Ending line: 'Madame, I want to be white too'. My other grandmother cried over the phone when I was born because she wanted a boy, and this, despite my mother's attempt to console her: 'The baby girl is white like snow' (*Bayda mitl el talj*). At 85, she used to protect her face from the sun while hanging her laundry out on the balcony.

Race as yet another 'excuse' for exploitation

Since the influx of foreign women from Africa and Asia particularly, the position of housemaid has become one which carries with it a particularly low status, not only because of the servile nature of the tasks performed and the difficult living and working conditions, but also, it is true, because of the new racial component attached to domestic work in Lebanon today. That the attitudes and behaviours of Lebanese employers towards their housemaids 'of colour' carry a strong racist element to them almost goes without saying. Racial stereotypes such as: they are dirty, stupid, liars, etc., are common. My argument, nevertheless, is that racism is only an 'added' factor within the employer/housemaid dynamic; it operates not so much as the direct cause of abuse but rather as an 'excuse' for further exploitation and mistreatment.

According to Rollins (1985: 203), the presence of domestics 'supports the idea of unequal human worth: it suggests that there might be categories of people (the lower class, people of color) who are inherently inferior to others (middle and upper classes, whites). And this idea provides ideological justification for a social system that institutionalizes inequality'. This 'ideological justification' is an important point on which I would like to elaborate. It is not my opinion that race is more important than class when it comes to explaining the type of power and control housemaids are subjected to. It is my view that both race and class are important determinants within this particular dynamic. Race, however, is used as a further 'justification' for exploitation (an exploitation that would have taken place anyway). This exploitation is deemed 'deserved', since these women are viewed as 'naturally' inferior and, if I want to push things further, almost 'non-humans'. As we have seen earlier, the employer is appropriating the 'personhood' of the housemaid and not just her labour. Total control is possible through the 'dehumanisation' process which is easier with housemaids who are (not only inferior by class but also) 'black'. The constant reminder by employers of the fact that, they are 'after all human beings', would not have been necessary otherwise. The equation goes like this: 'She is a maid, so by definition, she is under my control, she is only there to serve me and her being stops and begins with this obligation. The fact that she is a coloured maid ("naturally" inferior and fit for that place) not only supports my right over her but gives me a further excuse (should I need one) to exercise this control almost guilt-free'. It is by stressing the 'innate inferiority' of the dominated (in this case house-maids) that one justifies the domination (Phizacklea 1983). Further-more, I feel that the 'ideal employer' claim ('She is lucky to have me as an employer') comes logically to corroborate this attitude. 'She is not only poor but black [i.e. 'innately inferior']; I am, therefore, doing her a favour by employing her'. Following this logic, *any* employer would be the 'ideal' one. The control is not only maintained but justified; hence, the lack of self-reproach or guilt.

In his book *White Nation* (2000), on multiculturalism in Australia, Hage talks about the two rather opposing immigration debates amongst 'white' Australians: the first concerned people who wanted the 'ethnic other' to stay; the second, those who wanted the 'ethnic other' to leave. Both currents, he argues, perceived 'ethnics' as objects. 'Both the "multiculturalists" and the "racists" shared in the conviction that they were, in one way or another, masters of national space, and that it was up to them to decide who stayed in and who ought to be kept out of that space' (Hage 2000: 17). What appeals to me in Hage's words is the reduction of ethnics or migrants to 'passive objects' to be governed, as well as the 'conception of ethnics as people one can make decisions *about...*' (Hage 2000: 17; emphasis in original). If we play on words and replace ethnics by Sri Lankan housemaids and the 'one who one can make decisions about' by Lebanese employer, we have a summary of what is really going on in Lebanon. The employer can, and often does, decide when the housemaid should work, rest, sleep, eat (and what to eat), take a shower, cut her hair, talk to others, go out, answer the phone or make a call, send money to her family in Sri Lanka or not, cry or smile, leave the country or stay (even in an endangered zone during the July 2006 war on Lebanon)... and the list stretches to even the most unthinkable details (shave her legs, wear a uniform or regular clothes, use a specific type of deodorant or sanitary pad, meet men or forget about her womanhood...). I am purposely insisting on the large scale of daily-life details which employers 'decide about' to show the de-gree of 'appropriation' taking place. What concerns me the most, how-ever, is the reason or reasons behind such a tight control: Why do em-ployers believe they have an absolute right to 'decide about' almost everything when it comes to their housemaids' lives in Lebanon? Could

racism be a simple answer? I believe not. As I mentioned before, negative racial stereotyping is used as a 'justification'. The numerous 'excuses' given by Lebanese employers for such a tight control are indeed
racially anchored: 'Not allowing them out? But of course, they are stupid, naïve, I don't let her go out for her own sake... Why am I tough
with her? But because you simply *cannot* be nice to them, these people
are ungrateful, if you are kind they take advantage of it (*biyerkabouh
ala dahrik*: they climb on your back)...'. One would think, while listening to Lebanese employers, that they have no other choice *but* to control. The justification, therefore, follows racial terms, but racism alone
does not explain such implacable domination.

Moreover, even if racism is being 'used' at times, the question remains: 'Is the main aim the assertion of the superiority of the race
every time there is a racist classification in usage or are different goals
targeted here?' (Hage 2000: 31). Even if actions are 'racially motivated'
in appearance, it remains important to uncover how they can be, in
fact, related to other motivations. Hage (2000) gives the example of a
white footballer uttering racial insults to a black opponent in a football
match. Is his action 'racially motivated' or 'football motivated'? The fact
that he racially insulted his opponent does qualify him as a racist, but
was he trying to merely assert the 'white race' superiority or was his
real motivation simply to win a football match? Some 'white' Australians, for example, can believe that their race is superior to the 'black'
or even the 'yellow race'. This belief might not necessarily be followed
by any imperative for action. They might believe 'others' are inferior
but do not necessarily care about where they live, work, etc. As soon as
they start worrying about the presence of 'too many' Arab Australians,
they are becoming concerned about what they consider to be a 'privileged relationship between their race and a territory' (Hage 2000).
Would their motivation be qualified as a nationalist or a racial one
(even if their idea of territory has a racial component to it)? Hage believes that these apparently 'racially motivated' practices are in fact defined by other (less obvious) motivations such as nationalist ones or
even simpler ones like winning a football match.

As demonstrated above, racism, even if irrefutably present, might
not be the real issue at stake. Just as 'white Australians' feel they have
the right to control their territory, Lebanese employers feel they have
the right to control the 'personhood' of their housemaids. The issue is
more one of 'appropriation' than racism, even if the 'appropriation' carries with it a racial component.

More importantly, just as both the 'multiculturalists' and the 'racists'
decided *about* the 'others' (Hage 2000), Lebanese did (and still do) decide 'about' maids, whether Arabs ('white') in the past or African and
Asian ('black') today. A similar point is made by Constable (1997)

about Chinese employers. She notes that Chinese domestic workers employed in Hong Kong in the past had the same ethnic, racial and national background as their employers and yet they were abused, just as Filipinas are today. Before the war (1975), maids in Lebanon were Arabs (Lebanese, Syrians, Palestinians, etc.). Maids were controlled, treated as 'invisible', just as Sri Lankans or Filipinas are today. There might be a difference in the degree of 'dehumanisation' which, according to me, is not based on race but on the different circumstances involved. Contacts between the Lebanese family and the Arab maid's family were common at the time. Maids were on 'familiar' grounds, they had visible referents. Moreover, girls came to work relatively very young (some at nine or ten years old). They were 'raised' by their employers, and so it was easier for them to fit the mould preset for them. Sri Lankans, on the other hand, are totally isolated in a foreign country, contact with home is difficult, their support system (whether by their government in Sri Lanka or their embassy in Lebanon) is weak, their legal status is dependent on their employers. In a way, they are totally at the mercy of their employers who, consequently, can act with more latitude with them than they did with previous Arab maids.

Finally, is it sufficient to feel superior and consider others to be inferiors; or is it rather a matter of being able to 'act' as a superior? It is true that 'The belief that there is a hierarchy of races or cultures, is not in itself a motivating ideology. Racism on its own... does not carry within it an imperative for action' (Hage 2000: 32). In fact, is not the real issue one of power? While 'Everyone can entertain prejudiced fantasies about a variety of "others", it is the power to subject these "others" to your fantasies that constitutes the social problem' (Hage 2000: 34). Racism is not anybody's exclusivity; in fact, as Hage notes, Arab Australians, too, have negative stereotypes about 'white Australians'. The crucial difference is that they do not (or cannot) act upon them because the power is held by 'whites'. Reducing the other into a passive object of government is only possible because it *could be*. I am using here Edward Said's (1995) rhetoric on *Orientalism* in which he describes the relationship between the Occident and the Orient as one of domination and power. The Orient was 'orientalised' he claims, 'not only because it was discovered to be "Oriental" in all those ways considered commonplace by an average nineteenth-century European, but also because it *could be* – that is, submitted to being – *made* Oriental' (Said 1995: 5-6).

Therefore, if racism is not the direct cause of exploitation, but comes 'second' to it, what is? While there may be issues of race and class operating in this particular context, it is primarily the unequal relationship in terms of power (the weak or the strong) and of being able to exercise this power that determines the Madame/housemaid relationship. Exploitation and abuse 'could be' because of the inferior class status of the housemaid, her extreme vulnerability (whether economic, legal or moral), low position within the household and within the host country, total isolation on unfamiliar grounds, limited choices in the home country ... And it 'could be' done easier today because, on top of it all, these women are 'black'.

5   Symbolic power

'Le plus fort n'est jamais assez fort pour être toujours le maître, s'il
ne transforme sa force en droit et l'obéissance en devoir.'
'The strongest is never strong enough to always be the master,
if he/she does not transform his/her strength into right
and obedience into duty.'
Jean-Jacques Rousseau (*Du Contrat Social*)

Introduction

When I first started working on the subject of Sri Lankan housemaids
in Lebanon, I was taken aback by the empathy I felt towards them. The
bad guys, I was told by many (scholars, officials, NGO members), were
of course the Lebanese, and the good guys the Sri Lankans. And I did
see injustice, abuse, violence, on the one hand, and innocence, naiveté,
helplessness, on the other. I was, however, not totally convinced that
reality could be drawn in black and white. Many of the Lebanese who
abused their housemaids were in fact decent women; many were my
friends. Moreover, the fact that this abuse was so common and spread
across most Lebanese communities made me wonder: Are Lebanese
simply barbaric human beings who take advantage of the poor and are
unable to apply a minimum of decency, or was there more to the subject than met the eye?

The emphasis on the human rights abuses of Sri Lankan housemaids and their portrayal (in Jureidini & Moukarbel 2004) as 'contract
slaves', following Bales' (1999) analysis of contemporary slavery, were
important. Sri Lankans were indeed exploited and some of their living
and working conditions did resemble those of slaves. This approach,
however, and despite its more or less 'objective' account of the delicate
issues involved beyond the sensational and emotive discourse, was not
complete and left many questions unanswered. Were Sri Lankan
housemaids really passive or did they 'resist' with the means available
to them? Were choices available to them, even if these were indeed limited? Could the Lebanese go on exploiting and abusing their housemaids if the latter did not in some way 'consent' to it? Were poverty
and weakness enough to explain this compliance? And why do the Lebanese who choose to employ Sri Lankans instead of Filipinas consider
the former to be 'easier to mould'? Many other questions need to be
asked and answered but the one recurrent in my mind was: What was
really happening here (it was indeed reprehensible) and why?

No matter how the concept of modern slavery is used and how careful one is in contextually defining it, it carries with it an emotional and moral weight that can be, and perhaps intentionally is, shocking. Moreover, the modern use of the term 'slave' implies somehow the absence of choice. The choice to migrate in the first place is not simply based on economic reasons. Other considerations (discussed in more detail in Chapter 3) come into effect, such as a desire for independence away from the control and abuse of husbands, a pull for adventure and a quest to attain a better life. The choice to stay on, in the second place, does exist, whether for financial, moral or emotional gratification. I have encountered Sri Lankan housemaids in Lebanon who, despite harsh working and living conditions, humiliation and abuse, choose to renew their contracts. Many do stay because they no longer feel at home when they go back for visits to Sri Lanka, or because they want (but do not necessarily need) more money. Some, in contrast, decide to leave after only two or three months spent in Lebanon. Ramia, a freelancer who worked for me and my mother, has wanted to go back to Sri Lanka for years now. Every year she tells me it's her last. The money she earns is spent on her mother, her sister – whose husband abandoned her, leaving her and her children without resources – her friend in Lebanon who borrowed $1,000 from her, her stepmother and the house she is building but which is not finished yet. Where does one stop? If the house is built, one needs appliances, then one needs to save money for the future, to invest in a small business, to care for extended family members, etc. Ramia had a miscarriage last year because she did not stop working when the doctor advised her to. She thought: 'I'll work just a few more months then leave'. She is now trying to get pregnant again without success. 'This time', she says, 'as soon as I know I'm pregnant I will leave'. After thirteen years, Ramia has finally decided to go home.

Power is not this absolute authority imposed as an unavoidable course of destiny. Why is domination practiced on one group and not another, why do some groups submit to it more than others, or by the same token, resist and fight it more than others? Can the answer to domination simply be: because they can? Not just because they are, in reality, able to exercise their power but also, and above all, because they can easily get away with it when their behaviour is accepted by society as normal, as part of 'the natural order of the world'. If there is no law threatening you with punishment to discourage you from abusing your housemaid, if your friends, peers, family members or society as a whole do not condemn or judge you, if, rather than blaming you, they encourage you and actually do exactly the same as you, then you go on abusing without needing to either hide or change. In any case, in your eyes, this is not abuse; only human rights activists or university researchers see in your behaviour something condemnable. But who are they to judge and after all, what do they know?

It is my argument that violence is dominant within the Lebanese employer and Sri Lankan housemaid relationship. Yet, unlike what is reported in Lebanese newspapers, cases of extreme and regular physical abuse by employers are not very common and remain the exception. What have become 'normalised', however, are the more insidious forms of violence that are used to control each and every aspect of the lives of Sri Lankan housemaids in Lebanese households. Using Bourdieu's notion of 'symbolic violence', I argue that Lebanese employers use 'symbolic violence' as a means to deal with their housemaids rather than 'real' violence. This chapter first develops Bourdieu's (1991) theoretical framework on 'symbolic violence'. It also draws a profile of the 90 housemaids interviewed, in an attempt to understand the 'baggage' these women carry with them to Lebanon. This, in turn, follows Bourdieu's concept of habitus, in which he explains that, in order for 'symbolic violence' to be effective, it has to be applied on people who are *predisposed* by their habitus to adhere to it. The chapter finally demonstrates, by using a number of my key findings retrieved from both my quantitative and my qualitative data, how 'symbolic violence' (and not physical violence) is commonly practiced upon Sri Lankan housemaids working in Lebanon.

Bourdieu's notions of 'symbolic violence' and 'habitus'

Bourdieu initially developed the notion of symbolic violence in reference to the gift exchange in North Kabyle society. Unlike Lévi-Strauss, who analysed this exchange in terms of reciprocity, he read in it an expression of disguised power and domination. Relations of domination are sustained through various 'soft and disguised' strategies that camouflage domination with a semblance of innocence and gratuity. One way to exercise power over others is to put them in a situation of debt. More subtle ways would be the exchange of gifts. By giving a gift to people who cannot return the favour, one would be subjecting the receiver to a situation of personal debt and obligation. In fact, generosity can also be an instrument of possessiveness. As Bourdieu (1980: 216) notes: '*On possède pour donner. Mais on possède aussi en donnant*' (We possess to give. But we also give to possess).

In a society like the Kabyle society, where domination has to be maintained for the most part through interpersonal relations rather than institutions, symbolic violence becomes an adequate means of exercising power. Symbolic violence, in contrast to overt violence, is 'gentle', invisible violence, 'unrecognized as such, chosen as much as undergone, that of trust, obligation, personal loyalty, hospitability, gifts, debts, piety, in a word, of all the virtues honoured by the ethic of honour' (Bourdieu 1991: 24). Bourdieu uses the term 'symbolic power' to describe not one particular form of power exercised in daily life but, rather, almost all aspects of power. Using the term 'symbolic' in opposition to 'real' might mislead one to think that symbolic violence, as a purely 'spiritual' form, has no real effects. This, of course, is a complete fallacy. The effect of symbolic violence is as real and as dangerous as other forms, if not more so, as it uses insidious channels that are harder to detect.

By using the notion of symbols, Bourdieu refers to the tools of communication and knowledge that contribute to ensuring that one class dominates another and leads, in Weberian terms, to the 'domestication of the dominated' (Bourdieu 1991: 167). The dominant class engages in a symbolic struggle to impose on others its own definition of the social world, a definition that suits most its self-interests but that is presented as universal. This, in turn, 'contributes to the fictitious integration of society as a whole, and thus to the apathy (false consciousness) of the dominated classes' (Bourdieu 1991: 167).

Power is present everywhere, according to Bourdieu (1991). The fact that power is dispersed in various fields does not render it less forceful, just less easy to find. '[W]ithout turning power into a "circle whose centre is everywhere and nowhere", which could be to dissolve it in yet another way, we have to be able to discover it in places where it is least visible, where it is most completely misrecognized...' (Bourdieu 1991: 163). He believes that modes of domination shifted from open coercion and physical violence to forms of symbolic manipulation in advanced societies. Power, according to him, is rarely manifested in everyday life through the use of physical force; instead, it is channelled into a symbolic form and thus is conferred a 'legitimacy' that it otherwise would not have. For domination to be successful, it has to be hidden and invisible to the eyes of the dominated. Pure violence puts domination at risk by triggering a rebellion or flight on the part of the dominated, whereas symbolic violence allows for the duration of domination – just as pure retaliation is risky for the subordinates who rely instead on forms of resistance that are difficult to decode and repress, as we shall see in the following chapter. The advice of a Lebanese employer to her relative on how to punish her housemaid illustrates perfectly the point made above: 'The daughter of my husband's aunt brought one [Sri Lankan housemaid], she stayed six months, she told me the maid doesn't want to work. She works like she's been taught in Saudi Arabia. She told me: "She's dumb". She hit her more than once and told her: "I want to send you back to Sri Lanka". The housemaid told her: "Yes, I want to go back, Madame, you hit, you no good". And she sent her back. But she lost the money paid [to the agency], nothing was returned to her. I used to tell her [her relative], "Be patient, no need to hit, make her repeat things". According to me it is a bigger punishment if you make her repeat things more than once, she gets tired like this'.

Symbolic power is an invisible power 'misrecognised' as such and therefore 'recognised' as legitimate. Individuals are subjected to various forms of violence (limited in their social mobility, treated as inferiors, etc.) and can perceive it as pertaining to the natural order of things. Patriarchy, for example, cannot be apprehended simply in terms of pressure by one group (men) over another (women). Gender domination exists 'precisely because women misrecognised the symbolic violence to which they were subjected as something that was natural, simply "the way of the world"' (Webb et al. 2002: 25). They were complicit, in this way, in their own domination. Hence, symbolic violence compels the 'dominated' to accept their own domination by the internalisation of values defined by the dominants themselves and the diffusion of common knowledge and beliefs and unexpressed rules adhered to by all.

To comprehend the true nature of symbolic violence, it is essential to 'see that it presupposes a kind of *active complicity* on the part of those subjected to it' (Bourdieu 1991: 23; emphasis in original). Symbolic power exists, therefore, within a particular relationship between people who exercise power and those who submit to it. It can only be exercised with the complicity of people on whom this violence is practiced, who 'misrecognise' this form of power through a state of denial of the economic and political interests present in a set of practices. People who are dominated by others are not just passive individuals accepting subjection. By tacitly accepting and legitimising the hierarchical relations of power they adhere to, those who least benefit from this power fail to see that 'the hierarchy is, after all, an arbitrary social construction which serves the interests of some groups more than others' (Bourdieu 1991: 23).

As mentioned before, symbolic violence is efficient on people who legitimise it and adhere to the set of values and beliefs of the dominant group. Moreover, '... *intimidation*, a symbolic violence which is not aware of what it is (to the extent that it implies no *act of intimidation*) can only be exerted on a person predisposed (in his habitus) to feel it, whereas others will ignore it' (Bourdieu 1991: 51; emphasis in original). Bourdieu argues that reaction to violence differs depending, in part, on one's habitus. Symbolic violence needs, in order to be efficient, a habitus inclined to respond to it and indeed accept it. The notion of habitus might help answer the following questions: Why do Sri Lankan housemaids accept, rather passively, the living and employment conditions

imposed on them? Why are they generally perceived as abiding and docile by their Lebanese employers, and chosen and controlled accordingly? And, more importantly, why does symbolic violence 'work' better
on them than on others? 'The habitus is a set of *dispositions* which in-
cline agents to act and react in certain ways... Dispositions are acquired
through a gradual process of *inculcation* in which early childhood experiences are particularly important' (Bourdieu 1991: 12; emphasis in
original). Our 'dispositions' towards certain attitudes, actions and values follow a certain pattern guided by common cultural trajectories
and types of existence. Knowledge (the manner in which we comprehend the world and assemble our beliefs and values) is composed –
and not passively stored – through habitus. Habitus operates in a moment in time, when a set of dispositions meets in everyday life a specific problem or choice or 'feel for the game'.

Habitus is the partly unconscious 'taking in' of rules and values. It is
an infinite capacity to construct in a conditional freedom ('regulated
improvisations'), products (practices, perceptions and attitudes) that are
limited in their production by various historical and social conditions.
People are 'written' by their class habitus. Class affiliations influence
one's habitus without entirely determining it. Dispositions necessarily
reflect the social conditions within which they were acquired. They let
us react to cultural rules and settings in various ways – as they allow
for improvisations – but 'the responses are always largely determined –
regulated – by where (and who) we have been in a culture' (Webb et al.
2002: 44). It is important to note that habitus is somewhat analogous
across persons from similar backgrounds. A person from a working-
class background, for instance, has acquired different dispositions to
one from a middle- or high-class environment. The social conditions of
existence of people, therefore, whether similar or different, are expressed in their habitus.

Habitus directs people's actions and responses in their daily lives.
This orientation helps them find appropriate responses to particular situations, or, as Bourdieu calls it, to have a feel for *le sens pratique*, the
'practical sense'. Factors that form the habitus are transmitted 'without
passing through language and consciousness, but through suggestions
inscribed in the most apparently insignificant aspects of the things, situations and practices of everyday life' (Bourdieu 1991: 51). This power
of suggestion is hard to resist particularly because it intervenes
through situations of everyday life as 'silent', suggestive and persistent.
It acts best in the domestic unit, beneath the level of consciousness.
For instance, instead of telling a child what he should do, those practices tell him who he is or should be. One person might, for instance,
impose on the other without even saying anything nor having a desire
to control. This power of suggestion is the condition for symbolic

power to be effective on people disposed, in their habitus, to respond to such practices.

For a specific habitus to function properly, 'Individuals must normally think that the possibilities from which they choose are in fact necessities, common sense, natural and inevitable' (Webb et al. 2002: 38-39). The rules and perceptions pertaining to one's habitus are viewed as 'civilised' while others are rejected as simply barbaric. One revealing example pertains to Western eating habits. Cows, pigs and chickens are consumed after slaughter while domestic animals (cats, dogs) are rescued. Stories of others eating dogs or cats are beyond comprehension and met with total disgust. The animals we eat are 'depersonalised' while other domestic animals are regarded as pets and cannot be considered food (Webb et al. 2002). The Lebanese somewhat 'depersonalise' or 'dehumanise' their Sri Lankan housemaids and treat them in a way they consider to be normal or 'natural'. Westerners, by contrast, might view Lebanese attitudes and behaviour towards their housemaids as 'barbaric'. The most important aspect of habitus, therefore, 'is that it naturalises itself and the cultural rules, agendas and values that make it possible' (Webb et al. 2002: 40). In the words of one Lebanese employer:

> I gave the maid the day off. I take advantage of the absence of X (the employer's husband) because when he's here he has a tendency to treat her like a slave. Anyway, foreigners think that we do treat them like slaves. A friend of mine living in Beirut who is English married to a Lebanese says that she thinks that we are awful with our maids, that we treat them like slaves. She has an English nanny for her daughter. The nanny does nothing but take care of the daughter. She won't even wash the dishes after the little girl eats. Can you imagine?

Habitus is subject to modification and is not constituted once and for all but evolves through various adjustments in time and place – it is durable and transposable. It can only be changed, however, through a gradual process. The change takes place:

> when the narratives, values and explanations of a habitus no longer make sense... or again, when agents use their understanding and feel for the rules of the game as a means of furthering and improving their own standing and capital within a cultural field. (Webb et al. 2002: 41)

Lebanese employers do not face yet the need to change the rules of the game and act differently towards their housemaids. They do not feel guilt or shame, and if they do, they convince themselves that, in the end, they are doing their housemaid a favour by employing her and that, they, as 'ideal employers', should be thanked. In a way, the constant norm within Lebanese society is that the ill treatment of housemaids 'is acceptable, if not necessary'. This norm is diffused by Lebanese governmental institutions, recruitment agencies and police agents who accept, participate and often encourage the abuse of housemaids. Unless the set of dispositions is changed from the inside, i.e., unless the Lebanese start to believe that it is contradictory to common sense and accepted behaviour to mistreat their housemaids, no rules or regulations can be rigorously and successfully applied to resolve the issues at stake. This is a point I pick up in my concluding chapter.

It is important to note here that people's actions take place in a particular social setting. Therefore, specific practices or thoughts are not the mere product of the habitus but the product of the relation between a particular habitus as such and the social setting (or *champ*, as Bourdieu calls it) in which it takes place. Bourdieu (1991) does not imply that social settings are 'determining' in their actions and choices. On the contrary, individuals have different strategies at their disposal to act in one way and not another and live their lives as 'reflective beings'. Bourdieu emphasises only that specific social contexts ('fields') do influence people's actions in ways that are not always apparent. Habitus works not through a mechanical determinism but within constraints and limits set out in history. The concept of habitus goes beyond the usual antinomies (determinism and freedom, conditioning and creativity...) to generate products (thoughts and actions) that are limited in their production by the historical and social contexts. They are neither completely new nor mechanically reproduced. The notion of symbolic violence, therefore, like any other in Bourdieu's work, is flexible and better understood in a specific setting. In this case, the setting or *champ* is the unique context brought about by the presence of Sri Lankan housemaids in a foreign country which is Lebanon. In this particular setting, symbolic power dominates the employer/housemaid relationship in private households. Moreover, Lebanese governmental institutions and public spaces are grounds for the perpetuation, if not the encouragement, of such insidious forms of violence.

However different people's aims might be, they all share one important presumption: an unconditional belief in the way the game is played. Those engaging in the struggle within a particular field are united by a common 'complicity'; they all genuinely invest in and trust the rules of the game. Quoting Bourdieu (1991: 164) again: 'For symbolic power is that invisible power which can be exercised only with the complicity of those who do not want to know that they are subject to it or even that they themselves exercise it'. It seems that Sri Lankans and Lebanese alike accept the rules of the game they find themselves engaging in. But before I disclose those rules and shed some light on the ways this complicity operates and the symbolic violence exercised, it would be useful, following Bourdieu's notion of habitus, to draw a general profile based on the background and lives of the 90 housemaids I interviewed. I already introduced some characteristics of the sample of interviewees at the end of my 'methodology' chapter (see Chapter 2). Below, I extend this profile discussion, linked more explicitly to the notion of their habitus.

Profile of the housemaids

The profile of the 90 Sri Lankan housemaids I interviewed is organised as follows: general demographic information (age, marital status, etc.), details regarding their living conditions in Sri Lanka, information regarding education (including language skills), and their previous employment experiences. Finally, I felt it was important to discover whether these women had experienced violence within their own families, as a possible hypothesis or precondition to their acceptance of abuse at the hands of their employers.

Demographic information

The average age of the women I interviewed was 32.7 with a minimum age of nineteen years and a maximum of 63. Only 20 per cent of the housemaids were never married, 44 per cent were married, 20 per cent separated/divorced, and 14 per cent widowed. Most women (90 per cent) who were or had been married have children: 2.2 children as an average. The average age at marriage was 18.7 with a lowest age of thirteen and an oldest of 29. Husbands usually stay behind in Sri Lanka; only a few were in Lebanon with their wives. Most children also were left in Sri Lanka (95 per cent). Those who live in Lebanon were born there. Women who have their children with them in Lebanon are also accompanied by their husbands. The children who live in Sri Lanka are usually looked after by the housemaids' mothers (56 per cent). When husbands are in charge of the children (13 per cent) they are helped by women within the family (usually mothers and mothers-in-law). Other children are looked after separately by relatives (sisters, aunts, etc.). Housemaids in general come from large families – the average number of brothers and sisters is 5.8. Their mothers are deceased in 18 per cent of the cases, fathers in 54 per cent.

Living conditions in Sri Lanka

Just over two-thirds (68 per cent) of the Sri Lankan housemaids I interviewed lived in a village in Sri Lanka, and only one-third (32 per cent) came from a city. Less than half had electricity in their Sri Lankan homes. Many electricity instalments resulted from the work of the migrant women. As one housemaid told me: 'Now I have electricity, before no. Two years ago I pay for electricity'.

The average number of residents at home was 5.2, with a maximum of eleven people living together and a minimum of two. Generally, homes are rather rudimentary, with one or two rooms; the bathroom is usually outside. In the words of two housemaids I interviewed:

> Lived in a small house in a village with my sister, the husband of my sister, their four children and my son. Small house, one room, hall, well for water, kerosene lamp (no electricity), bathroom outside. I was living before with my husband but when he died, his family kicked me out.

> In Colombo, I stay with my mother, husband, brother, sister. All in a small house, two rooms. No electricity, bathroom is outside, water outside.

One Lebanese employer related to me how her housemaid was scared to go inside the bathroom; she had no clue as to how it should be used. The employer had to teach her everything, even how to use the toilet paper roll. Electrical house appliances are also a big mystery to many migrants. Acknowledging this fact, the Sri Lankan government (as pointed out in Chapter 1) created a training programme that would initiate these women, among other things, in the use of these appliances. The effect of such programmes cannot be precisely defined. It is my opinion, however, that they are helpful to a limited extent.

Many women come to Lebanon with a specific aim: making money in order to build a house. Those who were married wanted a house on their own to be able to have privacy with their husbands and children. Below are three testimonies from housemaids on this topic:

> I lived in a small house in city, Kandy, next to my mother house, small house: one room, one living room. No electricity. Not really my own, that's why I want to build my own house for me and my husband and children.

Live in village, husband and daughter, in house, alone. House built since we [she and her husband] came to Lebanon. Electricity, two rooms, bathroom outside, one salon, kitchen.

Live in small village with husband, father husband, mother, one brother of husband and me. House of father of husband. Electricity, one room, one salon, kitchen, toilet inside, no phone, no TV. I am building a house, not finished yet.

Education and language skills

None of my interviewees had ever attended university (unlike many Filipina housemaids working in Lebanon); 21 per cent of the 90 Sri Lankans interviewed had no or very little schooling; 30 per cent reached levels 6-9, 28 per cent, level 10, 7 per cent, levels 11-12 and 6 per cent, high school. The average age of leaving school was thirteen years. Could this lack of education contribute to the way the Lebanese view Sri Lankan women as 'stupid'; and, therefore, more 'controllable' than, for instance, Filipinas? In the words of two Lebanese employers:

This one [housemaid] is Filipina. She understands, she speaks, she is smart. She studied accounting. She has a Bachelor degree. Smart. But those who are like this give us a hard time.

Filipinas are tougher but they are educated. At least now I speak English. With the Sri Lankan, I did not speak any language. But Filipinas answer back.

Lebanese employers often complain about their Sri Lankan housemaids who 'just do not understand what is asked of them'. This language barrier, according to employers, makes the 'training' of housemaids even more difficult, especially during the first couple of months of the housemaid's stay. Of the housemaids I talked to, 43 per cent spoke little Arabic, meaning they only understood and spoke a few words; 12 per cent (those who had recently arrived in Lebanon) spoke none; 44 per cent managed well. Only 13 per cent managed to speak English rather well, 46 per cent knew a few words and 41 per cent almost none. The CIA World Factbook (2006) states that English is commonly used within the Sri Lankan government and is spoken 'competently' by about 10 per cent of the population. My result regarding spoken English (13 per cent) seems therefore to be quite realistic despite my doubts about the adjective 'competent'. Three-quarters of my sample could not write in English. When asked for their name or address, most were reluctant to write them down; and the few who did, wrote in a meticulous and rather 'childish' way. Two-thirds could, however, (they claimed) write in their own language.

My results show that language could be a barrier for most of the women interviewed (only 44 per cent managed in Arabic and 13 per cent English), especially in the early stages of migration. Those who spoke Arabic well have been in Lebanon for more than eighteen months.

Employment

Nearly two-thirds of my interviewees had never held paid employment in Sri Lanka prior to coming to Lebanon; only 36 per cent had. Housemaids often answered: 'No jobs there'. Those who worked were employed in the garment industry, mainly in factories (seventeen of the 32), seven in agriculture, six had clerical jobs and two, teaching jobs. One of the two teachers was sheltered and educated by Catholic nuns and later taught in the convent. As one housemaid told me: 'Never worked when finished school at thirteen or fourteen. Brother wouldn't let me go outside'.

Of the 90 housemaids interviewed, 73 per cent had no fixed income or no income at all. Four-fifths of the housemaids' mothers never had paid employment, 20 per cent worked in the fields or sewed clothes. Hence, they had no regular income. The fathers' previous or current line of work is as follows: 40 per cent primary activities (farming and fishing), 27 per cent in a shop, clerical or factory work, 15 per cent in construction and allied trades (carpenter, electrician, etc.), 5 per cent in the government or army, 3 per cent as drivers and 9 per cent never worked. Nearly all the respondents' fathers had no fixed or regular income (87 per cent); those who had, received very low wages, an average of a little over $7 per month.

The employment of husbands (for the housemaids who are or were married) is as follows: 29 per cent in agriculture or fishing, 19 per cent in a shop, store or clerical work, 15 per cent in construction and allied trades, 8 per cent as drivers, 5 per cent in the police or army, 2 per cent as *concierges*, and finally (and tellingly) 23 per cent unemployed. The income of the husbands ranged from a maximum of $320 (this figure is for one husband who was employed outside Sri Lanka) to a minimum of practically nothing, with an average of $37. For those who live in Sri Lanka (86 per cent of the husbands), the average available income was $25: but 60 per cent had either no fixed income or no income at all. Eight of the husbands live and work outside Sri Lanka, seven in Lebanon and one in Turkey; for this subgroup the average monthly income is $243. Clearly, the highest salaries ($200 and above) are of those who reside in Lebanon and Turkey. Husbands in Lebanon usually work as cleaners or *concierges* and gain on average $235 per month. The one in Turkey works in a cargo company and earns $300 per month.

Violence within the family

Six in ten of the sample respondents said they had a good relationship with their husband, while the rest claimed it was not good. The reasons given by housemaids for unhappy marital relationships were 'other women', husband's drinking problem, and physical abuse. The Sri Lankan ambassador confirmed that women do face problems in their marital relationships: 'Some husbands divorce them. There is alcoholism, drug, heroin, unemployment...' Or in the somewhat different words of two Lebanese employers:

> Sri Lankans are good-hearted, sweet with kids. If we hit them, they forget. Because they are beaten in their homes too. Their husbands are drunk. They send their wives to earn money... Sri Lankans lie like they breathe, maybe because they are beaten there.

> Some are tempted to run away, work outside [as freelancers], live with a man.... Because they are mistreated by their husbands there. Most of them. Men stay at home, and make their wives work, they beat them. So they run away from their husbands and come here [to Lebanon]. I know four, five here from my neighbourhood... The husband was drunk, she said: 'I don't want to go again, I prefer to stay here'.

And in the words of two housemaids:

> People are tired in Sri Lanka. They work a lot, no money, so they drink. My husband drank, hit. I left him. Got married at fourteen, left him at sixteen. Now I am 26.

> Father died when I was young – sick, stomach cancer. Husband works land, little money. Husband hits me sometimes. He drinks whisky. I say: 'Don't drink', he hits me.

When asked about their relationship with their parents, 86 per cent of the housemaids interviewed said it was good and 14 per cent not good. A few admitted that they were beaten by a drunk father, some to being hit as a child, but they all seemed to be embarrassed by the question; they blushed, looked down and responded very quickly: 'Parents good'. I witnessed the same reaction when I asked whether or not they were physically violent with their children: 73 per cent very quickly said: 'No, no'.

In one conversation I had with Ramia (the freelancer who used to clean my flat), I asked her whether there was domestic violence in Sri Lanka. Below is one part of this conversation:

Me: Is there violence in Sri Lanka? Husband hits wife...?

Ramia: Yes! *Ktir ktir* (a lot).

Me: In Sri Lanka, if a woman goes out....

Ramia: Never they go out, in Sri Lanka, a woman, if I married, and I go Sri Lanka, husband no let me go anywhere, no...

Me: Husband goes with woman...

Ramia: Yes, but wife no.

Me: Did your parents fight?

Ramia: No, no, no, noooo. When I was little father hit me yes.... [laughing]. Father did not like me going on a bicycle. Once he hit me.

Me: Mali [Ramia's sister who used to work in Lebanon too] hits her children?

Ramia: Yes, Mali hits them a lot. *Ktir* (a lot). I hit Mali too...[laughing]...

Me: You hit each other?

Ramia: Yes [laughing]...

Most Sri Lankan housemaids I interviewed came from outlying rural villages, were relatively uneducated and did not have paid employment in Sri Lanka. The same goes for their parents and husbands. I do not claim that Sri Lanka is a country where domestic violence is common and women undergo abuse by husbands or fathers. It is my impression, however, that the housemaids I interviewed experienced some sort of violence in their home country prior to migrating.

Before I end this section, I wish to hand over the debate to a number of Sri Lankan housemaids I spoke to, to give a more vivid picture of where they come from and what kind of 'baggage' they carry with them to Lebanon:

Age 44. Widow, six children: 23, 20, 19, 18, 16, 15. Four boys, two girls. They are in Sri Lanka, alone in house, husband dead. Married at fifteen. Husband died three years ago. He was crazy. He stayed sick a long time and then died. He was fisherman. Sometimes 50 rupees per day or 100 ($1.3). Sometimes nothing. Not enough for big family. Mother dead, heart, long time ago, maybe 25 years ago. Father dead 30 years ago. Raised with sister. I have three brothers, one sister. Brothers all married, alone living. One boy [brother] fisherman, one like mechanic, one just anything... School Level Five, I left at ten, parents dead. Didn't work after school. I live in village, alone with children, not my mother's place, my place. Small house, one room, no electricity. I work two years in Saudi Arabia. Good. Long time ago, maybe 1983, before my husband died. Here no good. After two months, Madame take me to agency, they hit me. I make *pipi* on myself when they hit me. Hit one time only. Husband was good. Good together. Only when he is crazy he hit me. When he is good, he is good with me. Sometimes he hit me, not always, he drinks sometimes. No hit my children... sometimes when they are naughty. Not too much.

Age 36. Separated from husband. One boy, seventeen. In Sri Lanka with mother. Married at fifteen. Left him after one year of marriage. He is no good. He hit me a lot. Problem. Drinks a lot. Before I married he had mother and children. I found out after I left him. Mother 80, never worked. Father died ten years ago, stomach ache. He was a clerk. He died, no more money. School Level Eight. Left school at fifteen, got married, I loved him a lot. Never worked in Sri Lanka. I live in Colombo, two rooms, one living, bathroom outside, no electricity. With mother, two sisters, husbands of sisters, children.

Age 32. Married, five children, ages five to thirteen. In Sri Lanka with mother and husband. Husband is 35. Unemployed, he drinks little. I marry at eighteen. Mother 55, Sri Lanka, no work. Father dead ten years ago. Sick chest. He worked in land. I have two brothers, one sister. All married, brothers work in land, sister no work. No school. No work in Sri Lanka. I live in village, mother, husband, children. Two rooms, one salon, bathroom outside, no electricity.

Physical violence

As mentioned several times in this book, extreme cases of physical violence by employers remain the exception. As Sister Angela, the Sri
Lankan nun in charge of the Laksehta centre, pointed out to me, physical abuse in its ugliest forms does take place:

> We had people who were very badly treated. People who attempted
> suicide, beaten. Many, many stories of people who jumped off or
> came down the sheets from the sixth, seventh floor. People who
> missed and had a broken leg or injuries... People who have tried
> to take things like Flash or *Eau de Javel* [bleach]. Left in hospital
> and we had to take care of. People who were raped, pregnant.
> Burned with the iron, or bitten by the employer. Bitten. I wouldn't
> have believed it if you had told me this. But because I saw it I be-
> lieve it. I won't be surprised if you can't believe it. Because it's in-
> credible that these things can happen...

However, she adds:

> But, there is a big but, this is only one side of the story. There are
> many who go and they come back quite thrilled. With their hopes
> fulfilled, everything's OK, family is OK. Nothing wrong. And this
> is also true. There are also others who have built their house, put
> aside something for the education of their children. The women
> abused like I described are very small percentage of people who
> come here [to the shelter]. Our experience is only a tiny experi-
> ence. But my opinion is that even if it's one [abused housemaid]
> this should not happen. So it's serious. Number-wise, it may be a
> small number. But problem-wise, it is serious...

It is serious indeed. But my aim is not to dwell on those extreme forms
of violence, no matter how atrocious they are. My plan is rather to highlight forms of violence that might be less intolerable but are, nonetheless, much more widespread and, in their own way, just as unacceptable.

Freelancers' abuse

Before I elaborate on the forms of physical violence housemaids endure in Lebanon and on the regular and insidious strategies of domination (or 'symbolic violence') used by employers to, in short, hijack the
housemaid's personhood and fit her into a convenient mould, I would
like to note that no cases of violence were registered with freelancers I
interviewed (or know about). The words of the Sri Lankan ambassador

corroborate my finding: 'I receive no complaints from the freelancers'. This only confirms my initial thought: abuse is prominent with live-ins and almost non-existent with freelancers. Freelancers do not *live* with the employer but only *work* there a few hours a day. Furthermore, they can change employers at any time. The freelancer who used to work for my mother never accepted to clean our neighbour's house: she simply did not like her. Komari, the freelancer who cleans my flat every week, worked for only three other employers: my sister, a friend of my sister's and another employer. She confided to me: 'I do not want to work for bad employers, I work only if employers are good'. Ramia (a former freelancer I employed) came straight to my place one day after working at another household. She was hungry. When I asked her: 'Why didn't you eat there, didn't the Madame suggest you have lunch?' she replied: 'Yes, she did, but I refused. See, Leila, they are dirty and I do not do the cooking there'. Ramia, as a freelancer, could refuse; live-ins, however, have no choice but to eat whatever is offered to them.

That is not to say that freelancers are immune from abuse but their problems are of a different nature. The most important problem freelancers face is the retrieval of their passport from their former employer. One has to keep in mind that most freelancers are former live-ins, who have left their employer to work 'outside'. Many have 'run away' to do that, leaving their passport behind with their employers (who of course held on to it so that 'she does not run away'). As the son of a Lebanese employer admitted to me:

> She ran away two years ago. She worked in many different places. Now she wants her passport back and money we owe her. The point is not about money, it is about principle. If she has good manners and asks in a good way, maybe I will give her the money and her passport. She was not happy when she was working for us. Maybe she didn't like the work. She wanted to be a queen maybe. Sure we locked her in. If you leave your place with all the things in it, you have to lock it.

Many freelancers and former 'runaways' have had to 'buy' their passport back. Employers, who feel they have lost part of their investment (they paid on average $1,500 to the Lebanese agency and were expecting in return the service of a housemaid for two and a half to three years), refuse to return the passport unless the 'runaway' pays for it. As this freelancer (former live-in who 'ran away') related to me when I interviewed her:

> First seven months *contrat*[1] house. No money except one month. I left. Madame said she wants $2,000 to give me back my passport. I worked one and a half years in another house. House good. I

paid her [the Madame] and got my passport back. After I change sponsor.

The Sri Lankan embassy does advise housemaids to report to the police the 'loss' of their passport in order to provide them with a *laissez-passer* that will allow them to leave the country or a new passport should they wish to remain in Lebanon. In the words of the Sri Lankan ambassador:

> For the past seven months, we gave about 300 *laissez-passer*. That is for people who lost their passport also. They go to the police and say they lost their passport. They say this but they are run-aways. We have to give them a *laissez-passer*. They use this strategy to get out of the country.

And the testimony of one freelancer:

> I came to Lebanon seven years ago. No visit to Sri Lanka since, passport problem. Madame [the current employer of the house-maid] told me about ad in newspaper, there is amnesty period now [periods given by General Security in order for undocumented migrants to regularise their situation]. I come embassy. He [staff member at embassy] said: 'Go bring police report that you lost passport and we make new passport for you'.

Freelancers who succeed in retrieving their passport have to look for 'fake' sponsors to regularise their situation, but often the latter disappear with the money and at times the passport.

> I give my passport to Pakistani man in Adonis [a coastal area out-side Beirut] four years ago to make visa with $1,000. He take pass-port. He ran, no passport, no money.

Freelancers' major problem, therefore, is the regularisation of their situation. Fourteen of the 23 freelancers (61 per cent) I interviewed were 'illegal' compared to only six of the 24 live-ins. The Sri Lankan ambassador admitted: 'Of the freelancers, 50 per cent are legal, 50 per cent illegal'.

Physical abuse within the household

Over one-third of the housemaids interviewed reported physical abuse by the Madame of the house. Hitting, slapping and pushing around were mentioned at times but mostly from runaways, and for many, this occurred on the same day housemaids ran away:

[Does Madame hit you?] Yes, Madame no good. [How?] Madame slap me, with hand. [How often?] Madame hit me, Madame no good. [Yes, but does she do it often, every day, from time to time...?] One time, she hit me, today, that's why I come to embassy.

I ran away because four months no pay me. Once she [Madame] hit me, slap me once.

Madame beat me once, slap. No day off, too much work. Madame always criticised me about my work.

Madame always shout at me. She hit me once. With a wooden spoon that her son was holding.

Housemaids complained less about being physically abused by 'Mister' – only 17 per cent in my sample:

Madame good, Mister hit me. When I iron, Mister wrinkles them so that I do it again.

Mister hit me with his hand.

In half of these cases, the physical abuse followed the housemaids' refusal of Mister's sexual 'offers':

Employers are Muslims [she is Buddhist]. Mister, Madame hit me all the time. With chair. Mister even tried to choke me. He wanted me to do a blow job for him. In Lebanon, one house good, ten not good. Christian people are not like this, only Muslims.

Mister give me $10 and say: 'Come with me'. I don't take it, Mister hit me.

As for physical violence by other members of the family they were rare, only 9 per cent of the cases. When it does take place, it is mainly by women (usually mothers-in-law) and sometimes children if they are old enough.

Physical abuse by agencies

Physical abuse by Lebanese agencies does take place, yet the numbers remain limited as my study shows: 15 per cent (unlike what the Sri Lankan ambassador had told me: 'Ninety per cent of the agencies hit the girls. Not too much, slaps on the face...'). These numbers may be low because not all housemaids have a contact with their Lebanese agencies (twenty of the 56 housemaids who came through the intermediary of a Lebanese agency and not through networking had no contact whatsoever with the people there: 'Never saw them'). It is only when Lebanese agents bring housemaids under their names and make them work for short periods of time for different employers that this direct contact occurs. Moreover, some housemaids (although not many, only nine in my survey) are deliberately taken by their Lebanese employers to the agency for disciplinary purposes (the housemaids were beaten there). In the words of two Lebanese employers:

> We took her in [to the agency] and they beat her well (*taamouah atle mrattabe*).

> I took her to the agency two or three times. But do you think they are efficient these agencies? OK, they [housemaids] come back, one or two days they are calm, then it's like before.

Not all employers, however, condone these 'disciplinary methods' but perhaps not for the humanitarian reasons one might expect. As two Lebanese employers explained to me:

> Now one [a friend of hers] told me, some agencies hit. If you complain about her and take her to the agency, they hit her there, threaten her. If she [the housemaid] is not good. But this does not convince me... How is the one who is beaten going to come back to the household against her will, how is she going to work? I mean, according to me, if she is going to be moody in the house, I wouldn't be able stand her. I cannot stand those who are moody. You understand?

> For example this one when I took her back to the agency, they hit her. I didn't hit her here and I never, never... I say, what for? Send her back. Yes, this I didn't like. I thought they wanted to talk to her. I didn't think they were going to hit her. They hit her. Then I told them: 'I don't want her. After you hit her I don't want her anymore'. Because... how is she going to work after that? They thought I took her to the agency so that they teach her a lesson and send her back with me. I said 'No. No way'.

Some agencies hire Sri Lankan women to do the 'disciplinary' job on their behalf. As one Lebanese staff member at the Sri Lankan embassy told me:

You just have to go and see that in each agency there is a special woman whose special job is to hit the girl. Who is usually from the same nationality and they [Lebanese agents] do this for the purpose of not hitting them themselves and have problems, they let somebody else hit them. And if you come and tell them: 'Why did you allow... why did you hit the girl?' 'No, I didn't hit her, it's the Sri Lankan who hit her. She's like her and she hit her, it's not me who hit her'. You know... they always put on somebody else. But you are paying this girl to hit the maids who are coming and working. Some of them [Sri Lankans who 'discipline' at agencies] are men, some of them women... Most of them are women. Sri Lankan women are very strong. Much stronger in their own way than Sri Lankan men, you know. They are the ones who take care of the family, they are the ones who build a house, they are the ones who pay for everything.

Lebanese employers I talked to also spoke of Sri Lankans who beat housemaids in agencies:

I heard that they [agencies] treat them [housemaids] like animals. Her sister [the housemaid's sister] told her she was beaten by the agency. But I don't know which agency. And that there is a Sri Lankan there who beats them. They hit her in front of me. Violently, yes. It's a Sri Lankan man who hit her, not a Lebanese. It is not Lebanese who deals with maids. In general it is either Sri Lankan women or Sri Lankan men. The two agencies I dealt with, yes, the two times, it was Sri Lankans who dealt with Sri Lankan maids, not Lebanese. The Lebanese talked to us. The Sri Lankan talked to the Sri Lankan maid. This happened with me.

These 'disciplinary measures', however, are not common. Most employers only threaten to use them. Again, this is a sign of the 'symbolic violence' I refer to throughout my research.

Extreme cases of violence that at times required hospitalisation were in general the agencies' doing. I have personally seen the results of three cases of women who were cruelly beaten at their agency (one had bruises all over her body, the second had her chest burned by boiling coffee and the third was hospitalised for a few days). In one particularly severe case of brutality and physical abuse perpetrated against a young Sri Lankan housemaid by a Lebanese agent, the ambassador personally complained to the Minister of Labour, resulting in the suspension of the agent's licence for three months after which he resumed his operations. The agent, however, was not banned and no charges were brought against him. Negotiations recovered only part of the wages the housemaid was owed, even though further compensation for injuries was claimed on her behalf. I interviewed the victim before her departure for Sri Lanka. Even though my research is on symbolic violence rather than physical brutality, I cannot, from a personal but also professional stand, avoid one example of the sort of atrocities some of Sri Lankan housemaids (fortunately not many) endure in Lebanon. Here are my notes on this case:

D. is Sinhalese, Buddhist, age 24, single. She has three brothers and one sister, all in Sri Lanka. Two of the brothers are married and live on their own. They work the land. One still goes to school. The sister is also married and lives with her husband, she does not work. After school (at eighteen), D. went to work in the garment business (sewing). She lived in a house in a small village in Sri Lanka with her father, mother and one brother: two rooms, one living room, no electricity, no phone, bathroom outside. Her mother is 50, she never had paid employment, the father is 51, unemployed. She came to Lebanon 'to feed mother and father, they did not want me to leave'. It was the first time she travelled outside Sri Lanka. The agency in Sri Lanka advised her to go to Lebanon. She was accompanied by a friend. Neither knew anything about Lebanon before arriving. D. attended a training course in Sri Lanka: she was taught how to use electrical appliances, cook... et cetera. D. did sign a contract in Sri Lanka before coming. It only detailed the length of the stay and the salary: two and a half years for $100 per month. The agency charged her 70 dollars. 'I made money from sewing. I bought gold. Then, since I had no money and wanted to come to Lebanon, I went to the bank, put the gold and got money for it'. She also signed a contract in Lebanon, but is not sure in what language it was written. 'Maybe English. He [notary] did it, I just signed. He never explained to me anything'. On arrival at Beirut airport, the mother of the agent was waiting for her. Her passport was taken from her and given to the woman. 'Now I do not know, maybe it's here [at the embassy]'. From the airport, D. was taken to the agency where she stayed for three days. She was then sent to Faraya [in the mountains] to work for Mr T., his sick wife and their twelve-year-old daughter. The family is Christian. She spent eight months with them. Mr T. is about 40 years old. He works in a bank. In Faraya, the door was not locked but still, she could not go outside. She was allowed out to the supermarket but only accompanied by the daughter. She was instructed to refrain from talking to anybody on the way. As for food, it was not enough. Rice, bread, salad and tea. Labné [Lebanese type of yogurt], cheese and meat were also available, but she did not like them. 'I could not eat on my own, open the fridge and eat, they would give me the food. I was hungry but I did not tell them'. She worked twelve hours a day, from seven in the morning till seven in the evening. The housewife being sick, she was in charge of everything, cleaning, cooking, looking after the daughter... Her only contact with her family in Sri Lanka was through letters. Her parents do not have a phone. Mr T. mailed the letters for her. She did not confide in her parents, preferring to keep her negative experience in Lebanon secret from them. 'Haram (poor them), my father and mother, I do not want to worry them. I will not tell them. I will tell my brother. I do not tell my sisters. Only my brother. Girls are more sensitive, not strong like men. My mother might get sick and go to the hospital. My father is old I cannot tell him. I love my parents very much. They never shout at me. I always did what my mother wanted. My sisters sometimes got punished. Not me. I was different. I always said "Yes"'. At various moments of the interview, I asked D., who was obviously in pain, if she wanted to stop. She insisted, a sad smile on her face, on proceeding with the interview. Mr. T was harassing her sexually. 'He is no good'. When she refused his advances, he beat her and stopped feeding her. 'I tell him to stop. "I am a girl, you are like my father". He did not. I told him I want to call the agency. There was no phone in the house, he would not give me his mobile. Then I called from his mother's place in Beirut. I did not want to work anymore. I told Madame what was happening. Madame is sick. She is very nice'. D. was then sent back to the agency with only $300. The agency owner beat her for the first time, slapping her and beating her feet with a metal rod. The agency owner is a '30-year-old, rich, handsome, small Muslim man, he has a beautiful wife and two young children'. After that, D. was placed with a 'good family' and was happy. This, however, did not last. She was taken back to the agency upon the request of the agent who wanted more money from the employer. She was told that she was to be taken to work in Syria (this is illegal). When she protested, D. was beaten again. In Syria, D. was not paid. After six months, she claimed her money and refused to work. This is when she was beaten. She fled her employer's house and went to the police. 'You know why they weren't paying me? Because the agency guy was collecting the money. I did not know that. Then I went to the police. They came and asked my employer why they weren't paying me. He told them that he was paying the agency'. The police then called the Beirut agency and the agent had to pick her up at the border. The owner was so angry and this time, wounded her severely. He beat her with a metal rod. He walked on her body repeatedly, grabbing her long hair as he went on, pulling it along. 'He was so large, I couldn't breathe'. He finally ended up cutting it, to the despair of D. She was tied up after that for six days. The women at the agency [other Sri Lankan housemaids] tried to feed her, but she could not swallow. On the seventh day, her hands were untied and she managed to run away. She knotted two saris together and went out from the window of the third floor. She took a taxi to the Sri Lankan embassy where officials hospitalised her immediately. D. is going back to Sri Lanka. 'I am sick now, I need to rest'. If she feels better, she is willing to go to another country 'but not Lebanon'. The agency paid her $1,500 (which were only her fees), and the ticket back home. A $5,000 compensation was claimed but not given. 'There are very nice people in Lebanon and very bad people. He wants money [he is only interested in money]. You do not have money, you ask, they hit. For one and a half hours he hit me. He cut my hair. My hair was that long (crying). I cannot eat, my stomach hurts. When I walk my leg hurts. Do not be sad. Thank you very much'.

Sexual abuse

Sexual abuse (sexual harassment, not rape) does not seem to be widespread in Lebanon; 11 per cent of my sample complained it was taking place. As expected, 'Mister' was responsible for seven of the ten cases, as described by housemaids below:

> Mister was taking me to bathroom to touch me.

> Mister twice came to touch me. I wouldn't allow it. He threatened to beat me.

The other three cases were either perpetrated by the 'agency man' or the sons of the employer. Only one case of alleged rape was noted. I met the Sri Lankan housemaid who accused the son of her employer of rape (she was a runaway and had taken refuge at the embassy). I am not sure, however, how credible her testimony was; she seemed very disturbed, or 'mentally ill', as the ambassador described her.

One-fifth of the housemaids I interviewed complained of being harassed on the streets, mainly by men, in an insulting and generally sexual way. Below are some examples given by housemaids:

> When I walk on streets some shout: 'Dicky dicky one dollar'.

Lebanese in general? Don't like Lebanese, only like *contrat* house...
I took passport photo, he said: 'Open your blouse'.

On the streets, not good. Man, army man, he showed me his pe-
nis on the street. Some people say Sri Lankans no good. A lot of
Lebanese say so. This is wrong. Sri Lankans are good, not bad.

On the street, they say: 'One dollar, one dollar'. Lebanese boys no
good.

Some people good, some people not good. Some people see us
like no good, they want to make sex with us.

If a Srilanki girl is on street, some boy tell: 'Come, I give you five
dollars... two dollars'. Lebanese boys. I heard two or three times.

Despite the alarming incidents described above, it is important to note
that physical and sexual abuse are not common practices in Lebanon,
as my survey shows. On the other hand, more 'acceptable' or 'symbolic
violence' seems to be the norm. The following section details the ways
in which Lebanese employers control their Sri Lankan housemaids
with less reprehensible tools.

Symbolic violence

'Symbolic violence' takes indirect routes that lead towards a close control of housemaids. These means are justified by Lebanese employers
(or Madames, as it is mainly the Madames who deal with and therefore
abuse their housemaids) as necessary. Lebanese employers, while
claiming to be 'ideal employers', do not believe (and I think it is genuine – which incidentally makes the problem even harder to solve) they
are mistreating their housemaids: they are just protecting their own interests and those of their families. These various means of control (or
'protection') are described below and are developed as follows: shouting
and constant criticism, withholding of passport, withholding of payment, food control, work duties, and supervised contact with the outside world.

Shouting and constant criticism

Half of the housemaids interviewed claimed that their Madames were
not treating them right (excluding the physical violence mentioned
above). One might expect a higher percentage of housemaids to com-

plain about their Madames. However, one should keep in mind that employers define the employer/housemaid relationship in a way that best suits their own self-interests. This definition is generally accepted by all: Lebanese agencies obviously as well as governmental bureaux, but also Sri Lankan agencies which have their own financial interest at heart, as well as the Sri Lankan government wary of jeopardising the much-needed remittances (the Sri Lankan ambassador told me: 'There are violations but we can't speak because we lose the market'). And even (and more importantly) by the housemaids themselves, following what Bourdieu (1991) calls 'active complicity' on the part of the domi- nated. Symbolic violence is 'misrecognised' (i.e. non-recognised) as vio- lence and the rules of the game are generally abided by rather than questioned by housemaids. For example, one Lebanese employer, when asked why she kept her housemaid's passport with her (a housemaid who has been working for her for the past 21 years), said:

> I never gave it to her. I give her her residency papers. Because first of all I am scared she might lose it. But if she takes it I have no problem, I can give it to her. But from the very beginning she got used to the idea that her passport is with me. For example she went to the embassy the other day to renew it and came back, she gave it to me: 'Madame, put it with you'.

And in the words of another Lebanese employer:

> I live with my mother-in-law. You know, every year the maids have to renew their residency. So she [the mother-in-law] gives her her passport to go and do it. So the maid, I don't know, during one week or ten days, she has the passport and my mother-in-law for- gets about the passport. The maid comes and says: 'Madame, this is my passport'.

Moreover, many live-ins, when asked whether they were given a day off per week, replied: 'Nooo, *ana contrat* (I am contract)'. It was not so much the answer but the tone that struck me: it was said like a state- ment of the obvious, without anger or resentment. Coming over as *'contrat'* meant no days off. The housemaid did not question the rule set by agencies and employers, she was *contrat* and therefore could not go out. On the other hand, those who are not officially *contrat*, mean- ing those who are live-ins but are themselves paying for their yearly pa- pers (work and residency), know very well that this rule does not apply to them. When Candy, the Sri Lankan housemaid who was working at my grandmother's, was asked to stay with the old lady on Sundays, she replied with a touch of pride and anger: 'I am not *contrat*, I can go out on Sunday'. Candy's sponsor was not my grandmother but a 'fake' one. She paid for her papers herself and did not feel, therefore, obliged to abide by the standard live-in rules.

Even Sister Angela, director of the Laksehta centre, talks about the housemaids' acceptance of the 'rules of the game':

> Even those who think they have no problem don't even realise it. They have accepted that situation. And they are happy because they are not physically harassed. But even that is slavery. Their passport is confiscated. This is a kind of slavery. They have no holiday, this is slavery. They cannot go out, they have no freedom of movement. This is slavery. And overworked. They are not conscious of that. They say, 'We were not beaten, we were given to eat, Madame is kind'; they're happy. They were given the promised pay. They are happy. They are not conscious themselves of their rights.

When I asked 'runaways' the reason that led them to take such action, 'no salary' was mentioned in 73 per cent of the cases, while only 14 per cent talked about abuse. On a similar note, when I asked housemaids (all categories) about their future plans, more than two-thirds of those who said they wanted to return to Sri Lanka complained about wages not being paid.

Moreover, employers often tell their housemaids that they should be lucky to have them as employers, by comparison to other employers who are 'bad employers'. This type of 'mental pressure' (another form of symbolic violence) can affect the way housemaids view their working and living conditions. I asked one Lebanese employer if she ever shouted at her housemaid. She replied:

> One time. I shout. Do you think I will hit them? [in an angry voice]. Never [laughter]. But I can tell you that there are people that hit their maids. Oh, a lot. No? [asking her housemaid who had stepped in to serve us coffee]. But she's very lucky to work for me. Speak *wli* (you) [laughter]. Do you know, other Sri Lanki, when they come to Lebanon, what happens? [asking her housemaid]. The housemaid answered: 'Some employers they are not good. Some employers they are good'. The Lebanese employer (talking to me but with the housemaid still present): 'She buys magazine every week, and from the Sri Lankan magazine maybe she knows that many Sri Lankis are abused here, they write, yes? [to her housemaid] Every week she goes and buys from here. And I let her to go by herself, for example to the shop. I am not searching her. Because they say, 'Oh! You don't lock the door'. 'Oh! You

let her go and throw the garbage'. 'Oh! You let her go and bring magazine'. I say 'Yes of course, because I trust her' [making sure the housemaid heard her].

Going back to the 'abuse by Madame', constant criticism and shouting (as yet another way to keep housemaids cornered in their 'servile' role) seem to be the rule rather than the exception. As housemaids noted:

I ran away from *contrat* house five months ago. No pay money, no hitting, just Madame shouts.

I worked with Muslim family. No food, no toothpaste, no bedding. I was stinking. I slept in the living room. The couple was good together. But not with me because I was Christian. Madame shout at me, no beating, no going out.

Even Lebanese employers admit to it and the reasons they give are pretty unanimous: housemaids do stupid things, but also, one simply *cannot* be too nice to them; this race *needs* to be controlled. Three Lebanese employers illustrate this:

Yes, of course I shout at her. When she does stupid things... No later than yesterday, it's been a year since she's with me, it has been one year I explain to her the generator system, electricity. 'Before you do anything, unplug one fridge'. I have two fridges. The counter was disconnected, she went down... ten times, the counter is far from the house. She went up and down and the two fridges were still connected. She was going to burn them. 'It has been a year; haven't you learned that you need to disconnect one fridge?' Nothing, she stood in front of the counter like this. You cannot not shout, not get angry. When she does that, after one year, standing in front of the counter and looking at it, how is it going to be fixed when both fridges are connected? Do I feel like hitting her, yes I feel like hitting her [laughter]. But I never did, I don't know why...

The only houses I saw where there was no problem were where the employer was strict. The maids were always scared. That's the only way it works. *La Tashtari el abda illa wel asa maahou*: do not buy a slave without the stick with it.

Tallaetly daghtey (she made my blood pressure go up). I'm always after her, I can't leave her. I told her to use a sponge to scrub the tub and another to clean the toilet. She used the sponge of the toilet on the bathtub. Even though they are the same. But I put them in different places and explained to her. No use. She did a lot of things from six this morning till noon. She put the laundry out, mopped, et cetera. But when I told her to mop here, she didn't understand what I was saying. I had to go bring the mop myself. *Toushmeh* (stupid). I don't think she has a lot of brain. Today I shouted at her and I felt bad.

Withholding of the passport

It is common practice for Lebanese employers to hold on to their housemaid's passport as another means to control their lives and future actions. As one housemaid told me: 'I need my passport, this is my life. If there's no passport I cannot travel anymore'. There is no clear law in Lebanon forbidding the confiscation of passports according to lawyers working with various Lebanese NGOs dealing with issues of migrant workers. To the question: 'Where is your passport?', the 90 housemaids interviewed answered as follows. Only 29 per cent said they had their passport with them, 52 per cent said it was with the employer ('Passport with Madame'. 'Why?' [Shy laughter]... 'Maybe she is afraid I leave the children, I go. Maybe afraid, that's why') and 10 per cent with the agency. The remaining answers included: 'I lost it', 'The passport was destroyed' ('Madame tore my passport in front of me') or 'I do not know where my passport is'. The Sri Lankan ambassador, when asked about this issue, said: 'It is OK for Lebanese employers to keep the passports of their maids; there is always a risk that the maid runs away and the employer is responsible for her by law'. No one else, however (the agency, for example), has the right to do so.

Holding on to the housemaid's passport is 'misrecognised' as violence and redeemed as 'necessary' (just like the shouting and constant criticism described above). In fact, agents, employers and even the Sri Lankan ambassador claim that this measure is only a preventative one, discouraging housemaids from running away. In the words of one agency director, then three Lebanese employers:

Once she [the housemaid] has the passport, she can run away anytime. Anyway, she doesn't need it. If she wants to go out, she can use her residency visa.

I put her passport in my drawer at my office, locked. Her passport is here, look [she opens the drawer], I hide it here. I don't even want to leave it in the house. What if she [the housemaid] found it and ran away?

> Her passport is always with me. Let's say for instance she thought of running away, it will be easier for her [to run away], so I keep it. In any case she doesn't ask for it.

> The agency gives us instructions: Don't leave your drawer open, lock in with keys... Lock her in, take her passport, don't leave any money in front of her. It's just not to tempt her, no more no less. I leave the passport in the closet and lock it. I don't leave it in front of her. I am not really scared that she might take it and run away. But why risk?

One Lebanese employer takes that risk but without conviction:

> The other day I renewed her papers, I put them in the drawer with the passport. They are in front of her. She can take them. And I haven't put it away. It's a mistake on my part. But she's honest.

Withholding of payments

Nearly six in ten of my sample respondents complained about wages not being paid. It is mainly runaways who do so (34 of the 52 who answered positively). Actually, and as mentioned previously, the principle reason for running away, as they themselves claim, is the withholding of wages (73 per cent). As one Lebanese staff member at the Sri Lankan embassy in charge of runaways who go there for help, told me: 'The girls make problems [and run away] only when they are not paid. Not even when they are beaten'. One should keep in mind that these women came here with a primary goal, to make money. What is ironic is that employers say they are not paying the housemaid in order for her *not* to run away. Agents at times advise employers to avoid paying their housemaids' wages in cash. 'She ran away three times. The first time they [employers] gave her $500, then she ran away. The sponsor then agreed to transfer money only and not give cash'.

   Not paying them what is rightfully their due is, therefore, a form of violence aimed at maintaining control over them. However, should employers decide to not pay the housemaid in cash every month (for her not to run away with the money), that does not always mean that they are not paying her at all. Employers transfer money to Sri Lanka usually every three to six months, but more often than not they do not give or show the housemaid any receipt. The housemaid who does not 'see' the money nor the proof of the transfer assumes, therefore, she is not being paid. A Lebanese employer explains:

All of them I give them directly. From hand to hand. Never, I told her later or... They [agencies, employers] all say keep money aside. Maybe she runs away. No, I always give on time. When she wanted to make a transfer, I did it for her. This was a reason for problems between us. She thought I wasn't sending the money. The money didn't arrive. There was war in their country. What can we do? So she got crazy how the money didn't get there.

The Sri Lankan ambassador often advises Lebanese employers to show their housemaids any money transfer receipts, just as he did in this particular case with an employer who had come to the embassy looking for her runaway: 'You have to pay her every month. And if you transfer money you have to show her the receipts. These women are poor, they left their families, their children in Sri Lanka. The children need to eat...'

Money is withheld not only to make sure the housemaid does not run away but it is also used as a means of control. As I said many times, employers have power over every aspect of these women's lives. Yet again, they claim and believe that they are doing the right thing on behalf of their housemaids, only deciding what is best for her. As a result, housemaids are at times not even free to spend their own money as they please, as this Lebanese employer relates:

Now for instance it's been eight months I didn't pay her [her wages]. Because she is not sending [money to Sri Lanka]. The basis of the contract stipulates that I don't give her her salary unless she sends it to Sri Lanka. Depending on what she wants I give her a cheque and I put it in an envelope and she sends it. I don't give her cash every month, no. When she leaves, I'll give her everything at once. That way the money is not spent. She wanted to take the money [wages], she said: 'Give me, I need to buy gold, give me....' I didn't accept... Now she told me: 'I want a cellular'. I didn't accept to buy one for her. They start being jealous of each other. Her friend has a cellular. I told her: 'What for? The phone is not forbidden [the house phone] you can use it to call your cousin [in Lebanon]'. So, what for, just to spend money? I don't accept. She saw with my neighbour gold she wanted the same, I didn't allow her to bring. I told her: 'When you're ready to leave, the money is here ready. But you worked all this time at least so that you have money when you leave, not that you spend everything on nothing'. She was supposed to go one month and come back. But now she says her husband and son don't want her to come back...

Another form of control relating to wages concerns housemaids who 'in principle' agree to renew their contract, i.e. go for a visit to Sri Lanka upon the termination of their three-year contract and come back to Lebanon for another three-year contract with the same employers (I say 'in principle' because many use this as a strategy of resistance – discussed in the next chapter – to secure their departure). Often, employers do not pay housemaids in full but keep part of their wages with them to *ensure* they will indeed come back as promised. In the words of two Lebanese employers:

> She [her housemaid] is going for a month and coming back, but I want to make sure she comes back so I will hold on to some of her money here.

> My maid is due to leave in six months. I asked her to come back, she hasn't answered me yet. I will keep part of her salary, friends told me to do so to make the maid come back. Sometimes they tell you: 'We want to come back', you buy a return ticket then they don't and you lose your money. So if she tells me: 'Yes I want to come back', I will keep part of her salary with me. If she doesn't want to come back, I will pay her everything and send her. I will then have to look for somebody else. But I want somebody who doesn't go out...

Food

Most housemaids interviewed (73 per cent) claimed they had no problem with food, but when probed, over two-thirds said they were mostly given leftovers and did not have the freedom to eat whenever and whatever they wanted. Here are two brief extracts from housemaids' interviews, followed by two longer narratives, the first from a Lebanese employer, and the second from a Lebanese employer's daughter:

> Madame say: 'Don't eat anything before you ask me'. She give me food.

> I open fridge and take something, if old food, OK; if cake, Madame shout.

> Some [housemaids] eat in hiding, some steal food, for example a neighbour of mine called me and told me: 'Come and see'. I said: 'What?' She [the housemaid) had hidden cans in the closet, cans of sardines, tuna, soap, et cetera. 'But why does she do that? Why does she hide things?', I asked her [the neighbour]. She answered:

'I don't know, even though I serve her food'. I told her: 'Maybe she's still hungry, she needs to decide how much she wants to eat'. Me, I finish eating, I tell her: 'Serve yourself, but do not put your spoon in and return it into the pot. Put as much as you want but your spoon in your plate, like we eat'. Because I'm scared they might eat directly from the casserole. That's all. But I leave the casserole in front of her, she wants to eat twice or three times, it's OK... too bad (*tant pis*). You see? On the issue of food, I am strict about one thing only – it is forbidden to put your spoon inside the food, it is forbidden to make a mess with the bread inside the food; you serve yourself with your own spoon into your own plate. I used to, I'm not going to lie to you, I used to hide and watch her to see if she was applying this. Only then did I trust her. Because if you see them eating from the casserole you get disgusted, nauseated. But the quantity of food is not an issue for me. They [other employers] serve them once only. So she [the housemaid] is hungry maybe. The neighbour locks the fridge. There is a key for the fridge. It is not always their [Sri Lankans] fault.

You know what happened today? Something very stupid. I had some things to wash by hand. She [the housemaid] loves me very much. Really. So, when she sees me doing something, she's very annoyed, like why am I doing it. She has to do it. So, I was doing my things and she came and said: 'No Madame, I'll do it, please, I'll do it'. And she really pushed me away. I said: 'OK'. My mother was preparing her lunch. She was making her [the housemaid] French fries. You see, she's contradictory my mother. She's preparing her lunch. And she [the housemaid] was cleaning my clothes. And the meal was ready. And she [the mother] said: 'Lata, come and eat'. Lata said: 'I finish this and I come Madame'. 'I told you to come now', my mother says. Lata: 'I finish and then come'. My mother: 'No. You hear what I said. You come now. Why don't you understand what I say? Why don't you come? Why do you want me to get angry at you? Just come now...' She [the housemaid] left everything and went to eat. You see. I don't know how to explain this. It's white or black with her [the mother]. I think this is violence. She's [my mother] making her do what she wants. She [the housemaid] doesn't have the freedom even to choose. When to eat, or what to eat. Because my mother decided to make her French fries and something else, I don't know. But maybe she [the housemaid] doesn't want to eat that. She's always telling her what to eat. 'Take this and eat it'. Why? Once I really shouted at my mother not a long time ago. I had to prepare spaghetti for my son. And he didn't eat it. He ate a little bit. She [my mother] said: 'It's

OK, Lata will eat it'. Why Lata will eat it? This was for my son and it's awful. 'Why does she have to eat it? Why don't you give her the choice to eat it or not to eat it?' This is something that I cannot accept. So, I threw it away immediately. But she does that from time to time. Another story, sad one. You know the syrup [sugar diluted with water and rose water] that you eat with *kneffé* [Lebanese pastry]. We had *kneffé* once and we had some syrup left. And my mother called Lata and said: 'Lata, this is sugar, put it in your tea, it's like sugar'. This is unjust. I don't know. I think this is not fair. And I went really mad. But my mother didn't understand why I was mad. She got mad also. And I got mad... This is unjust... 'Don't throw it away. You put it in your tea'. Why does she have to put it in her tea? You see what I mean...?

It is my opinion, from observing Sri Lankans for years now (those I interviewed, saw at friends' or relatives' flats, or employed myself), that housemaids are too shy to ask for food and generally accept what is given to them. They usually abide by the 'rules of the game' set by employers while 'not recognising' any type of control as violence perpetrated against them. In the words of one housemaid: 'Yes Madame let me cook for me. But later she don't like it a lot. She said allergy and something. But I eat rice, twice a week like this. They are good people, right'? Even those in my sample who claimed: 'Food OK, no problem', when probed on whether they could simply open the fridge and eat, said: 'No, no... not like this'. A Lebanese employer explained to me why, in her opinion, Sri Lankan housemaids were 'better' than Lebanese: 'They [Sri Lankan housemaids] are not demanding at all, at all. If you don't give her or do things for her she doesn't ask. For example whatever you make her dress she dresses, whatever you put on her plate she eats, if you don't specifically tell her do what you want, no way, she won't'.

Again, Lebanese employers who, in a reversal of roles, are 'serving' their housemaids, only do it, they claim, for 'her own good'. In the words of one Lebanese employer:

Mine is very sweet, she always asks: 'Can I eat?' She was never insolent. The other [friend's housemaid] opens the fridge and eats... Me, for instance, I prepare the meal, she has her own bowl, I put for her and I put a lot. Then I put for her dessert or a fruit. The other one no, she opens the fridge and eats... Mine has a freedom to eat as much as she wants, even between meals, but I make sure I serve her so that she eats well. When we go to eat at my mother-in-law's, I serve her first, *haram* (poor her). Many Lebanese treat their maids bad, they make them suffer, not just hit. I don't, I could never do that. I treat her very well.

Regarding the type of food, most of the housemaids interviewed (69 per cent) were are not allowed to cook their own type of food but were expected to eat Lebanese food. Here is a trio of views on this:

> Housemaid: 'You know, Leila, I come your country, first time I don't want to eat your food, I cannot eat your food. I how can I stay? How eat this? One month, Leila... I want to think, *chway, chway* (little, little) I try. Yes? After OK'.

> Lebanese employer: 'No spicy food though. I didn't let her because her odour is very strong, you know, disgusting. She doesn't cook for herself. She eats from our food'.

> Agency director: 'Some [employers], especially *nouveaux riches,* treat them like a fridge. Many think, she will come, the next day, she will eat our food, speak our language'.

Once more, Lebanese employers do not think they are mistreating their housemaids; quite the contrary, as one claims: 'Usually, they do not cook. They eat from our food... I never treated her less than us... She doesn't appreciate the fact that I am treating my daughter for example like her'.

Work duties

When asked about their work tasks, all housemaids answered systematically 'everything'. 'Everything' means: cleaning, taking care of the children, walking the dog, taking out the rubbish, cook or help in the kitchen, some also clean the employer's relatives' houses... In short, they are on call 24 hours a day. In the words of one Lebanese employer: 'She gets me nervous sometimes. Sometimes, I call her. She doesn't come. I call and call. I get angry. She ends up being in the bathroom'. The General Security director I interviewed did not like the fact that Lebanese women were relying so much on their housemaids: 'Now a maid does everything. You bring her as a maid, soon she becomes a nanny, then the cook, finally she is the wife. What is the role of the wife in that case?'

Lebanese employers are, however, wary of losing their role as housewives and so try to 'manage' the duties of their housemaids in a way that does not give the latter too much power. Again, this is about keeping the housemaid 'in her place', very much distinct from the place and role of the 'lady of the house'. Housemaids do 'everything' in the house except for the few tasks Lebanese employers hold on to. Two examples are given by Lebanese employers:

> I cook. No, not the maid. No. But she helps me a lot. Let me tell you how. For instance we want to make *tabboulé* [Lebanese salad]. I bring the products, I go on Saturdays and buy things for the whole week. She cuts the vegetables for me, does the dishes, things like that.

> For example, Nayla, the fridge, I do it [clean it], from inside. You find some [employers], they start screaming, for example, 'Did you see, the rice is smelly, why do you leave it?' I find that this is my work. The maid, she's going to do everything? And me, what is my role of housewife? I think that way. There are things that I have to watch. Not her. Her, she has things to do. She knows them. Some of the women, if their maids don't tell them that there is no more rice in the house, they start shouting: 'Why didn't you tell me?' No, I'm not like that. Sometimes you find this kind of women [employers]. They want a maid and a housewife. You bring her to help you, not to run the house for you.

It is common for Lebanese employers to take their housemaids to work for their relatives (mothers, mothers-in-law, brothers, etc.) or friends. Housemaids are usually not paid for this extra assignment just as they have no say in the matter. One housemaid told me she worked in three houses: 'Madame house, Madame mother house and Madame friend house'. One Lebanese employer said her mother-in-law made her housemaid work whenever she took her there:

> She [housemaid] loves my mother a lot but she does not love my mother-in-law. If I tell her I'm going to my mother, she is very happy, like going to a party. Because my mother treats her very well. My mother-in-law makes her work [laughing]. My mother-in-law has someone coming to clean just twice a week [freelancer]. So she makes her work, I don't say anything.

Needless to say, housemaids are overworked. Housemaids in my sample worked on average fifteen hours a day. The majority woke up between six and seven in the morning and went to bed between ten and eleven at night. Bedtime varies, of course, depending on whether the Madame is having guests over or not. Between the time they are up and their bedtime, housemaids have little time to rest, especially if employers have young children. When asked what they do during their leisure time, answers varied: care for children, rest/sleep, write/read letters, watch TV, ironing or sewing for Madame, take a bath, massage Madame or simply nothing. Only very few can go out, visit friends or just walk outside.

I will leave it to Lebanese employers to explain how their house-maids spend their days (and at times nights):

> She wakes up around six-thirty or seven o'clock. It depends on my little boy because now she sleeps with him in the room... she doesn't start work [household chores] before my other son goes to school, because he leaves here at a quarter to eight. She works till two-thirty. Time we come back at. In the afternoon she is with the kids. At night after we eat she does the dishes; she has two or three days per week ironing; she irons at night, not during the day. No, she doesn't cook. She does take care of my kids, I can leave them with her and go out. No time off according to the agency. On Sunday she doesn't go. Effectively, she has no right [for a day off]. But Sundays there is no work. Unless we have guests....

> Some Lebanese employers do not treat their maids right. Some of them make them work ruthlessly. Mine works a lot too. She doesn't sit on a chair starting six in the morning till maybe mid-night. She doesn't sit. She doesn't know what is to rest her but-tocks. But it's not me who ask her to do this. I tell her: 'I want everything impeccable'. She works on automatic. I leave, I go to the pool, go for visits, I come back... She is slow, very slow. But I leave her, she knows that she has to clean everything, clean very well, slowly or not slowly... it doesn't matter. Some for example ask them to do every day the house, if there is work or not, just to keep them busy, to make them work. I don't.

> When I go out at night, she [the housemaid] is not allowed to go to bed in case the baby wakes up and she doesn't hear her. She has to wait up for me. This is quite normal and rather fair since my neighbours receive guests at least three times a week and the maid is awake to help.

> I explained to her her duties so she knows how to divide her work. Monday she cleans the living room, Tuesday the bedrooms, but when she cleans I mean everything is cleaned including windows, Wednesday is kitchen, Thursday and Friday is *retouche* [cleaning everything again but not thoroughly], every day she should dust the house, no matter what. So even if she's doing the bedrooms, she dusts here too. Always the dust. If she's doing the kitchen the

dust is taken off too. So the house is dusted every day plus the
bathrooms and then she goes on to do what's on the schedule.
But there is something essential to be done every day, dust and
bathrooms, these are to be done every day. Sunday there is no
work, just dishes...

Supervised contact with the outside world

Nine out of ten of the housemaids interviewed had no days off per week;
only one out of ten did (usually Sundays). Eight out of ten also stated
that they were not free to leave the house of their own accord. They may
do so under supervision (accompanied by a member of the household)
or merely just to buy things from the neighbourhood store. Even then,
they are advised not to speak with anyone on the way. Many employers
explained that their housemaid did not wish to go out anyway:

> No, she doesn't go out. But she doesn't like to. We always take her
> out with us, twice a week. She has no one here. But there is the
> Sri Lankan of our neighbour, when she goes down with the kids
> down to play she sits with her, they talk...

> She is not given a day off but she does nothing on Sundays, and
> anyway, she does not ask to go out, she knows no one.

As mentioned before, agents usually advise their clients (employers)
not to allow the housemaid outside the household without supervision,
as evidenced below in quotes firstly from an agency director, then from
two Lebanese employers.

> We advise the sponsors not to let the girls out. It is risky. They
> meet many girls on the street. If there was no chance of them run-
> ning away, it would be better to let them go out. We all need our
> freedom.

> Our agent told us: 'Do not let her go out because she'll change.
> Take her out from time to time with you'.

> No, no day off, not at all. In the contract [agency contract], it says
> three years, days-off forbidden.

Even the Sri Lankan ambassador, when I asked him about this issue,
seemed to condone such attitudes: 'Many women present in Lebanon
encourage others (through balcony talks, etc.) to run away and introduce them to the sex business. Many raids took place in Beirut arrest-

ing Syrian, Egyptian workers, with Sri Lankans working as prostitutes'. So, I replied, when the Lebanese claim that they do not allow their housemaids out to protect them from bad influence, they are not totally wrong? His answer was: 'No'.

Six out of ten of the housemaids interviewed said that they were 'locked in' (meaning, employers lock the household door when they leave). Some agencies even do not 'guarantee' a housemaid (meaning replacing her within three months in case the employer is not satisfied) if she is not 'locked in' and is allowed out on her own. In the words of one Lebanese employer: 'She has no key to the house. I lock her in. Precaution. I am not really scared of her, I am scared she might open to someone'. Housemaids who were not 'locked in' were still not free to go out as they wished, and in a sense, it is as if they were. Employers who do not 'lock in' their housemaids have their reasons (and means to ensure she does not open the door). As one Lebanese employer explained to me:

> I told this one [housemaid] when I brought her that she can't go out. Anyway, the contract stipulates that she doesn't. But I don't lock the door on her, I have kids. I tell her all the time that it's not safe for her to go out, that maids are raped, et cetera. I made her so scared to open the door to anybody, I tell her stories about people knocking on the door, getting in, raping, beating and stealing. She believes me and gets so scared. Whenever I leave, I hear her locking the door from inside after me. I do this so that she doesn't open to anybody or bring any of her friends in.

Seven out of ten of the housemaids were not given house keys. A housemaid testifies: 'Madame no work. I had my own room and bathroom. No key. She even took the key of my room so I don't close the door. No go out. Always with Mister and Madame. Never leave me alone. Outings with them, sometimes I'm tired, I don't want to go'. Those who were given keys could use them only in emergencies, or just to go and buy things and come back, wait in front of the building for the children's school bus... In the words of one Lebanese employer:

> I give her a key. For emergencies not for her to go out. If I'm late for my daughter, so that she could be waiting for her coming from school... Things like that. It is forbidden that they go out anyway. But I don't lock the door. But in the agency, it is not allowed. Where do you want her to go? She comes with me, she goes out with me. Not with their friends or going out themselves.

The reasons employers give for not allowing their housemaids to go out in general (no day off, lock her in, no key) can be summarised as follows: since Sri Lankan housemaids are naïve they could easily fall under the bad influence of 'others'. 'Others' might be freelancers who could encourage them to run away and work outside or men with whom housemaids could end up being sexually promiscuous (she could therefore catch diseases or get pregnant) and even allow them inside the household in the absence of their employers. Here are a few of these reasons:

> No, she doesn't have a day off. You know, I am afraid if I send her, maybe she will meet another girl, she will tell her: 'Come and run away', or she will meet a man. Most of them they teach them to run away...

> I don't let her out. No I don't. Even if she wants to go upstairs she has to ask me. I don't let her out. No I don't. Even in the house if at night we're sitting in front of the TV she wants to take a shower she comes and tells me: 'I want to take a shower, do you need anything?' When they are a group they start encouraging each other. The group here who work as freelance. They have a room and work in many houses. They have freedom. And if there are men too, this scares me. And she has the house key in case something happens, God forbid. She might then receive somebody. This is what scares me. I have a baby in the house.

> She's not allowed out, no. The maid of a friend of mine caught syphilis. I have kids. What if she goes out with men, what if she brings men over. The other day, a Syrian man followed back a maid who works in the same building. He kept coming and waiting for her downstairs in front of the building. If she wants to go to see her sister or a friend for instance, I'll take her. I'll wait for her in the car if need be but I will never let her go on her own. I'm too scared she'll catch something. This is why I want a maid who has never been here and knows nobody. My Sri Lankan has an address book full of names and numbers of people she knows in Lebanon. What if she gets hooked with a man? When I leave I never lock the door on her, I have kids in the house. What if she brings her boyfriend while I'm away and takes him inside the bedroom, leaving my kids unattended?

Moreover, employers believe they are not only protecting their own families but they are also concerned about the well-being of their housemaids and are, in a way, protecting them from themselves. In the words of one housemaid: 'I can't go out. If I go maybe somebody see me [ironic tone]... [laughing]. I am not afraid of myself but she [the employer] is afraid of myself... [laughing]'. One Lebanese employer told me about the vulnerability of her housemaid:

> I didn't allow her to go out. No, never, not even Sunday. Maybe I didn't have enough confidence in her. She was young, maybe vulnerable. I don't know. Maybe she would meet somebody and all the stories that we heard about... Many things that happened... You know maids who were in contact with people, thieves or something like that and they used to bring at home, steal things. I didn't have anything at the time to steal at home but (laughter) it was the fact that she would be in contact with people like this and maybe bring them home when I'm not at home. I wasn't comfortable with the idea. Maybe because she was too young [the housemaid is 21]. For me, she wasn't... I never thought of her as a person... strong person. She was more like a child. Naïve. And I think she was the kind of... she was scared. Because I remember sometimes I used to tell her: 'Go and bring this', for example, when we are in the car and I say 'Can you go and, I don't know, bring something from the shop?' 'She used to say: 'Alone?' It was like... 'I don't want to go alone'. She gave me this impression of being naïve and scared.

These fears, in my opinion (and despite the fact that unfortunate incidents – diseases or robberies – of some sort do take place from time to time), are not justified and have turned into a kind of obsession amongst Lebanese employers. They can in fact be convenient alibis (just like racism) to isolate and hence control further the housemaids. It is my belief that the inherent fear underneath all these restrictions is that the housemaid might be influenced by others and therefore 'change', i.e. become less submissive and more demanding. Public spaces can be privileged 'sites of resistance', places where 'offstage performances' or 'hidden transcripts' can take place, but more importantly, these 'sites' are out of the reach (and control) of employers (Scott 1990). Gatherings of subordinates (housemaids) are therefore unwelcome by the dominant group (employers). The rule of the game is one of control, complete control over the housemaid's 'personhood'. 'Demanding' housemaids are to the dislike of Lebanese employers, as one told me:

> She [her housemaid] came to me the other day and said she wanted to go on Sunday with her Sri Lankan friend (woman) she knows from the building. They start teaching and spoiling each

other, that's what happens. I said: 'No way. It is said in the contract that you are not allowed out. And you don't have a day off'.
Can you imagine? She wants to go out now!

Conclusion

As mentioned earlier in this chapter, people's actions (and reactions)
are not merely determined by one's general or 'lifelong' habitus but
rather by the particular relation stemming from a certain habitus and
the social setting in which it takes place. Housemaids feel totally isolated in a new setting where employers, agencies, government regulations and institutions (of both host and sending countries) conspire to
perpetuate (or even to encourage) the exploitation of migrant women
working as housemaids. Lebanese employers have (and are given) the
power needed to set the rules of the game as they see fit. To be able to
achieve their goals, they use – instead of straightforward violence – less
reprehensible means ('symbolic power') to keep Sri Lankan housemaids under their tight control. These means, are, more often than
not, 'misrecognised' by housemaids and justified as necessary by
employers.

However, this does not mean that Sri Lankan housemaids are merely
'passive prey'. To simplify the discourse would be to do injustice to
them. As Scott (1990) has noted, similar forms of domination more often than not lead to similar modes of resistance. To counter the 'symbolic violence' of the 'superordinates' (Lebanese employers), 'subordinates' (Sri Lankan housemaids) cannot afford to engage in open and
confrontational acts of resistance (for fear of violent repression). In
fact, attempts by housemaids to openly question their employers' orders and negotiate work duties are automatically overpowered. I witnessed one of these attempts at my grandmother's place. My grandmother told the housemaid to mop the floor. The housemaid replied:
'Not now mama'. My grandmother kicked the bucket of water onto the
floor and said ironically: 'Well, now you have to'. Housemaids choose
instead various 'detours' or safer means of resistance. Using Scott's notion of 'everyday forms of resistance', I will describe in the next chapter
how Sri Lankan housemaids in Lebanon resist their employers' domination and how effective this resistance is.

6 Resistance

'When the great lord passes,
the wise peasant bows deeply and silently farts.'
Ethiopian Proverb (in Scott 1990)

It is my opinion that Sri Lankan housemaids in Lebanon are neither passive victims stoically enduring abuse and exploitation, driven by misery into migration and onto the stake of abuse, nor are they these strong and courageous women who have decided to take control of their lives, empowered by their migratory experience away from abusive husbands and despite authoritative employers. In fact, the general image lies somewhere in between the dark or bright accounts of migration. Sri Lankan housemaids do not just suffer in silence. Their 'resistance' might be inaudible to some, but it does nonetheless resound to persons who choose to listen more carefully. Just as violence is 'symbolic', insidious, yet powerful, taking unusual routes that are harder to detect and overcome, resistance occurs in the same 'discrete' pattern, through almost imperceptible yet influential acts.

'Everyday forms of resistance'

As Scott (1990: 128) claims: 'If the logic of a pattern of domination is to bring about the complete atomization and surveillance of subordinates, this logic encounters a reciprocal resistance from below'. As employers, therefore, use strategies to exercise power, housemaids construct their own to resist this power. Here I use Scott's notion of 'everyday forms of resistance' to explore the systems of resistance Sri Lankan housemaids construct in response to the 'symbolic power' and control strategies used by their Lebanese employers.

In his co-authored study of peasant groups in South Asia (Scott & Tria Kerkvliet 1986: 1), Scott emphasises behaviour that lies 'between passivity and open, collective defiance'. Rebellion, he asserts, has been very much emphasised at the expense of the 'ordinary weapons' of subordinate groups. Yet, less ostentatious and dramatic but subtle and persistent forms of 'everyday resistance' do have an important impact on class and authority relations. Subordinate groups' subtle ways of resistance are often mistaken for acts of deception and ruse by dominant groups. Just as Bourdieu concentrates on everyday forms of 'symbolic violence' that are harder to detect than 'real' violence, Scott analyses insidious forms of resistance practised by the weak at the expense of the powerful. Both forms of violence and resistance analysed by Bourdieu and Scott take indirect and unsuspected paths to attain, nonetheless, irrepressible and tangible results. This interesting parallelism is at the core of my conceptual framework.

Scott draws his material from studies on slavery, serfdom, colonialism and highly stratified peasant societies to analyse general patterns of resistance in response to domination. He chooses forms of domination (where status is, in principle, attributed by birth) that are similar in their construction and consequences. Scott does not mean to assert that all 'superordinates' and 'subordinates' share immutable characteristics. His claim, however, is that 'similar structures of domination, other things equal, tend to provoke responses and forms of resistance that also bear a family resemblance to one another' (Scott 1990: 21-22).

Scott (1990) also talks about forms of domination that are, despite their institutionalisation, subject to 'personal rule'. 'Here I have in mind the great latitude for arbitrary and capricious conduct by the master toward his slave, the lord to his serf...' (Scott 1990: 21). As much as Lebanese employers allow themselves to change their minds, give conflicting orders, alter their moods, Sri Lankan housemaids are, on the other hand, denied any 'capricious' behaviour or attitude. They are supposed to act like robots, follow orders with a smile, not feel homesick or just sick...

Elites elaborate different styles of speech, dress and etiquette as a way of distancing themselves from lower classes. Terms of address vary with power. For example, in the past, the dominant class in France used to address their servants with the pronoun *tu* while they were approached with the polite *vous*. Another example of the asymmetrical use of address was the common practice by ruling groups to call their inferiors by their first names or simply 'boy' (while the latter used 'Master' or 'Mister'). As mentioned earlier (Chapter 4), Lebanese employers, when they do not call their Sri Lankan housemaids by their first names (or the name of a previous housemaid), generally use the term 'girl' (*binit*). Elites also distance themselves physically from subordinates. 'In racial, colonial, or status-based social orders, this cultural segregation also discourages unofficial contact between orders for fear of contamination' (Scott 1990: 133). Lebanese employers' fear of contamination from their Sri Lankan housemaids takes multiple forms: washing clothes and eating separately, using different cutlery, denial to come too close to babies and kiss them on the face, etc. Housemaids also are often obliged to wear a costume, increasing the feeling of segregation.

Just as elites create a culture that is closed to lower classes, subordinates elaborate their own, hermetic and resistant to the dominant group. This culture is based on isolation and mutual dependence, the sharing of similar experiences and the fear of a common 'enemy'. Sri Lankan housemaids in Lebanon do have their own 'public quarters' (for example, the Dora area described in Chapter 2) that employers usually do not (or do not want to) access. They also benefit from a strong informal networking system whereby women help each other through personal loans, food and shelter, search for sponsors, etc.

Scott and Tria Kerkvliet (1986: 1) analyse forms of resistance that share common features: 'They require little or no co-ordination or planning; they often represent forms of "self-help"; they typically avoid any direct symbolic affront to authority; and they are generally underwritten by a sub-culture of resistance'. These forms of insubordination or 'weapons of the weak' are not to be confused with survival strategies. Resistance acts are those directed towards or against superordinates only. They are conscious and are, therefore, acts '*intended* either to mitigate or deny claims asserted by superordinate classes' (Scott 1985: 290; emphasis in original). This approach expands the domain of politics to practices of everyday life (to what Scott calls the 'infrapolitics of the powerless'), beyond formal organisations and collective mobilisations. These forms of resistance cannot really change the overall situation of domination but are not, however, without effect. Small acts added to others might initiate an avalanche according to Scott. Unproductive work, for example, can, on a large scale, hinder the success of an enterprise, just as peasant tax evasion can endanger the state.

According to Scott and Tria Kerkvliet (1986: 6), the everyday forms of resistance of peasants consist of 'footdragging, dissimulation, false-compliance, pilfering, feigned ignorance, slander, arson, sabotage and so forth'. An Afrikaner's views are cited as such in Scott (1990: 133): 'The coloureds have learned one thing: to play dumb. They can accomplish great things this way... They talk to me but there's always a wall between us – a point beyond which I have no understanding. I can know about them, but I can't know them'. Subordinates use stereotypes that are aimed at stigmatising them to their own benefit. If they are considered stupid, and if, for example, a direct refusal to obey an order is unacceptable, they pretend not to have understood the order in the first place. Refusing to understand (faking ignorance and dumbness) becomes a form of resistance and class struggle. Sri Lankans are often accused of dumbness. In the words of one Lebanese employer: 'She never understands, I tell her one thing and ask: "Did you understand?" She says: "Yes Madame". Then she doesn't do it'. Another Lebanese employer commented, 'Intelligent? Not at all. This one, not at all. The other, the Ethiopian, super-intelligent. But this one not at all. Obedient? Euh, like I told you, depending on her moods'. Are these examples of 'feigned ignorance'? Did Sri Lankans fail to understand or did they simply choose not to? Or are they, sometimes, simply 'not in the mood' to obey?

Scott (1990) gives the example of a form of resistance difficult to repress. In Poland, supporters of the union *Solidarnosc* decided to go for a walk everyday at the exact time of the official government television news broadcast. This mass promenade was not illegal and was, therefore, hard to suppress by the regime. Taking an ordinary activity and changing it into a scene of political meaning for the opposition is a typical example of resistance. Gossip, spreading rumours, sending anonymous letters or circulars, groaning, singing and dancing are other forms of resistance. Another example, according to Scott (1990), is theft. Thefts were encouraged amongst the slaves themselves and were considered to be a mere re-appropriation of one's labour products. Sri Lankans are often caught stealing. Do they feel that it is their due? Do they consider that the Lebanese have a surplus of things that might be of better 'use'? Do they feel that being poor gives them the right to take away from the rich? Is it payback day when they leave and take with them things that are not theirs?

As mentioned earlier, acts of resistance are subtle and disguised. For example, a peasant can insult a noble in a way that is difficult for the latter to comprehend. 'By the subtle use of codes one can insinuate into a ritual, a pattern of dress, a song, a story, meanings that are accessible to one intended audience and opaque to another audience the actors wish to exclude' (Scott 1990: 158). The dominant group might understand some of the hidden messages present in the performance but find themselves unable to react, as nothing ostensible emerged from underneath the apparent innocence of the subordinates.

A question worth asking here is: Why resistance instead of open confrontation? I often wondered why Sri Lankans (especially freelancers who had more margin of freedom) did not simply say 'No' instead of lying. How many times have I asked Ramia (the freelancer who used to work for my mother and at a later stage for me): 'But why didn't you simply say "No"? She'd answer: 'But, Leila, *haram* (poor) mama' (about my mother)...or 'Mama will get upset'. The only way for Ramia to refuse a job was to say 'Yes Madame, of course Madame...' and not show up. Why the lying, why not simply decline the offer? My mother was neither despotic nor violent. It took me some time to understand: Ramia did not say no because she thought she simply could not say no to any form of authority. Her position as a maid, her history or 'habitus', her experience in Lebanon probably taught her that the best way was to lie and avoid confrontation. Submission does not mean lack of resistance and is sometimes a way of resistance. Ramia's way to resist authority was to resort to lying. What is most interesting here is that Ramia applied this form of resistance without discernment. She could have said no to my mother who posed no threat to her. In fact, my mother often repeated: 'Please Ramia, if you can't come, it's OK, just tell me, but don't say you're coming and not show up'. 'Yes Madame...' I have a member in my family who used to use, and still does use, this strategy with her brother (the eldest in the family). She used to say "Yes" to his constant 'advising' with a big smile on her face... to only do in the end exactly as she pleased. Her brothers and sisters stood up to their eldest and faced unending crisis. Which is the best way? Open conflict or discrete resistance?

The debate about power has concentrated on the reasons behind the conformity of ordinary people when no obvious use of violence was detected. According to Scott (1985), subordinates are prudent by tactic. The vulnerability of subordinates leaves them with no other choice but to use indirect means, as direct confrontation can be dangerous. Rituals of subordination suggest that the only realistic choice is that of 'public' submission and deference and 'private' resistance. These forms of resistance are safe expressions of aggression and act as substitutes for direct aggression. They are not simply a way of expressing anger behind the scenes but also aim at minimising appropriation and domination. 'If the personal aspect of submission is crucial to relatively impersonal forms of wage labor performed by workers who enjoy political rights and who are formally free to quit their job, then it ought to be far more relevant to those forms of domination that are more direct and personal' (Scott 1990: 112; emphasis in original). Being constantly under command creates a huge resentment. Greater frustration stems from the fact that subordinates believe that they are not treated as human beings on the job. Domination, unlike material appropriation, is directed towards the person; it does not only touch the body but also the soul. Systematic humiliation and denigration can affect one's personal sense of dignity. The natural impulse, led by rage and injustice, would be to respond violently. But within all forms of subordination and oppression, subordinates are denied the 'ordinary luxury of negative reciprocity; trading a slap for a slap, an insult for an insult' (Scott 1990: xii). Subordinates, therefore, faced with the urge for survival, choose to conform to what is expected of them and repress their rage in their own self-interest or the interest of their families.

Housemaids in Lebanon, for example, cannot 'answer back' and, on the rare occasions when they do, this so-called stepping out of place is immediately repressed. Quoting a Lebanese employer:

One time she [the Sri Lankan housemaid] came, H. [the employer's son] was here. She went from the morning on Sunday and only came back at eight pm. I was sitting watching TV. She came in and sat on the chair in front of the TV. The sink was full of

dirty dishes. I told her: '*Wli* (Hey you!), instead of sitting, go do
the dishes'. She said: 'I don't want to'. Me [raising her voice]:
'What, you don't want to do the dishes?' She said: 'Yes, I don't
want to'. I don't know what H told her in English and she responded. He slapped her on the face. I stood between them. She
started moaning: Euh, euh, euh... I went inside and shut the door.
I said to myself when F. [the employer's other son] comes, he'll
settle things. When F. came she went to his room and started telling him: 'He [H., the son who slapped her] pointed the knife at
me and I don't know what'. I told him: 'Listen, this one if she is
to stay here, she will create problems between you and your brother'. He told me: 'Why did he hit her?' I said: 'Hit her? Because
she answered me. He told her: "Go and do the dishes", he told
her one word, she answered with ten'.

This example portrays a case of open confrontation where open resistance (namely refusing to submit to an order) led to open violence and
retaliation. The attempts of housemaids to directly question the supremacy of the dominant group (employers) remain rare and are usually
violently repressed in Lebanon. Employers, it is my guess, do grasp the
importance of such open confrontations and are quick to repress them:
what is really at stake here is not just tasks undone but the legitimacy
of the domination itself that was put at risk. Housemaids, after their
failed rebellious attempts, often revert back to more subtle forms of resistance. The housemaid mentioned in the example above did just
that... until she went one day to buy groceries for her employer and
never came back (running away can be the ultimate act of resistance).
Resistance is not static, it shifts from covert to open confrontation.
Domination, also, can vary from indirect repressive means to more direct ones. This 'flexibility' is important to note. Both strategies of resistance and domination are in fact interactive ones, 'shaping each other
in a dynamic trajectory. The dynamic interplay between [them] imposed reciprocal constraints on each other, resulting in a net balance of
forces...' (Adnan 2007: 222). I have watched my grandmother and Candy, her housemaid, 'interplay' in that way many times. But in the end,
the major force is always the employer's. Candy could try, and at times,
did 'win', but it was my grandmother who had the upper hand in this
relationship.

When subordinates, therefore, fail at their open attempts, they usually 'adapt' and resort to another form of retaliation, 'secretive' by definition. A 'hidden transcript' (a critique of the powerful spoken in the absence of 'powerholders' and for a different audience) is created and
used as a counteractive tool since the 'public transcript' (the discourse
of subordinates spoken in front of the dominants) is denied to them.

'It is this systematic *frustration of reciprocal action* in relations of domination which... helps us understand much of the content of the hidden
transcript' (Scott 1990: 37; emphasis in original). The practice of domination, in itself, generates the hidden transcript. The more severe the
domination, the bigger the dissemblance between public and offstage
discourse and the richer the hidden transcript that gives the illusion of
reprisal and acting out one's violence. Scott analyses forms of subordination whereby public and hidden transcripts are greatly divergent.

Scott (1990) notes that it is difficult to assess the impact of power
on action when power is almost uninterrupted. He claims, for example,
that one can only begin to estimate the extent of a teacher's influence
on a classroom when that teacher leaves the room. A public transcript
might be misleading while the hidden one can be more in accordance
with reality. 'The motives behind acts of deference will remain opaque
to us until and unless the power that prompts it weakens or else we
can speak confidentially, backstage to those whose motives we wish to
understand. It is particularly in this latter realm of relative discursive
freedom, outside the earshot of powerholders, where the hidden transcript is to be sought' (Scott 1990: 25). This is what I experienced
when I tried interviewing Sri Lankan live-in housemaids at their employers' households. All I got was a polite discourse that I felt was not
the true expression of reality. I decided to carry on with my interviews
at the Sri Lankan embassy which provided a secure setting for 'hidden
transcripts', away from the source of threat and power, i.e. employers.[1]

In public life, subordinates put on an 'act' more often than powerful
groups need to. For instance, when a boss enters a room, the employee
changes his or her poise and activity. 'Power means not *having* to act
or, more accurately, the capacity to be more negligent and casual about
any single performance' (Scott 1990: 29; emphasis in original). Subordinates, in contrast, are more devoted to performances that encompass
conformity and obedience to orders even if degrading. I mentioned this
'performance' with regards to housemaids and the children they are
caring for in Chapter 3. Housemaids cannot show anger, fatigue, bore-
dom or hatred, but have to act according to rules and desires set by
their employer even if this means pretending to love the children they
are caring for. One cannot assume, however, that the subordinate's actions before his/her 'powerholder' are imperatively fake and based on
pretence, nor that his/her behaviour when surrounded by friends and
family is always sincere and authentic.

It is important, according to Scott, to avoid looking at subordinates
as mere puppets enduring domination passively, and to acknowledge
their agency as actors. 'What may look from above like the extraction
of a required performance can easily look from below like the artful
manipulation of deference and flattery to achieve its own ends' (Scott

1990: 34). Deference and flattery may be used by subordinates as strategies to avoid suspicion just as a criminal might walk calmly in front of the police. Dominant elites are sometimes aware of such 'performances' and try to decode these 'rituals of subordination'. Just as a Japanese landlord might wonder: 'Does anyone lie as much as a peasant?' (Scott 1990: 35), Lebanese employers often complain about the constant lying of their housemaids.

> They all lie. They lie because... *haram* (poor her)... if she breaks something she hides it. Because she knows you're going to shout at her. I like her a lot, I think when she's going to leave I'm going to cry because I love her a lot. We got attached to her. A person with you in the house... But they all lie, all, all, all... They lie. They lie a lot. They pretend they are miserable. And they bond together, you understand what I'm saying?

> Like you bring a dozen glasses, you are left with three. How? They break, true. But that much? One time, I doubted, I opened her bag and I discovered things. I told her. But they lie. You show them the stuff and they still lie. Sri Lankans lie.

The 'offstage' performance takes place in a different social space or privileged 'site' of resistance not monopolised by powerholders. Spatial parameters are defined, according to Scott (1990), as separate spaces for power and resistance. His spatial dichotomies resemble those of public/private social spaces charged with notions of control, exclusion and subordination. Social spaces of relative autonomy are essential to the subordinates. Sites for the 'hidden transcripts' are locations where people who share similar experiences meet and confide in each other. Moreover, these sites have to be as much as possible out of the reach of the dominant's control and repression. 'The least patrolled, most autonomous sites would presumably be the most likely locations for recovering the hidden transcript' (Scott 1990: 120). Slave quarters, woods or ravines where family and friends met safely outside the master's big house, could be examples of suitable unmonitored sites. Hidden transcripts can also be exchanged in the privacy of homes or in chapels, pubs, inns or taverns in Europe where the working class met after work in an ambiance of freedom and alcohol. In medieval Europe the market place was the most common location for hidden transcripts. In Lebanon, and since Sri Lankan housemaids are limited in their movements, sites are created such as balconies, meeting places while throwing out the rubbish or going to the shops, church on Sunday if allowed. For freelancers and live-ins who are allowed out on Sundays,

Dora (a district on the outskirts of the city) is the most important social site.

A location could also be transformed into a safe site if watched and secured from any kind of outside surveillance. 'The creation of a secure site for the hidden transcript might, however, not require any physical distance from the dominant so long as linguistic codes, dialect, and gestures – opaque to the masters and mistresses – were deployed' (Scott 1990: 121). In Lebanon, balconies are used as social sites for Sri Lankan housemaids who are not allowed outside their employers' households. Balconies become a location for social encounters whereby housemaids meet and talk to others working in the same building. This site, even though within the employer's property, is safe and suitable for hidden transcripts as the Lebanese do not understand the Sri Lankan language(s).

Speaking in private cannot be controlled, unlike printed words (whereby typewriters, letters, can be confiscated, etc.). Talking is sometimes the only way of expression left to Sri Lankans and, even then, this activity is controlled. Who do they talk to? Friends, family, strangers on the streets. Where? Over the phone or from one balcony to another. For how long and what are they saying? Letters sent to or by them can also be confiscated. Since Lebanese employers cannot read Sinhalese, they sometimes use the services of a 'translator' (another housemaid or even the Sri Lankan embassy staff) trying to decipher in this way the hidden transcript.

Gatherings of subordinates are often unwelcome by the dominant group. 'The political symbolism of most forms of personal domination carries with it the implicit assumption that subordinates gather only when they are authorized to do so from above. Any *unauthorized* gathering... has therefore been seen as potentially threatening' (Scott 1990: 61; emphasis in original). All structures of leadership – feudalism, slavery, serfdom – are based on a dyadic relationship, the slave serves his master for instance while the latter feeds him, etc. This form of hierarchy assumes, contrary to reality, that 'there are no horizontal links among subordinates and that, therefore, if they are to be assembled at all it must be by the lord, patron or master, *who represents the only link joining them*' (Scott 1990: 62; emphasis in original). Lebanese employers, in general, do not allow their housemaids to go out on their own. The assumption is that meetings like these lead to insubordination. In the words of one Lebanese employer:

> It is forbidden that they go out anyway. But I don't lock the door. But in the agency, it is not allowed. Where do you want her to go? She comes with me, she goes out with me. Not with their friends or going out themselves... By the end, yes, I do let them. Finally

you cannot own them. You have to limit. Because, in their outings they start: 'Ah, you, how much do you earn?' 'Now I want to work on my own'. 'Now I want to go'. 'Now I want to come'... And everyone who goes and comes, be sure that something goes with her. She takes things and brings back diseases. This is not good for me.

To summarise, a subordinate is neither entirely submissive nor rebellious. He or she resorts to various strategies of resistance that are 'hidden' yet powerful. Those forms of retaliation are in general misread and need to be 'decoded' to be fully understood. They are meant to be opaque to the dominant one in order to outlast. These 'everyday forms of resistance' are expressed through 'hidden transcripts' within secure social sites. Forms of resistance of Sri Lankan housemaids in Lebanese households are numerous and complex. They can stretch from small acts such as being late, misunderstanding an order or lying, to more serious ones like stealing and ultimately 'running away'. The next section explores these strategies in more detail.

Resistance patterns used by Sri Lankan housemaids in Lebanon

Before I highlight the ways in which Sri Lankan housemaids resist their employers, it is important to note that their lack of reaction to violence (whether physical or symbolic) can be misleading and does explain, in part, why employers view Sri Lankan housemaids as passive and easy to control. Housemaids follow orders, eat the food handed to them, get up when they are told, etc. When criticised, shouted at or even hit, they usually do nothing to stop the violence... except cry. In the words of two housemaids and three Lebanese employers:

Agency Madame always hit me. With her hands. I cry. If somebody hits me in Sri Lanka, I kill him. But if my husband hit me I never hit him. Outside the family, yes. But here not my country. Nobody here to help.

Madame no like my work, always tell me: 'No good'; I cry.

When I shout at her... *haram* (poor her), this one is very good, she doesn't answer back. But I am always right [not jokingly], I do not just shout to shout.

I liked her a lot [her previous housemaid]. Yes, but sometimes she used to make me really angry. You know even your own mother if she's living with you 24 hours a day, as much as you love her, you're going to somehow yell at her or shout, I don't know. It's normal. What's not normal is that she thinks that she doesn't have the right to answer. This makes you uncomfortable with the fact of yelling at her. After you have regrets and... You know, and they cry... they cry, because they don't dare react.

The other day I yelled at her. Her reaction? [laughing] She couldn't say anything. She wasn't going to yell at me. When I get angry I start you know... I don't stop. No, but she understood very well what I was saying. And when I get angry she looks at me like this... no reaction at all. Like this: big eyes and that's it, no expression. She used to do a sort of 'blockage'. Like: 'I'm not going to react, I'm not going to say anything'. Probably she was scared. Because she was young [laughing]. Maybe she was scared. I used to talk and she used to look at me like this... As if I was talking to myself. You feel like you're talking to no one.

Not reacting, however, does not mean not 'resisting'. Generally, housemaids avoid open confrontations; they might not answer back but they do resist with their own means and in their own time. Housemaids, for example, feign ignorance, pretending at times they did not understand their employers' instructions. Two Lebanese employers explain:

But sometimes she [the housemaid] was, maybe because of her age [21] or something, but sometimes I was very angry with her. She was very intelligent and sometimes I think she used to do things on purpose, acting like she didn't understand or something like that. This was the bad part of our relationship. But otherwise, she was very clean, very nice... I remember once I was really very angry at her because I asked her not to give, I don't know, something to my oldest daughter and I was in the bedroom and she was with her on the balcony and, then I don't know, after ten minutes. Fifteen minutes. I went and I saw her giving her this thing and I got very angry but I don't remember what it was. But I remember that, what I thought at this moment was that she understood what I said but she didn't want to listen. Just to keep her [the daughter] quiet she gave her this thing and this is what made me very angry. I knew that she understood what I said.

The agent man is tough with them, he is obliged to be with them for one reason: they teach them there to go to the house and say 'I don't know how to do things'. Even though they know. So that not a lot is asked from them. They try to take advantage in the beginning like this. That's why he is hard on them.

Housemaids can also choose to work at a slow pace, as many Lebanese employers complain they do:

> Two months ago I had an argument with her. It was ten, she was awake since eight and had done nothing yet. I told her: 'Please... if you don't like the work here, you don't like to stay here, leave'. She started telling me in the kitchen: 'No Madame, please, I like this house...'. I was going to send her to the agency. She is very slow. She drives me crazy, the bathroom takes three hours. And I am very quick. My house needs three hours and it's done. She works the whole day and finishes only two rooms. She used to say: 'X [employer's two-year-old son] does not let me work'. We sent him to day-care. Still the same. Still as slow.

> When there is school, we need to be up by six-fifteen. But when there is no school, sometimes seven, seven-thirty. Even if my husband wakes up earlier, she is not up to see if he needs something. Even though there are many who do that, I see them who start cleaning the house at six. Before nine, she doesn't start. Even though I tell her, 'Start early, finish earlier and sleep in the afternoon'. But because she is very slow, she doesn't do this. She is supposed to finish earlier. No, she doesn't finish. She stays the whole day. From day to night... She has always excuses. Even if they are not true excuses.

However, how can one know for certain that 'working slowly' is yet another act of resistance used by housemaids to counter-effect the power employers have over them? I do not believe one can; working at a slow pace can simply mean... working at a slow pace. It is possible that some housemaids are used to doing things slowly or that they are just tired from working around the clock. One Lebanese employer explained to me the pros and cons of hiring a Sri Lankan housemaid instead of a Lebanese one: 'Sri Lankans are more submissive than the Lebanese. The Lebanese are more healthy. These girls [Sri Lankans] come more tired. At 40 they are old'. So 'these girls' can simply be tired, hence performing household tasks slowly. Where 'working slowly' can indeed be described as an act of resistance is when housemaids change their working pace, especially at the very end of their contracts, to ensure that they are sent home and not 'retained' in Lebanon. One Lebanese employer (among many others) complained to me about that:

She is leaving in two months. I cannot stand her anymore. They start good but then they do not work as hard as before. She is not working anymore. My husband suggested that I pay her only half her salary since she is working half the load.

Pretending to be sick (Agency director: 'Sometimes, they [housemaids] pretend they are sick because they want to return') or claiming that a family member in Sri Lanka is seriously ill or even dead in order to be able to leave the country are also common acts of resistance. At times, housemaids use letters received from Sri Lanka as a possible exit excuse. As one Lebanese sponsor (male employer) related to me:

After two years, Komari wanted to go back to Sri Lanka, claiming that her contract was over, that she would go for just a few weeks and come back. I told her the contract was for three years and refused to let her go. Komari told us after a while that her husband died. Then, a week later, she said she got news from Sri Lanka that her son fell on his way to school and he's injured his head. My wife believed her and felt sorry for her. I knew she was lying all along. I asked a Sri Lankan housemaid working for my relative to read one of the letters Komari received from Sri Lanka. It turned out it was a letter from her husband telling her that they were all fine, that the children were OK, that he was not seeing other women and asking her not to go with other men in Lebanon. When confronted with her lies, Komari claimed that this is what they had told her, probably to get her to go back. She said she's ready to go and come back to Lebanon. My wife refused saying: 'If you go you don't come back'. We were very disappointed with her lies. We always treated her right, never shouted at her. My wife (using here an ironic tone) used to tell her in the evening: 'Komari, if you don't like the food, there is steak and *kafta* [Lebanese type of meat] in the freezer, you can fry some for yourself...' We sent her away a few days after we confronted her with her lies. We could no longer trust her and felt hurt. I made her pay for her ticket back since her contract was not due for another year.

Moreover, housemaids who have finished their contract and do not wish to renew it often tell their employers they will go to Sri Lanka for a visit then come back, while planning all along not to return. In the words of a Lebanese employer and an agency director:

My girl [housemaid] went home after the end of her contract and said she wanted to come back. She didn't, she phoned me saying:

'My mom is too sick'. I didn't believe her, she just didn't want to come back.

Filipinas and Ethiopians are clear. They say if they want to go back or not. Sri Lankans are liars. You never know with them. They have no God. The Ethiopian embassy is better. They meet us half-way. They are not with us nor against us. The Sri Lankan embassy here is biased.

The strategies of resistance described above would not have taken place if housemaids felt they could return home whenever they wanted (whether in the midst or end of their contracts). As discussed in Chapter 5, employers have been known to 'hold on' to their housemaids, even after the latter's full completion of the three-year contract, to avoid having to pay for and 'train' another one. Housemaids who feel entrapped come up with excuses (such as sickness or death) to be able to leave.

As also noted in Chapter 5, Lebanese employers do control their housemaids' outings and contacts with the outside world. Housemaids, however, find ways to get around these bans by finding pretexts to go out. Candy, for example, my grandmother's housemaid, used to tell her: 'Let me go, Mama, light a candle for Farid' (my dead uncle)' My grandmother could not refuse. Candy would go to church and disappear for a while (the church is just around the corner). Upon her return, my grandmother would greet her angrily: 'Wli (Hey you!), where have you been?' Candy: 'I couldn't find candles so I had to go from shop to shop'. My grandmother often complained to me about her: 'She is the best except for one thing: she goes out of the house pretending to go for errands and is late coming back. Sometimes she waits for me to sleep during the day and leaves. When I get out of bed I find her gone. When she comes back she tells me: "Mama, I went to buy bread or something for the house". She is a liar. She wants to talk to her friends on the street...'

I witnessed a scene once when I was at my grandmother's. Candy was out supposedly to buy something for the house. She was very late coming back (over two hours) and when she did, my grandmother, as predicted, started shouting at her. But Candy had prepared herself, she had a bouquet of flowers in her hand and showed them to my grandmother: 'Here, Mama, this is for adra (Virgin Mary), the flowers there are not good anymore, I went from shop to shop to find you nice ones'. Candy knew that my grandmother liked having fresh flowers in front of her Virgin Mary's icon. The incident that day ended quickly: the flowers were beautiful and my grandmother, happy.

Pretexts to go out or simply talk to others can be various. Apart from running errands (that might include candles and flowers), or going to church, housemaids find ways to make friends while throwing out the rubbish. In the words of one Lebanese employer:

> I was at my brother's place, and she [the housemaid] told me I'm going down to throw out the rubbish with my brother's maid. It was a coincidence that my niece went out. And she saw her speaking with somebody. When she came back I told her [the housemaid], 'Shanty, to whom were you speaking?' She said: 'Nobody, a girlfriend of mine'. 'Shanty, X [the niece] saw you speaking with a man. Why are you lying?'

Housemaids can even make friends without having to leave the employers' households: 'balcony talk' or talking from the balcony to other housemaids in the same or opposite building (and despite the fact that it is forbidden by employers) is very common in Lebanon, I see it almost everywhere I go. 'Fouté la jouah' (come inside), how many times have I heard this sentence? One employer told me about her housemaid as the latter stood on the balcony to talk to Sri Lankans on the street: 'She can smell them from far... Hey [calling her housemaid], come inside'. One agency director I talked to said: 'Every building has two or three Sri Lankans; they speak from the balconies. Many girls jump'. Many, in fact, who 'run away', can only do so from the balcony, as doors are often locked on them. They use sheets or ropes to go down, some fall and are injured, some sadly die. When I raised this subject with a Lebanese employer, she simply stated: 'Sri Lankans like to kill themselves'.

Many Lebanese employers will not even let their housemaids go to the nearby grocery shops or even put out the rubbish. They will, however, allow their housemaids to go to church on Sundays as the only 'acceptable' outing for them. Some housemaids use this hour per week to socialise; others even take this opportunity to 'run away'. As one sponsor (male employer) I met at the Sri Lankan embassy told me:

> I live with my mother. One day, two years ago, my mom told me: 'She [housemaid] went to church in the morning and didn't come back'. We checked the hospitals, we were worried about her. After two years some lawyer called me. She was working in a factory in Zalka. I said: 'You can keep her'.

Other resistance modes used by Sri Lankan housemaids working in Lebanon – such as being indispensable, pleasing the employer, emotional attachment – can be viewed (as discussed in Chapter 5) as private attempts to change the rules of the game. Sri Lankan housemaids do at times take advantage of the 'attachment' (whether emotional or practical) which employers have towards them.

The dependency which some employers have on their housemaids can empower the latter. My grandmother, who lives alone with Candy and is, therefore, totally dependent on her, could not really upset her. She once told me about a fight she had with her. Grandmother had asked her to prepare a dessert. Instead of spreading the preparation into a pan as my grandmother usually does, Candy divided the pastry into small pieces in order to make cookies. Grandmother did not like it and asked her to start again, spreading the small pieces of pastry into the pan. Candy got angry, grandmother said, and told her: 'What's this, always work, work!' Grandmother replied: 'What, you're talking to me like this?' Candy: 'If you don't want me, just say so and I'll go'. Grandmother told me: 'I thought of telling her to leave but what will I do without her? So I remained silent and went to my room'. An interesting role reversal in the strategy of silence!

Housemaids, at times, do praise their employers to get them perhaps to bend the rules a little. One example is given by a Lebanese employer I interviewed:

> She [the housemaid] tells me: 'Madame, I have never seen a mother like you'. She was in Singapore, worked for a family with three daughters; she used to take them to school, to the paediatrician. The mother worked a lot so she used to sleep on their side, wake up at night, even for the newborn. The mother was tired and wanted to sleep when she got home. She tells me: 'Madame, you are not like this, poor you, go out with Mister'. Sometimes I don't go out for two or three months, she goes crazy for me. She tells me: 'Madame, how do you wake up for X [the employer's one-year-old girl]?' I don't sleep well so I become touchy, because of lack of sleep. I tell her: 'You sleep more than I do'.

Abiding by the rules, doing what is expected of them (and maybe more) are also ways to attain employers' acceptance and at times favours. As one Lebanese employer relates:

> I went to the airport. Her hair was white, she had no teeth, all her teeth here (in front) were gone. She wasn't old then, she was, I think 39. So I saw this image in front of me I started crying, I told him [the employer's husband] 'What is this one going to do with me, skinny as a thread, no teeth, nothing...' She couldn't help me and I used to work then. You see? So I brought her home and I started teaching her. I found that she understood. If she has some-

thing she has a brain. She started learning. Two months later I fell and broke my leg. There was nobody like her. Taking the sheets from below me, giving me a bath every day. Took care of the baby, cleaning him, bathing him... She did as I told her to, followed my instructions. Impeccable! So I was very pleased with her and she got used to the children, she became attached to us, loved us. And it worked from here (*mishyit*).

Housemaids can take advantage, at times, of the emotional attachment employers (and especially employers' children) have towards them. I have seen many housemaids doubling their efforts to please their employers' children, knowing that employers are bound to become more lenient. Of course, no one doubts that genuine feelings are also involved here, but the way these feelings are used are aimed at gaining power *against* employers. A housemaid who has an 'ally' within the household (in the example below, the employer's son whom she, in a way, raised) can have more leverage within the household, as this Lebanese employer revealed to me:

This one [the housemaid], nobody can shout at her here. For example yesterday when she made her scene, my son's reaction was: 'Leave her alone Mom'. She knows that she is loved. You see? She was great with the kids, took good care of them. Because I used to work. She didn't wake me up, didn't bother me, she fed him, cleaned him, changed his clothes... She kept him very clean. Then she put him back to sleep. I felt that the baby loved her, this meant that she was not bothering him, not hitting him, not pinching him... She has a lot of patience. You see, if she is dusting she needs to wear glasses now. She doesn't see. Not everyone keeps one like her but because she adores the kids. My son in the morning tells her: 'Bye *habibi* (my love)'.

Other less 'correct' strategies of resistance (away from emotional involvement) involve lying, stealing and 'running away'. Most Lebanese seem to agree that Sri Lankans are generally 'liars'. As one Lebanese staff member at the Sri Lankan embassy ascertained during the interview:

They lie. I have never seen so many liars. When I started working here one and a half years ago, I used to go to the General Security detention centre and cry. I thought the girls were crying and I felt sorry for them. Then after a while, I saw they were liars.

And one Lebanese employer:

One day I remember, I was at the swimming pool, I was calling her [on the telephone] to tell her to prepare something because my brother was here, and I was calling and calling, it was busy, busy, busy, busy. I was five or ten minutes away by car from my house. I left the swimming pool, I popped into the supermarket, calling her, the phone is busy. I arrive here, I reach here, I stand outside the door, I call her, the telephone is busy. I ring the bell. You know what she does? She holds the bucket with water and she pretends she's cleaning the carpet. I told her: 'You were on the telephone'. Her: 'No'. I told her: 'Listen, don't lie to me, you were on the telephone for almost two hours'.

Another negative stereotype Lebanese employers have of Sri Lankan housemaids is that they steal. Housemaids have been known to steal, especially when their contract is over and they are about to leave the country. I know of many employers who discovered many things missing from their house soon after the housemaid's departure. Many Lebanese 'search' their housemaids before taking them to the airport. Lebanese employers see in this a pattern of behaviour and become suspicious of every housemaid they employ, even the 'good' ones. As one Lebanese employer confessed:

My maid is very good. She doesn't steal. I 'tried' her many times. We would leave money around to test her, in the beginning. But after all ... we never know. Many tell me they steal just before they leave.

I cannot but introduce a nuance here and wonder if stealing is necessarily an act of resistance? I know of one housemaid, for example, who was not abused, controlled nor 'managed' in any way. She had the key to her employers' household, she worked as she saw fit, she went out as she pleased, had even weekends off at times... and yet, she stole many valuable items before she left (needless to say she was not searched prior to her departure). Was she 'resisting' by doing that and what was she resisting? It is important to note that certain housemaids' actions are not necessarily resistance acts (or reactions) aimed *against* employers. They *can* also be mere opportunist manoeuvres.

Finally, the ultimate and more 'obvious' act of resistance is 'running away'. Many housemaids simply cannot take the abuse any more and leave their employers' households. As this 'runaway' I interviewed at the embassy said:

Today run away. Yesterday in the morning, I start to eat some bread and *labné* [Lebanese yogurt]. This time Madame came told me 'Clean underwear of children'. I said: 'When I finish eat, I will do it'. Madame slap me, took the bread and threw it in garbage. Because of that I plan to leave. Five o'clock in the morning, by bus to here. I pay one dollar. Only have one dollar left with me. Now I wait until clear problem from here [embassy]. If after that they allow, I want to stay in Lebanon to work for another family.

However (I open another parenthesis here), not every housemaid who 'runs away' does so because of abuse; some simply want to work 'outside' and take advantage of a more independent way of life (and work). Sri Lankans are indeed the largest number of migrant housemaids in Lebanon; they have also been there the longest. They have built networks over the years and 'learned the ropes'. This might explain why they run away more than others (and are detained in prisons and the detention centre more than other nationalities).[2] One freelancer told me:

There are too many Sri Lankans outside, runaways. Women go out and live with men, Hindus, et cetera. It's not good. Agencies are not bringing Sri Lankans anymore because they run away a lot. There are too many Sri Lankans outside. Those who are *contrat* go out on the balcony, Sri Lankans passing by tell them: 'Why do you stay in and work for just $100? You can make much more outside'. So they run away. But they don't know that there are a lot of problems outside. They leave without their passport and are then illegal. I know a girl who left like this, because somebody on the street told her she could gain more money outside. The Sri Lankan newspaper wrote an article on Sri Lankan women who leave their country to work outside, leave husband and children and stay sometimes ten or more years without seeing them. This is not good for the families.

Sister Angela was also worried about broken families:

Husbands are also the problem. Very often they get into alcoholism. Their families get broken. They [husbands] find somebody [another woman] who's there [in Sri Lanka]. Here sometimes women find somebody [another man] who's here [in Lebanon]. And more than in other countries I believe, in other Middle East countries. It is easy in Lebanon. They have some sort of freedom to be out. There are many who are not under a strict contract. They have their legal papers but they're [freelancers] living outside. So that leads to a lot of problems. Normally, they're supposed to be living with their employers [live-ins], which is what the government wants them to do. But that's only in theory. Most of them [freelancers] are out. And then, when they live in rooms, families get broken down because maybe a woman can't live alone in her room. So, there's another man also who also can't live alone. So, they join up here. And sometimes, they [housemaids] don't return...

Some also run away because they no longer want to work and wish to go home. The Sri Lankan ambassador has developed a strategy to 'test' runaways who seek the embassy's help: he asks them if they want to go to Sri Lanka or stay in Lebanon and work for another employer. If they say they want to go home, he assumes that the stories they are telling him about abusive employers are not truthful and that they are simply homesick. A Lebanese embassy staff member I interviewed also believes that not all runaways are abused: 'They at times come with a story: "Madame hit me, no food, Mister touch me...", just to be able to go home'. I witnessed one case of a runaway at the embassy where there seemed to be no abuse directed towards the housemaid. In the meeting were the ambassador, the Lebanese employer and her son, the housemaid and myself. The housemaid had been working for the employer for the past three months. She tried to run away once but failed. On her second attempt, she succeeded and took refuge at the embassy.

> Lebanese employer: 'Where do you find a Madame paying for two Sri Lankans? I gave her gifts of gold'.

The housemaid tells the ambassador she wants to go back to Sri Lanka.

> Lebanese employer: 'Come Komari. Come *mama* [mom – Lebanese mothers are called mama by their children but they also call their children mama], no why not? *Mama* paid money... They [meaning Sri Lankans] are liars'.

> Ambassador: 'You must not think these girls are educated like that'.

The Lebanese employer kept on trying to convince the housemaid to go back with her:

> Who took care of your foot when you got hurt? Didn't I kneel down every day to change your bandage?' Explaining to the ambassador: 'When I went to the agency to pick one, she was there sitting, her leg was hurt. I felt sorry for her, so I decided to take her

back with me even though I knew she wouldn't be able to work right away. I bought her medicine, took her to the doctor, took care of her. She has her own room, her own bathroom, she can cook and eat whatever she wants'.

The housemaid claims that there is too much work.

> Lebanese employer: 'Too much work? But I have two Sri Lankans. The other has been with me for years. She does all the work practically. It's not true... It's not fair. I didn't do anything wrong. I treated her well, took her to my own doctors, including my gynaecologist. Why should I lose all the money I paid on her? I pay her on time, I give her gifts, I treat her like my own daughter'.

The housemaid was standing in front of the ambassador's desk, hardly ever looking at her employer. The employer and son were sitting on chairs facing the ambassador (beside me). At one point, the employer asks the housemaid to come closer and takes her by her hands and asks her gently to tell her why she ran away. What problem did she have? The housemaid avoids answering and goes back to her previous spot. The employer pleads with the ambassador to at least let her take her back for six months (so her cost is not all lost). The ambassador refuses and asks the employer to come the next day with the housemaid's passport and belongings. There was no sign of abuse there (at least in my view); the housemaid herself never accused her employers of mistreating her. She, perhaps, just wanted to go back to Sri Lanka.

Concluding remarks

We have seen above how Sri Lankan housemaids in Lebanon use non-confrontational means or 'everyday forms of resistance' to resist their Lebanese employers' domination. However, the effects of such indirect actions remain to be assessed. Despite some direct benefits (being able to bend the rules at times, talking to other housemaids... or even going back to Sri Lanka earlier than planned), I believe housemaids have in the end more to lose than gain by using these modes of resistance. In a way, resistance 'backfires'.

Acts of resistance, especially lying, stealing and running away, are often misinterpreted by Lebanese employers. Employers do not view these acts as mere reactions consequent to their own violence (or symbolic violence); instead, they perceive them as reflective of the 'innate' characteristics of Sri Lankans. The more Sri Lankan housemaids resist with those means, the more 'alibis' they give employers to tighten even more their control.

Negative stereotyping is reinforced and a vicious circle created. Housemaids lie, steal, run away, in part, because they are controlled; employers reinforce their control, in part, because of these so-called Sri Lankan patterns. I am in no way asserting that resistance acts are the reasons behind the employers' controlling behaviours. I am only stating that the way these acts are perceived by employers leads more often than not to more control. Resistance can 'backfire' and lead to the exact opposite of what was initially targeted by housemaids.

As shown throughout this book, dominants (or superordinates) and subordinates have different goals: the dominants want to maintain their power and control while subordinates try to limit the appropriation and attain certain liberties. Both symbolic violence and resistance take complex and contingent routes to avoid direct confrontation (even if, at times, reverting to them). This interplay generates a stubborn group dynamic that seems to function and evolve over time. A type of 'equilibrium' is attained where the two protagonists (dominant and subordinate), each with the weapons available to them and with a measured strength, pull the rope in the direction that is best suited to their own self-interests; careful, however, not to break it.

Can this dynamic be stopped, and how? The next and final chapter attempts to answer this question by considering particular 'solutions' to this very complex and controversial problem. Though, I must say it upfront, my outlook is not very optimistic.

7   Conclusion

This research has attempted to invite its readers behind closed doors, inside Lebanese households. It has revealed how women – Madames and housemaids – still have a long way to go before relieving themselves of traditional expectations and responsibilities. It has explained how racism, despite all indicators, is not at the core of the abusive treatment of housemaids. It has given a detailed '*aperçu*' of the living and working conditions of Sri Lankan housemaids in Lebanon, and has shown how 'symbolic violence' is used by Lebanese employers to control their Sri Lankan housemaids. It also unveiled the way housemaids resisted this violence with the only means available to them and the limited (and at times negative) consequences.

Possible solutions?

Following this detailed analysis of the complex dynamics involved, what next? People often ask me what could be done to improve the living and working conditions of Sri Lankan housemaids in Lebanon. What 'solutions' to advocate? Amend the existing regulations? Change the attitudes of host governments and employers? Start with the sending countries by warning women about their rights or the absence of rights, or perhaps put more stress on development projects within sending countries by creating job opportunities for these women back home? I have no simple, one-shot answers. I will, in this concluding chapter, give a brief overview of various possible 'solutions' relating to the Lebanese side, although I am very sceptical about their implementation and outcome. But my main concern in this book has been to give a clear picture, as close to reality as possible, of a highly controversial and 'private' subject. My contribution might, I hope, guide others – human rights activists, NGO or international organisation representatives, and scholars – in their active commitment to helping migrant women in different parts of the world.

Ending sponsorship

Many suggestions have been made about finding a solution to the problems encountered by housemaids working in foreign countries. Most scholars agree that the immigration status (based on sponsorship) of migrant women working as housemaids and the consequent 'legal power' held by employers over housemaids (discussed in Chapter 4) are a fertile ground for abuse and exploitation. Therefore, and as Anderson (2000: 107) notes, '[b]y ending dependence on employers it [is] felt that a major source of abuse would be eliminated'. Housemaids have to have the right (and free choice) to change employers, end their contract or simply return home. If housemaids can cross this at-present-closed barrier whenever they want, their position in the host countries and inside households might very well be strengthened. Nevertheless, it is important to note – stressing again the ambiguity of the issues involved within this particular type of occupation – that the sponsorship system is also perceived as a problem by employers who view it as an added responsibility. A Sri Lankan embassy staff member explained to me why most employers hold on to the housemaids' passports and permits:

> They [employers] will never give the papers. They will never give the papers. Because when I am the sponsor of the girl, she should be always under my eye. If she's on the road, working somewhere, doing anything. If she had any accident, who will be responsible? I will be responsible. If she's dead, I'll have to pay. If she has an accident I'll have to pay. Nobody will say, 'Well no problem, she was outside the house, she will pay'. No. If I am the sponsor, I'll be responsible for her until she goes inside the plane and goes back to her country. Anything which happens during this time to the girl will be my responsibility whatever is the problem.

However, no matter how 'problematic' sponsorship is to employers, it is undeniable that its function is primarily disadvantageous to housemaids. Ending the sponsorship system, therefore, might rule out one determining aspect of abuse (and perhaps relieve employers from what they consider to be a burden). Does this mean that control and exploitation will stop? I believe not. As Anderson (2000: 107) observes, 'There continue to be problems around the nature of the transaction when domestic work is paid for, and within the employer/worker relationship...' The sponsorship system is only part of the problem. It did not apply, for instance, to Lebanese Shiites who worked as housemaids in the past in Lebanon. These women were citizens just like their employers and yet they were treated with the same injustice. The real problem lies behind closed doors, between the Madame and her house-maid. Whatever changes take place 'outside', through new rules or laws to improve the status of housemaids in a foreign country, the real issues at stake will not be fundamentally addressed.

Standardising contracts

Another possible area of intervention could be the setting up of a detailed and standardised contract that covers housemaids' basic rights (hours of work, weekly leave, suitable place to sleep, payment of wages on time, etc.). I am not confident, however, about the efficiency of such a measure. Contracts already exist in Lebanon, between (some) agencies and their clients (Lebanese employers), and between the Sri Lankan embassy and the Lebanese employers. These contracts stipulate the multiple responsibilities of employers towards their housemaids. But are they applied in reality? And how does one make sure they are? The Special Rapporteur, after her mission to Lebanon, suggested that Lebanese officials working for the Ministry of Labour inspect on a regular basis households where foreign housemaids are employed (Huda 2005). I very much doubt her recommendation will be applied at any point in time in Lebanon. New regulations can be passed, contracts drawn and signed, but their application, I am afraid, is very unlikely. One relevant example comes from Britain. In 1994, new regulations were established by the UK government, including the drawing up of a contract with terms and conditions of employment that housemaids helped to set up. One condition stipulated that employers provide a separate bedroom for the housemaid. This, however, was never put into practice: 112 out of the 181 housemaids interviewed by Kalayaan in 1996-1997 still did not have their own bedroom. As the civil litigation lawyer Jean Gould notes (in Anderson 2000: 103):

> I've seen many contracts in my office, some of them are brilliant, some say the women will be entitled to one day off a week, receive a reasonable wage, they'll be entitled to medical care and so on. But it doesn't happen, none of these things happen, they are not paid, they are not given time off, they work enormously long hours. Contracts are simply not, in this situation, worth the paper they're written on.

Moreover, if contracts are not enforced, would migrants in a foreign country denounce their employers to the police? And if they do, will they be heard?

In Lebanon, complaint offices for migrants were established by the General Security department and the Ministry of Labour. A circular

was distributed to agencies advising them to report back to General Security any housemaids' complaints of abuse. The Ministry of Justice issued a brochure (in English and Arabic) to be distributed to incoming
migrants informing them about their rights and providing them with
NGO contact numbers. However, and while acknowledging efforts
made by the Lebanese government to move ahead on human rights' issues relating to housemaids, the Special Rapporteur (Huda 2005)
noted that complaints were unlikely to be followed through. Assuming
housemaids ventured forth by denouncing their employers' miscon-
duct, officials would most likely side with the employer rather than the
housemaid.

Professionalisation of domestic work: 'public' within the private?

Domination is maintained in a family setting where work is not defined as such but rather as a 'service', a position of care and subservience. This domination could be lessened, according to Hondagneu-
Sotelo (2001: xix), by 'upgrading the occupation, a change ushered in
by systemic regulation and by public recognition that this seemingly
private activity is a job'. Could the 'professionalisation' of domestic
work be the answer leading towards the improvement of the status of
housemaids? By considering the housemaid as a professional who is
selling her labour and not her person, employers could end up treating
their housemaids better and start implementing specific employment
contracts (drawn up either by recruitment agencies or by foreign embassies). However, 'this is extremely difficult within the private domain
as it is currently imagined (Anderson 2000: 167). Delimiting tasks as
well as hours (doing 'everything' and being on call 'all the time' is how
housemaids describe their 'jobs') is problematic in the private sphere.
Where does work stop and life start (or life stop and work start) when
the housemaid is working for *and* living with her employers? Can the
public and private divide apply inside households? Employers control
the public space of their housemaids (by not allowing them out, supervising their phone calls, etc.) but also their private space (by deciding
when they should sleep, eat, etc.). Paradoxically, housemaids find privacy outside, in the public sphere (limited most of the time to balconies,
on the way to the shop or the rubbish bin...). Perhaps the most important difference between freelancers and live-ins is that the former sell
their service and not their personhood. The private/public boundaries
are clearly set for the freelancer: she goes to 'work' for a few hours then
leaves her workplace to resume her private life. As mentioned in Chapter 5, freelancers do not complain about abuse and exploitation. Their
problems are of a different nature (mainly pertaining to legal and spon-

sorship matters); they have no difficulty resuming their private lives once their 'public' (or employment) one is done.

Problems relating to lack of privacy are also raised by employers – and not just by live-in housemaids – which again confirms the complex dynamics and constant double-sidedness of the various themes discussed throughout this research. Many employers complained about their housemaids' constant presence: 'It is a presence at your place, and a presence which is not always agreeable because she has her moods; OK so do we but her, her moods are bizarre'. Another issue raised by employers is that of 'interference':

> They interfere in everything. The worst is that she sees the prices of everything I buy, clothes I buy. When I was pregnant, I did not tell people the first two months because a miscarriage is always possible. When I told her I was two months pregnant, she said: 'I know, Madame'. I asked how? She said: 'I saw the Clear Blue test'. I had thrown the test in the garbage bin. She sees everything, knows everything.

The fact that 'she knows everything' worries employers. At the beginning of my research, when I was still figuring out how and where to interview housemaids, I asked my sister to check whether her friend would agree for me to talk to her housemaid. The friend accepted at first then quickly changed her mind: 'No, it's not a good idea, she knows a lot'.

Some employers, to regain some sort of 'privacy' as they claim, choose to let go of the live-in maid and employ a freelancer: 'If she comes, cleans a few hours a day then leaves, I have no problem. It is a better formula... God, Nayla, having her [live-in] around all the time...' Most employers, however, do adapt to the constant presence of housemaids within their households: 'She is very discrete. I can spend more time with my husband. Sexually at first, it was a little difficult, what if she hears us? But now I got used to her'. It is my belief that, to be able to forget about the lack of privacy and constant presence of housemaids, employers render them 'invisible'; in other words, they 'dehumanise' them to be able to ignore them. The 'invisibility' of housemaids in the eyes of their employers does not just stem from the need to stress the inferior status of housemaids in comparison with the superior status of Madames. Employers, in order to nullify the physical closeness of housemaids, simply stop 'seeing' them after a while: 'when she moves in the house you don't see her anymore. And they [housemaids] are light [on their feet – discrete]'.

Issues of privacy are problematic for both employers and housemaids. They can be easier to manage for employers, however, as they have the power to 'ignore' their housemaids. But can housemaids manage their time, work and life with their employers? A 'public' divide within the private domain is extremely difficult to attain, if not impossible.

Abolishing agency fees or employers' 'investments'

Employers often justify the tight control they exercise over their housemaids by the 'investment' they made to get them into the country for a two-and-a-half- to three-year contract, i.e. the agency fees that average between $1,000 and $1,500. Employers feel housemaids are indebted to them since they paid a large amount of money to be able to employ them. I once attended a meeting between the Sri Lankan ambassador and a sponsor who came to 'reclaim' his housemaid who had run away:

> Ambassador: She's saying she was beaten by Madame.
>
> Sponsor: She is a liar. Nobody beats her.
>
> Ambassador: She says she is not paid.
>
> Sponsor: I paid her six months already [the housemaid has been working there for the past eight months]. And I paid $1,000 for her to come here. She says: 'I want to go to Sri Lanka'. I say: 'I paid $1,000'.

Even if this investment is overturned, the problem is not solved. There is another form of investment or 'human cost' that remains to be dealt with according to employers who claim that they put energy, time and effort into 'training' their housemaid: 'I have trained her you see, I don't want to waste my time teaching another one'. Moreover, in the past, Arab maids were treated the same despite the fact that agency fees then were very small (the same goes for Lebanese maids where no 'investment' whatsoever was involved).

Regulating agencies

Agencies are at times pointed out as the real 'traffickers' of human beings. As my data showed, they are also the principal source of physical abuse perpetuated upon housemaids. As one Lebanese staff member at the Sri Lankan embassy told me:

I think when you allow yourself to be an agent and when you allow yourself to play with life and sell human beings, you cannot
be humanitarian, impossible... Me, I can't give credit to any agent.
This is my experience. Even when you say that an agent is doing
his work perfectly law-wise, he cannot do it perfectly on a humanitarian level. It's impossible. When a girl makes a problem, you
cannot talk to her gently because for them [agents] she'll never understand in a gentle way. She should be hit. This is business to
them, they just want things done their way... This is what happens. I think they can't be human, it's impossible.

The Lebanese government has been taking steps to limit the mistreatment of migrant housemaids by employment agencies. In principle,
and following a 2003 decree from the Ministry of Labour, all employment agencies should obtain a licence from the Ministry of Labour.
The licence will be revoked if the agent fails to respect certain norms:
physical abuse is supposedly officially prohibited. However, as Huda
(2005) claims, it is 'often considered an acceptable form of disciplinary
action as long as a certain degree of intensity is not exceeded'. In reality, therefore, this measure is not enforced; only a few agencies have
had their licences temporarily suspended following certain 'extreme'
violations.

Regulating foreign labour

The absence of any real government policy regarding foreign labour in
Lebanon is obvious. 'The Lebanese economy is an open one, and this
has traditionally been interpreted by the authorities to mean, roughly,
easy access for economically beneficial cheap labor, in exchange for
limited responsibility on the Lebanese part' (Young 1999: 85). As Huda
(2005) states, the Lebanese government has 'failed to adequately orga-
nize and regulate the large-scale migration which Lebanon has experienced since the end of the armed conflict'. Challenging the present system in Lebanon is not easy. Political and social reasons have to be taken into consideration (Syrian workers can be affected by any
measures taken to improve the conditions of migrant workers in the
country). The presence of many Palestinian refugees adds to the complexity of the situation. This is, in principle, why the suggestion to regulate the presence of migrant workers by incorporating them under
the 1946 Lebanese Labour code (Huda 2005) is currently inapplicable
in Lebanon.

The role of NGOs

Despite efforts by international organisations – such as the European Community and the ILO office in Lebanon, and local NGOs such as Caritas and PCAAM – to work with Lebanese governmental ministries on various measures to improve the situation of migrant housemaids in Lebanon, and despite Lebanese officials' increasing will to help change the current situation, it is my view that things remain unchanged and that efforts are perhaps misdirected and of limited effect.

As the number of migrant housemaids increased in Lebanon over the years, and in view of the Lebanese relative 'disinterest' towards them, a number of assistance networks (local and international) were created to cater for their needs. As Speetjens (1998) pointed out, 'Lebanese governments have repeatedly turned their backs on refugees and migrants. The role of assisting them has been entirely offloaded onto NGOs such as the Middle East Council of Churches, the UNHCR, the United Nations Relief and Works Agency (UNRWA) and Caritas'. Assistance to migrants is diverse: visits to prisons and detention centres, legal and medical help, awareness seminars for migrant housemaids (which started in 2004), negotiations with employers to retrieve the passports of runaways, installation of safe houses or shelters, as well as the creation of a Migrants' Centre (opened in 1994 by Caritas Lebanon). As much as these measures are necessary and helpful, I do not believe they are dealing with the essence of the problem but, rather, merely treating the symptoms. First (with the exception of women detained), the help is only reaching those who have left their employers and are able to access the shelters and churches, etc. Those who are behind closed doors, this 'invisible' community who face numerous forms of abuse and exploitation and who, therefore, need help the most, are inaccessible to NGO members. Second, significant amounts of money are being donated to various NGOs by the international community to cater for the needs of housemaids in Lebanon (almost € 800,000 by the European Union in 2006 alone). Are these funds spent productively? I never understood why Caritas Lebanon sponsored the new General Security detention centre (where, I have to admit, the conditions of detention have indeed improved). This 'five-star hotel', in which detainees have no access to natural light or air, is located underground beneath a highway. The old detention centre could hold up to 100 persons, this one over 700. This means, in fact, that more people can be detained and for longer periods of time. Why legitimise what is in fact against the law, detaining people for months while they await deportation when the law states that they should be deported within days?

In March 2006, I attended the screening of the film *Maid in Lebanon*, sponsored by Caritas Lebanon and other international organisations such as the United Nations and the International Labour Organization. I will not discuss here the film itself (I have in part in Chapter 2), but I will comment on the various issues and 'solutions' raised after the screening by European Union delegates, Lebanese governmental representatives and members of Caritas. Speeches on human rights violations, injustice done to women, and the need for change and changes achieved, etc., were given. Very interesting speeches indeed but I could not help experiencing a sense of *déjà vu*. Since I started working on the subject of Sri Lankan housemaids in Lebanon (more than seven years ago) I have listened and re-listened to similar condemnations, promises and plans for upcoming changes. Have things changed? My experience is that they have not. I do not doubt the goodwill of all parties working on this issue but I cannot but wonder what has really been done and what in fact needs to be done in order for things to finally change?

The attitude of Lebanese employers towards their housemaids during the July 2006 war between Lebanon and Israel is yet another vivid indicator that things have not improved. Reports of employers fleeing the country and leaving their housemaids behind, or choosing to stay and not allowing their housemaids to join their embassies or the various NGO centres in order to be evacuated (the International Organization for Migration provided the financial and logistic support for such evacuations) were numerous. This is yet further proof, should there be need for any, that employers had actually appropriated the personhoods of housemaids – and in this particular case, their lives – as they were forcing (and thereby endangering) their housemaids to stay in a country at war. A friend of mine was annoyed by the Sri Lankan embassy's efforts to contact its nationals: 'I instructed my mother not to allow our maid to speak with the Sri Lankan embassy in case they called home'.

It is worthy of note here that the Sri Lankan embassy did not encourage (not to say discouraged) its nationals to evacuate the country (unlike other embassies such as the Philippines). When asked about those who had been already evacuated, the Labour attaché said: 'In fact, we want them to return to Lebanon' (in *L'Orient Le Jour*, 26 July 2006). The Sri Lankan embassy's position during the war made the headlines of a local French-language newspaper (*L'Orient Le Jour*, 26 July 2006): '*Le Sri Lanka appelle ses ressortissants... à rester*' (Sri Lanka calls upon its nationals... to stay). The newspaper article goes on to add that 1.2 million Sri Lankans work abroad and that, last year alone, these migrants remitted 1.5 billion dollars.

In fact, housemaids 'keep coming back', as the director of the film mentioned above told me. According to Sister Angela, they do so because the Sri Lankan government encourages this flow, following the dramatic situation in Sri Lanka:

> You see, the Sri Lankan government is only keen on the foreign exchange. Even though when I went back, I spoke at many conferences where there were government officials also. But they say we have an employment problem and people want to come. So, they let them come. And it is true. The problem there is acute. Even people who come here who have suffered, when they go back and they find the situation very bleak, the economic situation, then they want to work again. Even though they have suffered. So, they try to go to another country. Because the need is there for them. It's very sad, you know... I spoke at a workshop in Sri Lanka. I told them about the problems many women face in Lebanon. So they understood that but they said this is only a small percentage.

Stories of negative experiences encountered in host countries do circulate in Sri Lanka (whether through the local media or more directly through returnees themselves). As Brochmann (1993: 65) notes, 'Hardly any Sri Lankan woman would leave without knowing that the possibilities of running into serious trouble are fairly high'. Yet, and despite these 'warnings', women keep coming. I asked once Ramia (a freelancer who worked for me): 'Why do Sri Lankans keep coming here despite all the problems? Don't women warn them when they go back to Sri Lanka?' Ramia's answer was: 'Yes, we do, but they do not believe us, they think we are lying to keep them from coming here, they think we are jealous and are trying to discourage them from travelling and earning money'. To the same question, the Sri Lankan ambassador replied: 'Bad stories do reach Sri Lanka, media, TV, papers, etc., but people probably think: "It won't happen to us, our luck is going to be better"'. Whatever people think, the reality is that the migrant flows are constant. Brochmann (1993) seems to agree with Sister Angela that the problem lies in Sri Lanka. According to her, this migration flow is due to the numerous social and economic problems women face at home and the huge wage differential (about ten to one) between the Middle East and the local labour market (where most female migrants do not even have access to paid employment). This is undeniably true. Other gains and needs (discussed in Chapter 3) have to be stressed and do also act as incentives towards migration.

For as long as women 'need' to come, the problem will persist unless Lebanese employers change their attitudes and behaviour towards their Sri Lankan housemaids – which seems unlikely, at least in the short term. The literature on domination has underlined economic and material change as a means to render social systems more just, while ne-

glecting the 'importance of the *minds* of people in creating and maintaining hierarchical systems' (Rollins 1985: 5; emphasis in original). If
human exploitation is to be restrained, 'concrete' modifications can be
useful (such as changes in legal regulations and policies), but for them
to be effective, changes in attitudes, thoughts and emotions are needed.
'The conscious and unconscious minds of interrelating people and
their interpretations of the *meanings* of the forms of interrelating also
have the power to generate and perpetuate ideas of inequality' (Rollins
1985: 6; emphasis in original). How can one change the 'minds' of employers? Some have suggested that media campaigns would be helpful
in that regard. In fact, Caritas Lebanon, with the support of the European Commission and the Lebanese Ministry of Health and General
Security, initiated, in March 2007, a trilingual advertising campaign
(in the Lebanese press and on billboards, radio and TV) aimed at raising awareness of the problems migrant housemaids encounter in Lebanon (Azzi 2007). The campaign slogan ran as follows: 'Treat foreign
workers as you would like to be treated – regardless of race and status'.

Unfortunately, this campaign was launched after I had left Lebanon
to come to Sussex to finish writing-up my DPhil thesis. Meanwhile,
and as Patrick Laurent, chief ambassador of the European Commission
to Lebanon said, 'It is evident that these efforts will be in vain if the
general Lebanese opinion does not follow them' (quoted in Azzi 2007).

The special Madame/housemaid relationship

Why is the 'Lebanese opinion' (as well as the European, Chinese or
American one, as studies have shown) so convinced that it has the
right to direct, dominate and orient the lives of its housemaids as it
sees it fit? What is really at stake here? Could it be that there might
simply be no place for two women in the house, and, if one is to survive (the 'lady of the house'), the other needs to be rendered powerless
(I cannot but think here about the mother-in-law and daughter-in-law
living under the same roof in Arab countries – a subject I will not go
into here). Is this why Madames 'dehumanise' their housemaids and
render them 'invisible'? And, while doing so, or in order to do so, the
Madame needs to believe she is the 'ideal employer' having to endure
ungrateful housemaids. 'I treat her "like my daughter" (some even said
"like myself"), but she simply does not appreciate it. So I am, in the
end, *obliged* to be tough, one simply *cannot* be too nice with "these" women'. In an interesting reversal of roles, housemaids become the 'tor-
turers'. I once met with a male friend of mine and asked about his
mother. He replied: 'She's tired. She claims her maid is making her
sick. "*Marraditneh*" (she made me sick), "*Marradtini*" (you made me

sick), she keeps telling her maid... How can you stand having somebody in front of you that you cannot but torture? You will end up letting her go. My mother doesn't want to keep her anymore'. As I have
noted many times, housemaids have become 'salon subjects'. Lebanese
employers meet up and start 'comparing' their experiences with their
housemaids: 'My Sri Lankan is just driving me crazy (*Am bet djanene*).
How is yours?' And each Lebanese employer has to sympathise with
the other: '*Allah ysaadik!*' (God have mercy on you!).

Can 'these women' and the 'ladies of the house' ever peacefully coexist? Many incidents and testimonies come to my mind as I am writing
these words. First the words of a housemaid I interviewed:

> I cannot talk with the children, two boys: eighteen and fifteen.
> She's afraid of me. She say 'You are a girl'. It's OK, they are like
> my brothers, right? But she's afraid of me, I don't know. Husband
> tell me: 'Make coffee'. She say: 'Don't take you, I will take it for
> him'.

Could the employer be jealous, protective of her nest? My grandmother
used to go crazy when the 55-year-old son she was living with was nice
to their housemaid. I remember, once, he took the housemaid to buy
her a watch. My grandmother greeted him that day with bitter words:
'Why don't you buy her jewellery too?' I can also still recall the constant
bickering between Neemat (an Egyptian maid previously employed by
my grandmother) and Candy (her current Sri Lankan housemaid). Neemat kept coming to see (and help, especially with the cooking) grandmother even after the arrival of Candy. Neemat never missed a chance
to criticise Candy's work and Candy often complained about Neemat
making a mess in 'her' house. A relative of mine told me that my
grandmother had always been tough with her maids (Syrian, Kurds,
Lebanese). That I knew, but I was bewildered when she added that my
grandmother used to get very upset with *Jeddo* (my grandfather) because he used to call the maid '*binti*' (my girl) instead of '*binit*' (girl).
She said that one day she hit the maid and grandfather was very upset
with her. It led to a huge fight between my grandfather and
grandmother.

Another incident was related to me by a Lebanese employer who
had fought with her housemaid the day before the interview. She was
bringing a freelancer twice a week to help her current housemaid who
was 60 years old:

> Yesterday I had a crisis in the house with them [the two Sri Lan-
> kan housemaids]. She [her live-in housemaid] doesn't like her [the
> freelancer]. Because she's [the freelancer] good and capable. She

doesn't like her. She [live-in], while the other was ironing, told her: 'The children don't like your ironing'. This one [live-in] is jea-lous and protective of the house (*bitghar al beit*), she doesn't like anyone coming to help. She told me: 'Why do you bring her?' You see. She doesn't want anyone, doesn't allow for anyone to come. But the work doesn't end. You see. She thinks the house is hers (*el beit bayta*), she wants to give me orders and if someone comes to help she starts shouting at them, wanting them to work the way she wants...Things like that. She's become too familiar. Yesterday I fought with her, I shouted at her, I told her: 'I bring whoever I want and I decide who works and who doesn't work, who eats and who doesn't eat, you, can you do all the work? No, so that you stay up all night and you get sick on me'. She stays up all night to fin-ish ironing because I have a lot of ironing, three men. It's not ad-missible, the next day she gets up sick. You bring somebody [to help her], she doesn't like it... If you saw her shouting yesterday... you would have asked yourself how does she [the employer her-self] accept this, how come she didn't slap her? She was shouting and I was shouting, we were both shouting. And she told the other maid: 'Leave the ironing and get out'. I told her: 'How do you allow yourself to speak like this? Who is *maalmit el beit* (the lady of the house), me or you?' And she cried in the end, how I *kasartellah kilmetah* ['broke her word' meaning contradicted her]. She cried.

Another Lebanese employer explained to me when she started employ-ing Sri Lankan housemaids:

> Before, I had an Egyptian. She stayed 21 years. The Egyptian was very nice. Until she got accustomed to the house. I didn't have my word to say. It was either her or me. So I sent her away. Then I brought this one [the Sri Lankan]. First time I bring this race.

I cannot but stop at these words: 'It was either her or me'. If this is the case, one should not wonder how housemaids are treated. Nor should one believe that a contract or a law (and perhaps a media campaign) will make a difference. As long as, according to the Madame, it is 'me or her' and as long as the Madame has the power to decide who it is going to be... things will remain as they are.

When the two women – Madame and housemaid, from two different classes or even 'worlds' – live under the same roof, conflict seems una-voidable. But when the housemaid leaves, tension fades almost auto-matically, as this Lebanese employer told me:

> I had a maid, she left to work for other employers, friends of
> mine. Now she is another person, between me and her there is no
> more... I don't know, tension. I treat her as a friend and she treats
> me as a friend. Because she is totally another person now,
> whereas, when she was at my place, when I was her mistress, she
> created many problems.

The special Madame/housemaid relationship will never cease to surprise me. Even potential employers anticipate upcoming problems. A
female friend, who had just acquired the service of a housemaid confided to me:

> It is the first time I bring a maid to work for me. She just arrived.
> I'm a little bit afraid of that relationship. Why? Because I don't
> want to be a Mistress. You know what I mean [laughter]. The 'Ma-
> dame'. I would like to have like a friend at the house but I don't
> know if I can do this. Because... I don't know. I'm afraid not to be
> in control. It's exactly like when I went the first day at school [the
> employer is a teacher]. I was afraid not to be in control of the chil-
> dren, that one day the children will be in control of me. Anyway, I
> can't speak about my relationship with my maid yet. But I know
> I'm scared of it. I don't want to dominate her. Or be too gentle. I
> refuse the idea of having a servant. I prefer to have a relationship
> of an employer and an employee. Now I wish I can be as just... I
> wish. We will see. I don't know. I don't want to deprive her of her
> liberty or her right. But how to control her also, I don't know...
> Ask me in a year.

I recalled the words of an 'experienced' Lebanese employer: 'You learn
to become tough, you see? They become greedy (byitmaouh). But you
learn how to treat them with experience'.

In order to resolve the housework dilemma (and that of housemaids
in particular), a redefinition of reproductive work that is bound to result in the 'transformation of domestic service' is perhaps needed (Romero 1992) – instead of the formula whereby two women are trying to
coexist within one household. 'As a society we cannot continue to define reproductive labor as women's work... [E]quality must start at
home with the simple act of picking up ourselves. Beyond this, reproductive labor must be recognized as society's work, a responsibility that
requires collective responses rather than private and individual solutions. The goal must be to develop strategies to allocate the social burden of necessary reproductive labor in such a way that it does not fall
disproportionally on the shoulders of any group' (Romero 1992: 171).
This could be ideal but, until this is done, women will keep on carrying

the torch and housemaids in 'need' of a better life (again I stress the fact that this is not only limited to economic gains) will go on helping them.

A final reflection

In admitting to my lack of definite answers, I hope, instead, that I have raised the right questions and created the realisation that the 'problem' I have set out to analyse is much more complex than it initially appears.

There is a saying in French that goes like this: '*On a les défauts de nos qualités et les qualités de nos défauts*' (We have the faults of our qualities and the qualities of our faults). My focus on Sri Lankan housemaids in Lebanon has been deliberately narrow, and therein lie both its strengths and some possible shortcomings; the latter become potential avenues for future research. On the positive side, the quantity of data I gathered, the length of time spent 'in the field', the unusual positionality that my ethnographic research embodied and my theoretical focus on habitus, symbolic violence and everyday resistance all combine to yield a depth of insight and analysis that is perhaps rather unique. Certainly no other study gives such a detailed account of the living and working conditions of Sri Lankans in Lebanon (or the Middle East).

The particular scope of my own study leaves the door open for further research. Here are a few suggestions. The shifting of some Sri Lankans into sex-work in Lebanon is a trend I became aware of in the course of my fieldwork, but chose not to follow through. Other possibilities for future research could be comparative studies between Sri Lankans and the other main female migrant groups in Lebanon, Filipinas and Ethiopians. One of my hypotheses in this study has been that Sri Lankans are the easiest to 'break' or 'control' and 'mould'. A comparative study across these three groups of women would either support my hypothesis or prove me wrong. Another domain for future research could be a comparison of Sri Lankans' experiences in Lebanon with those in other destinations: in other Middle Eastern countries, or in Cyprus and Italy, where there are substantial Sri Lankan housemaid communities. In fact, a 'route to Europe' has been opening up for migrant housemaids in Lebanon. I have heard stories of housemaids (Sri Lankans and Ethiopians) 'crossing' from Lebanon to Italy – through Turkey – after paying smugglers a large sum of money ($2,500-$3,000). Europe seems to be the 'ultimate goal' of the job. Leaving Sri Lanka to work as live-in housemaids in Lebanon can be seen as the first step. The second is getting rid of the constraints of the 'live-in' condition to work as a freelancer. The third, after putting some money aside, is moving to Europe. This area of research is definitely worth pursuing. Finally, it would be instructive to carry the research back to the country of origin, in order to monitor more thoroughly both the setting from which migration takes place and the impact of return.

Post scriptum

I cannot end this book without a glimpse of hope. In October 2007, the general Lebanese public was shocked by the quasi-simultaneous publication of the article 'Bonnes à vendre' (Maids for sale) and broadcast of the documentary *Liban, pays des esclaves* (Lebanon, country of slaves) in the French media.[1] The author of both accounts, the French journalist Dominique Torrès, criticised, in rather harsh terms, the treatment of migrant housemaids by their Lebanese employers. Many Lebanese reacted angrily, mainly through letters to local newspapers. A Facebook group was even created in protest. Here are some of the 'outraged' reactions:

> Abuse does exist but only with a minority of employers whose social ideals have been somehow altered by years of war [in reference here to the 1975-1990 civil war]... We are very disappointed by this attack on our country, an attack which is totally baseless. Our country suffered the martyr as a defender of liberties and human rights in a region where obscurantism and totalitarianism prevail.

> This type of information is racist and unworthy of true journalism. The freedom of the press does not entail insulting a whole country with such ease.

> I advise Mrs Torrès to check what takes place in French cabarets before defining slavery.

> Not all the maids who come to Lebanon are *sold* and mistreated, Mrs Torrès... Their passports are not *confiscated* but held in a safe place. These women are not *forbidden* to go out nor are they *imprisoned*, they just need some adaptation time before circulating in a foreign country...

To put things into perspective, and before I move on to explain why one might perhaps be permitted to hope for an improvement in the living and working conditions of migrant housemaids in Lebanon, I must say that I found both article and documentary unprofessional to say the least. This 'sensationalist' journalism, based on generalisations and bias, is one form of information that I, as a researcher, condemn. But this is not the subject of this post-scriptum. What gives me a reason (even if a very modest one) to be hopeful is reading numerous 'other' reactions of the Lebanese people in response to the same French media reports.

> It is about time we call a cat a cat... The article and TV documentary are perhaps the last recourse to open the eyes of those who do not want to see.

> Let us stop with the self-victimisation and start confronting our reality, as dark as it is. It seems to me that we are more worried about our image than about the gravity of the problem. Our definition of mistreatment does not correspond to the basic norms of human rights. How would you qualify these very common practices in Lebanon: confiscation of passports, privation of days off, locking in, banning all private life?

> Mrs Torrès is right to denounce the abuses perpetrated against maids, because they very well take place... The road is still long in order to be able to call Lebanon a civilised country.

The road might still be long before things truly change for the better ... but there might just be light at the end of the tunnel.

Notes

1   Throughout this book I use the word 'housemaid' for Sri Lankan (and other migrant) women who are employed in domestic work in Lebanon today. Arab women working in this capacity in the past will be referred to as 'maids'. As I address domestic work in general terms, I also use the wording 'domestic worker', 'domestic' or 'maid', terms usually used in the literature on domestic work. I make this semantic choice for two reasons. First, I do not think 'worker' is an appropriate term to describe this position; a housemaid is not just working but living with her employers; her 'role' (or the one assigned to her), as I will show, goes beyond her work tasks. Second, this is the title of occupation written on the passports of Sri Lankan and other migrant women entering Lebanon.

2   Freelancers are housemaids who 'live out' as opposed to 'live in'. I will expand on these distinctions later in this chapter.

3   These writers are merely listed here by way of introducing some key names; their work will be more formally referenced in the rest of the book, especially in Chapters 3 and 4.

4   Housemaids call their female Lebanese employer 'Madame' (the French word for 'madam') just as 'Madames' use this term with housemaids when they refer to themselves or any woman in their company. If I am visiting a friend, for instance, she will call her housemaid and ask her to bring me coffee using these words: 'Nanda, bring Madame coffee'.

5   I use the word 'sponsor' instead of 'male employer', as it is generally Lebanese husbands who, as sponsors, take care of the administrative issues relative to housemaids. Their names are usually on the housemaid's passport. Their role, however, ends here, since it is their wives who manage the daily lives of these housemaids.

6   From herein all '$' signs refer to US dollars.

7   I had interviewed this person twice: during the first part of my fieldwork as the assistant to the labour attaché and then during the second part of my fieldwork after she had resigned (or was dismissed – depending on which version one chooses to believe, hers or the ambassador's).

8   For a reason I cannot explain, Sri Lankan housemaids called me 'Leila' instead of 'Nayla' (which is in fact my first name). I tried explaining to them that my name started with an *n* not an *l*, but I was Leila to them.

9   I chose not to draw a 'general profile' of employers for the reasons cited below. Abuse, as I describe it, is common to Lebanese employers or Madames from all classes. The only tangible difference is that high-class Madames usually employ Filipinas (at times two per household). A profile of the 90 housemaids I interviewed, however, was, in my view, possible as well as useful. Parts of this 'housemaids' profile' are disclosed at the end of this chapter; the remainder is included in Chapter 5, following the exploration of Bourdieu's concept of habitus.

10 I analyse the concept of 'everyday forms of resistance', as developed by Scott (1985, 1990), in more detail in Chapter 6.

11   French word for 'contract' that employers and housemaids use.
12   Of course, however, even the Sri Lankan embassy was not a completely 'neutral' place. It was a place of refuge, but also a place where power dynamics were at play (presided over by the power of the ambassador) as well as the site of open conflicts (where sponsors or agents came to 'reclaim' their housemaids).
13   For instance, 41 Sri Lankan housemaids were in holding, compared to just four Filipinas, when I visited the prisons as part of my early fieldwork (see Chapter 2); 163 Sri Lankans and only twelve Filipinas were in the detention centre I visited in the second fieldwork phase.
14   Article published in *Le Monde* (11 October 2007); documentary aired on France 2 in *Envoyé Spécial* (18 October 2007).

References

Abella, M. (1995), 'Asian migrant and contract workers in the Middle East', in R. Cohen (ed.), *The Cambridge survey of world migration*, 418-423 Cambridge: Cambridge University Press.

Adnan, S. (2007), 'Departures from everyday resistance and flexible strategies of domination. The making and unmaking of a poor peasant mobilization in Bangladesh', *Journal of Agrarian Change* 7 (2): 183-224.

Al Khouri, R. (2004), 'Arab migration patterns. The *Mashreq*', in *Migration Initiatives Appeal 2004*, 24-40 Geneva: International Organization for Migration.

Andall, J. (2000), *Gender, migration and domestic service. The politics of black women in Italy*, Aldershot: Ashgate.

Anderson, B. (2000), *Doing the dirty work. The global politics of domestic labour*. London: Zed Books.

— (2002), 'Just another job? The commodification of domestic labor', in B. Ehrenreich and A.R. Hochschild (eds.), *Global woman: nannies, maids and sex workers in the new economy*, 104-114 London: Granta Books.

Anthias, F. (2000), 'Metaphors of home. Gendering new migrations to Southern Europe', in F. Anthias & G. Lazaradis (eds.), *Gender and migration in Southern Europe. Women on the move*, 15-47 Oxford: Berg.

Azzi, I. (2007), 'Advocacy group kicks off campaign to spotlight plight of migrants', *The Daily Star*, 17 March 2007.

Baldwin-Edwards, M. (2005), *Migration in the Middle East and the Mediterranean. A regional study*, Geneva: Global Commission on International Migration.

Bales, K. (1999), *Disposable people. New slavery in the global economy*. Berkeley: University of California Press.

Birks, J. & C. Sinclair (1980), *International migration and development in the Arab region*. Geneva: International Labour Office.

Bourdieu, P. (1980), *Le sens pratique*. Paris: Les Editions de Minuit.

— (1991), *Language and symbolic power*. Cambridge: Polity Press.

Boyd, M. & E. Grieco (2003), *Women and migration. Incorporating gender into international migration theory*. Migration Information Source, Migration Policy Institute (Online edition).

Brettell, C.B. (2000), 'Theorizing migration in anthropology. The social construction of networks, identities, communities and globalscapes', in C.B. Brettell & J.F. Hollifield (eds.), *Migration theory. Talking across disciplines*, 97-135 New York and London: Routledge.

Brochmann, G. (1993), *Middle East Avenue. Female migration from Sri Lanka to the Gulf*. Boulder: Westview Press.

Buijs, G. (ed.) (1993), *Migrant women. Crossing boundaries and changing identities*. Oxford: Berg.

Burgess, R. (1984), *In the field. An introduction to field research*. London: Allen and Unwin.

Campani, G. (1995), 'Women migrants. From marginal subjects to social actors', in R. Cohen (ed.), *The Cambridge Survey of World Migration*, 546-550 Cambridge: Cambridge University Press.

Caritas Migrant Centre (2005), *Human Rights of Migrant Workers*. Beirut: Caritas.

Carling, J. (2005), *Gender dimensions of international migration*, Geneva: Global Commission of International Migration, Global Migration Perspectives No. 35.

Castles, S. (1995), 'Contract labour migration', in R. Cohen (ed.), *The Cambridge Survey of World Migration*. 510-514 Cambridge: Cambridge University Press.

Castles, S. & A. Davidson (2000), *Citizenship and migration. Globalization and the politics of belonging*. London: Macmillan.

Castles, S. & M. Miller (2003), *The age of migration. International population movements in the modern world*. London: Macmillan, third edition.

CIA (2006), *World Factbook Lebanon*, updated February 2007.

Chammartin, G. (2004), 'Women migrant workers' protection in Arab League states', in S. Esim & M. Smith (eds.), *Gender and migration in Arab states. The case of domestic workers* 7-23 Beirut: International Labour Organization.

— (2005), 'Domestic workers. Little protection for the underpaid', *Migration Information Source*, 1 April 2005.

Chang, G. (2000), *Disposable domestics. Immigrant women workers in the global economy*. Cambridge MA: South End Press.

Cheng, S.-J.A. (2004), 'Contextual politics of difference in transnational care: the rhetoric of Filipina domestics' employers in Taiwan', *Feminist Review* 77: 46-64.

Chin, C. (1998), *In service and servitude. Foreign female domestic workers and the Malaysian 'modernity' project*. New York: Columbia University Press.

Choucri, N. (1986), 'Asians in the Arab world. Labor migration and public policy', *Middle Eastern Studies* 22 (2): 252-273.

Cock, J. (1989), *Maids and madams. Domestic workers under apartheid*. London: The Women's Press Limited.

Constable, N. (1997), *Maid to order in Hong Kong. Stories of Filipina workers*. New York: Cornell University Press.

Ehrenreich, B. & A.R. Hochschild (eds.) (2002), *Global woman. Nannies, maids and sex workers in the new economy*. London: Granta Books.

Esim S. & M. Smith (eds.) (2004), *Gender and migration in Arab states. The case of domestic workers*. Beirut: International Labour Organization.

Fargues, P. (2002), *International migration in the Middle East and North Africa. A political interpretation*. Paper presented at the Third Mediterranean Social and Political Research Meeting, Florence: Robert Schuman Centre for Advanced Studies, 2-24 March.

Fernando, N. (2001), *Pre-departure, reintegrating and policy advocacy in the migration process*. Paper presented at the Consultative Workshop on Migration and HIV/AIDS, Colombo, 17 January 2001.

Gamburd, M.R. (2000), *The kitchen spoon's handle. Transnationalism and Sri Lanka's migrant housemaids*. New York: Cornell University Press.

— (2002), 'Breadwinners no more', in B. Ehrenreich & A.R. Hochschild (eds.), *Global woman. Nannies, maids and sex workers in the new economy*, 190-206 London: Granta Books.

Gardner, K. (1995), *Global migrants, local lives. Travel and transformation in rural Bangladesh*. Oxford: Oxford University Press.

GCIM (2005), *Report of a workshop on gender dimensions of international migration*. Geneva: Global Commission on International Migration, 23-24 March 2005.

Genet, J. (1976), *Les bonnes*. France: Collection Folio.

Giddens, A. (2001), *Sociology*. Cambridge: Polity Press.

Girgis, M. (2002), *Would nationals and Asians replace Arab workers in the GCC?* Paper presented at Fourth Mediterranean Development Forum, Amman, Jordan, 6-9 October.

Gmelch, G. (1980), 'Return migration', *Annual Review of Anthropology* 9: 135-159.

Godfrey, M., M. Ruhs, N. Shah & M. Smith (2004), 'Migrant domestic workers in Kuwait. Findings based on a field survey and additional research', in S. Esim & M. Smith (eds.), *Gender and Migration in Arab States: The Case of Domestic Workers*, 41-62 Beirut: International Labour Organization.

Gunatilleke, G. (1995), 'The economic, demographic, sociocultural and political setting for emigration from Sri Lanka', *International Migration* 33 (4): 667-698.

Hage, G. (2000), *White nation. Fantasies of white supremacy in a multicultural society*. New York: Routledge.

Hochschild, A.R. (2000), 'The nanny chain', *The American Prospect* (online edition), 11 (4): 32-36.

Hockey, J. (1996), 'Putting down smoke. Emotion and engagement in participant observation', in K. Carter & S. Delamont (eds.), *Qualitative research. The emotional dimension*, 12-27 Aldershot: Avebury.

Hondagneu-Sotelo, P. (2001), *Doméstica. Immigrant workers cleaning and caring in the shadows of affluence*. Berkeley: University of California Press.

Huda, S. (2005), *Integration of the human rights of women and a gender perspective. Mission to Lebanon (7 to 16 February 2005)*. Report of the Special Rapporteur on the human rights aspects of the victims of trafficking in persons, especially women and children, E/CN.4/2006/62/Add.3, 20 February 2005.

Indra, D. (ed.) (1999), *Engendering forced migration. Theory and practice*. New York: Berghahn Books.

IOM (2004), *Migration initiatives appeal 2004*, Geneva: International Organization for Migration.

— (2005a), *Migration and gender. Essentials of migration management. Volume two: developing migration policy*, Geneva: International Organization for Migration.

— (2005b), *Labour migration in Asia. Protection of migrant workers, support services and enhancing development benefits*. Geneva: International Organization for Migration.

Jaulin, T. (2006), *Lebanese politics of nationality and emigration*. Florence: Robert Schuman Centre for Advanced Studies, European University Institute (EUI) Working Paper No. 2006/29.

Jolly, S. & H. Reeves (2005), *Gender and migration. Overview report*. Brighton: Cutting Edge Pack, BRIDGE/Institute of Development Studies.

Jureidini, R. (2004), 'Women migrant domestic workers in Lebanon', in S. Esim & M. Smith (eds.), *Gender and migration in Arab states. The case of domestic workers*, 63-82 Beirut: International Labour Organization.

Jureidini, R. & N. Moukarbel (2004), 'Female Sri Lankan domestic workers in Lebanon. A case of "contract slavery"?', *Journal of Ethnic and Migration Studies* 30 (4): 581-607.

Kapiszewski, A. (2006), *Arab versus Asian migrant workers in the GCC countries*. United Nations expert group meeting on international migration and development in the Arab region, UN/POP/EGM/2006/02, 22 May 2006.

Kahale, S. (2003), *Exploratory study on foreign domestic work in Syria.* Damascus: International Organization for Migration.

King, R., M. Thomson, A. Fielding & A. Warnes (2005), *Gender, age and generations.* State-of-the-art report, IMISCOE Network of Excellence on Immigration, Integration and Social Cohesion in Europe.

Kofman, E., A. Phizacklea, P. Raghuram & R. Sales (2000), *Gender and international migration in Europe. Employment, welfare and politics.* London: Routledge.

Laksehta (2000), 'Annual report. Facts and figures, September 98-August 99'. Beirut: Laksehta Center, Dora, unpublished report.

Lofland, J. & L.H. Lofland (1984), *Analyzing social settings. A guide to qualitative observation and analysis.* Belmont, CA: Wadsworth.

Longva, A.N. (1997), *Walls built on sand. Migration, exclusion, and society in Kuwait.* Colorado: Westview Press.

Lueth, E. & M. Ruiz-Arranz (2007), *Are workers' remittances a hedge against macroeconomic shocks? The case of Sri Lanka,* IMF Working Paper 07/22.

Lutz, H. (ed.) (2008), *Migration and domestic work. A European perspective on a global dilemma.* Aldershot: Ashgate.

McDermott, M. (1999), *Afro-Asian migrants in Lebanon.* Report of the Committee on Pastoral Care of Afro-Asian Migrant Workers, Beirut (unpublished manuscript).

Migration News (2005), *South Asia,* 12 (3), July 2005.

Mirbeau, O. (1983), *Le journal d'une femme de chambre.* Paris: Flammarion.

Momsen, H.M. (ed.) (1999), *Migration and domestic service.* London: Routledge.

Moya, J.C. (2007), 'Domestic service in a global perspective. Gender, migration and ethnic niches', *Journal of Ethnic and Migration Studies* 33 (4): 550-579.

Mozère, L. (2005), 'Domestiques Philippines entrepreneures d'elles-mêmes sur un marché mondial de la domesticité', *Le Portique,* Carnet 1-2005.

Murphy, K. (2006), 'The Lebanese crisis and its impact on immigrants and refugees', *Migration Information Source,* 1 September 2006.

Nahas, C. (2001), in *L'Orient Le Jour,* 25 May 2001.

Najjar, S. (2004), 'Women migrant domestic workers in Bahrain', in S. Esim & M. Smith (eds.), *Gender and migration in Arab states. The case of domestic workers,* 24-40 Beirut: International Labour Organization.

Narula, R. (1999), 'Cinderella need not apply. A study of paid domestic work in Paris', in J.H. Momsen (ed.), *Gender, migration and domestic service,* 148-163 London: Routledge.

Nasr, S. (1999), 'Foreign labour', in *Investor's Guide to Lebanon,* 81-89 Beirut: Études et Consultations Économiques.

Palmer, P. (1989), *Domesticity and dirt. Housewives and domestic servants in the United States, 1920-1945.* Philadelphia: Temple University Press.

Pappas DeLuca, K. (1999), 'Transcending gendered boundaries', in J.H. Momsen (ed.), *Gender, migration and domestic service,* 98-113 London: Routledge.

Parreñas, R.S. (2001) *Servants of globalization. Women, migration and domestic work.* Stanford: Stanford University Press.

— (2005), *Children of global migration. Transnational families and gendered woes.* Stanford: Stanford University Press.

Pederson, M.H. (2003), *Between homes. Post-war return, emplacement and the negotiation of belonging in Lebanon,* UNHCR.Working Paper 79, News Issues in Refugee Research.

Phizacklea, A (ed.) (1983), *One way ticket. Migration and female labour*. London: Routledge and Kegan Paul.

Piper, N. (2005), 'Gender and migration', paper prepared for the Policy Analysis and Research Programme of the Global Commission on International Migration (GCIM), September 2005.

Rodrigo, C. (1992), 'Overseas migration from Sri Lanka. Magnitude, patterns and trends', *Asian Exchange* 8 (3-4): 41-74.

Rollins, J. (1985), *Between women. Domestics and their employers*. Philadelphia: Temple University Press.

Romero, M. (1992), *Maid in the U.S.A.* New York: Routledge.

Russell, S. (1990), 'Migration and political integration in the Arab world', in G. Luciani (ed.), *The Arab state*, 373-393 London: Routledge.

Sabban, R. (2004), 'Women migrant domestic workers in the United Arab Emirates', in S. Esim & M. Smith (eds.), *Gender and migration in Arab States. The case of domestic workers*, 85-104 Beirut: ILO.

Said, E. (1995), *Orientalism*. London: Penguin Books.

Sanjek, R. & S. Colen (eds.) (1990), *At work in homes. Household workers in world perspective*. Washington DC: American Anthropological Association.

Scott, J.C. (1985), *Weapons of the weak. Everyday forms of peasant resistance*. New Haven: Yale University Press.

— (1990), *Domination and the arts of resistance. Hidden transcripts*. New Haven: Yale University Press.

Scott, J.C.& B.J. Tria Kerkvliet (eds.) (1986), *Everyday forms of peasant resistance in South-East Asia*. London: Frank Cass.

Shah, N. (1994), 'An overview of present and future emigration dynamics in South Asia', *International Migration* 32 (2): 217-268.

Sharpe, P. (ed.) (2001), *Women, gender and labour migration. Historical and global perspectives*. London: Routledge.

Speetjens, P. (1998), 'Caritas provides help for migrants of all nations', in *The Daily Star*, 20 January 1998.

Tawk, R. (1998), 'Report on meeting with the Governmental Bureau of Foreign Employment of Sri Lanka'. Beirut: in conjunction with OXFAM, unpublished report.

Tilly, L. & J. Scott (1987), *Women, work, and family*. London: Routledge.

UNDP (1997), *Country cooperation frameworks and related matters. First country cooperation framework for Sri Lanka (1997-2001)*. DP/CCF/SRL/1, 24 June 1997.

Watson, J.L. (ed.) (1977), *Between two cultures. Immigrants and minorities in Britain*. Oxford: Blackwell.

Webb, J., T. Schirato & G. Danaher (2002), *Understanding Bourdieu*. Sydney: Allen and Unwin.

Williamson, H. (1996), 'Systematic or sentimental? The place of feelings in social research', in K.Carter & S. Delamont (eds.), *Qualitative research. The emotional dimension*, 28-41 Aldershot: Avebury.

Young, M. (1999), *Migrant workers in Lebanon*. Beirut: Lebanese NGO Forum.

Zlotnik, H. (2000), 'Migration and the family. The female perspective', in K.Willis & B. Yeoh (eds.), *Gender and migration*, 27-45 Cheltenham: Edward Elgar.

Zontini, E. (2002), 'Towards a comparative study of female migrants in southern Europe. Filipino and Moroccan women in Bologna and Barcelona', *Studi Emigrazione* 145: 137-159.

Other IMISCOE titles

IMISCOE Research

Rinus Penninx, Maria Berger, Karen Kraal, Eds.
The Dynamics of International Migration and Settlement in Europe:
A State of the Art
2006 (ISBN 978 90 5356 866 8)
(originally appearing in IMISCOE Joint Studies)

Leo Lucassen, David Feldman, Jochen Oltmer, Eds.
Paths of Integration: Migrants in Western Europe (1880-2004)
2006 (ISBN 978 90 5356 883 5)

Rainer Bauböck, Eva Ersbøll, Kees Groenendijk, Harald Waldrauch, Eds.
Acquisition and Loss of Nationality: Policies and Trends in 15 European
Countries, Volume 1: Comparative Analyses
2006 (ISBN 978 90 5356 920 7)

Rainer Bauböck, Eva Ersbøll, Kees Groenendijk, Harald Waldrauch, Eds.
Acquisition and Loss of Nationality: Policies and Trends in 15 European
Countries, Volume 2: Country Analyses
2006 (ISBN 978 90 5356 921 4)

Rainer Bauböck, Bernhard Perchinig, Wiebke Sievers, Eds.
Citizenship Policies in the New Europe
2007 (ISBN 978 90 5356 922 1)

Veit Bader
Secularism or Democracy? Associational Governance of Religious Diversity
2007 (ISBN 978 90 5356 999 3)

Holger Kolb & Henrik Egbert, Eds.
Migrants and Markets: Perspectives from Economics and the Other
Social Sciences
2008 (ISBN 978 90 5356 684 8)

Ralph Grillo, Ed.
The Family in Question: Immigrant and Ethnic Minorities in
Multicultural Europe
2008 (ISBN 978 90 5356 869 9)

Corrado Bonifazi, Marek Okólski, Jeannette Schoorl, Patrick Simon, Eds.
International Migration in Europe: New Trends and New Methods of Analysis
2008 (ISBN 978 90 5356 894 1)

Maurice Crul, Liesbeth Heering, Eds.
*The Position of the Turkish and Moroccan Second Generation in
Amsterdam and Rotterdam: The TIES Study in the Netherlands*
2008 (ISBN 978 90 8964 061 1)

Marlou Schrover, Joanne van der Leun, Leo Lucassen, Chris Quispel, Eds.
Illegal Migration and Gender in a Global and Historical Perspective
2008 (ISBN 978 90 8964 047 5)

IMISCOE Reports

Rainer Bauböck, Ed.
Migration and Citizenship: Legal Status, Rights and Political Participation
2006 (ISBN 978 90 5356 888 0)

Michael Jandl, Ed.
*Innovative Concepts for Alternative Migration Policies:
Ten Innovative Approaches to the Challenges of Migration in the 21st Century*
2007 (ISBN 978 90 5356 990 0)

Jeroen Doomernik, Michael Jandl, Eds.
Modes of Migration Regulation and Control in Europe
2008 (ISBN 978 90 5356 689 3)

Michael Jandl, Christina Hollomey, Sandra Gendera, Anna Stepien,
Veronika Bilger
*Migration and Irregular Work in Austria: A Case Study of the Structure
and Dynamics of Irregular Foreign Employment in Europe at the Beginning
of the 21st Century*
2009 (ISBN 978 90 8964 053 6)

IMISCOE Dissertations

Panos Arion Hatziprokopiou
*Globalisation, Migration and Socio-Economic Change in Contemporary
Greece: Processes of Social Incorporation of Balkan Immigrants
in Thessaloniki*
2006 (ISBN 978 90 5356 873 6)

Floris Vermeulen
The Immigrant Organising Process: Turkish Organisations in Amsterdam and Berlin and Surinamese Organisations in Amsterdam, 1960-2000
2006 (ISBN 978 90 5356 875 0)

Anastasia Christou
Narratives of Place, Culture and Identity: Second-Generation Greek-Americans Return 'Home'
2006 (ISBN 978 90 5356 878 1)

Katja Rušinović
Dynamic Entrepreneurship: First and Second-Generation Immigrant Entrepreneurs in Dutch Cities
2006 (ISBN 978 90 5356 972 6)

Ilse van Liempt
Navigating Borders: Inside Perspectives on the Process of Human Smuggling into the Netherlands
2007 (ISBN 978 90 5356 930 6)

Myriam Cherti
Paradoxes of Social Capital: A Multi-Generational Study of Moroccans in London
2008 (ISBN 978 90 5356 032 7)

Marc Helbling
Practising Citizenship and Heterogeneous Nationhood: Naturalisations in Swiss Municipalities
2008 (ISBN 978 90 8964 034 5)

Inge Van Nieuwenhuyze
Getting by in Europe's Urban Labour Markets: Senegambian Migrants' Strategies for Survival, Documentation and Mobility
2009 (ISBN 978 90 8964 050 5)

Jérôme Jamin
L'Imaginaire du Complot: Discours d'Extrême Droite en France et aux Etats-Unis
2009 (ISBN 978 90 8964 048 2)